25

Thomas Burt, Miners' MP, 1837–1922

Thomas Burt, aged 37, taken in 1874 at the time of his first election to Parliament.
Source: Thomas Cox Meech, *From Mine to Ministry: The Life and Times of the Right Hon. Thomas Burt, M.P.* (Darlington, 1908).

THOMAS BURT, MINERS' MP, 1837–1922
THE GREAT CONCILIATOR

Lowell J. Satre

Leicester University Press
London and New York

First published 1999 by
Leicester University Press, *A Cassell imprint*
Wellington House, 125 Strand, London WC2R 0BB
370 Lexington Avenue, New York, NY 10017-6550

British Library Cataloguing-in-Publication Data
A catalogue record for this book is available from the British Library.

ISBN 0-7185-0184-5

Library of Congress Cataloging-in-Publication Data
Satre, Lowell J. (Lowell Joseph), 1942–
    Thomas Burt, Miners' MP, 1837–1922 : the Great Conciliator /
Lowell J. Satre.
        p.   cm.
    Includes bibliographical references and index.
    ISBN 0-7185-0184-5 (hardcover)
    1. Burt, Thomas, 1837–1922.   2. Labor leaders—Great Britain—
Biography.   3. Coal miners—Great Britain—Biography.   4. Trade-
unions—Coal miners—Great Britain—Official and employees—
Biography.   5. Great Britain.   Parliament.   House of Commons—
movement—Great Britain—History.   I. Title.

HD8393.B84S38   1999
331.88'092–dc21
[b]   98-21734
                                                                                    CIP

Typeset by BookEns Ltd, Royston, Herts.
Printed and bound in Great Britain by The Cromwell Press Ltd, Trowbridge, Wiltshire

CONTENTS

Abbreviations

DLB	*Dictionary of Labour Biography*
DNB	*Dictionary of National Biography*
ILP	Independent Labour Party
LRC	Labour Representation Committee
MFGB	Miners' Federation of Great Britain
MNA	Miners' National Association
MNU	Miners' National Union
MP	Member of Parliament
NB–NUM	Northumberland Branch of the National Union of Miners
NDCOA	Northumberland and Durham Coal Owners Association
NMA	Northumberland Miners' Association
NMMCA	Northumberland Miners' Mutual Confidence Association
NRO	Northumberland Record Office
TUC	Trades Union Congress

To Ellen

INTRODUCTION

Thomas Burt was the most respected labour leader in Britain in the last quarter of the nineteenth century. His name was honoured, not only in the North East of England, but throughout the nation and on the European continent. Few men have gained and retained such respect over a career that spanned nearly fifty years.

Burt entered the coal mines in 1847 at the age of ten. In 1865, after eighteen years as a miner, he was elected executive secretary of the Northumberland Miners' Mutual Confidence Association, a struggling labour union less than three years in existence. He successfully guided the Association through its turbulent formative years, and by the 1870s the union was widely regarded as one of the most successful in Britain. This union, and the coal-mining communities of the North East, would be the foundation of Burt's power. In 1874 he was elected MP for the borough of Morpeth (the first member of the working class elected to Parliament), swept to victory by the votes of the recently enfranchised Northumberland miners. Tommy Burt, as he was affectionately known by the miners, remained the secretary of his union until 1913, and sat in Parliament until the end of the Great War in 1918.

Burt's life and values were shaped and moulded by the environment of North East England. He was born into a tightly knit Primitive Methodist family. Burt grew up in colliery villages and at an early age found his family subject to the disruption and economic deprivation caused by labour–management strife in the coalfields. He was also a product of the 'self-help' attitude prevalent within the working class, among miners in particular. Almost completely self-educated, Burt spent many hours poring over his beloved books at home and at the Mechanics' Institutes that sprouted up throughout the North East. He encouraged people of the working classes to better their lives through education and by the practice of temperance. None of these activities was unusual in the mining communities; Burt was one of many labourers working to improve himself and the community.

1

Burt's power and popularity were based on several elements. He was an extraordinarily effective speaker. Miners, Members of Parliament and the public were mesmerized by his talks. Deliberate in his speaking manner, he had a much-loved Northumbrian burr, a remarkable ability to quote poetry, and a ready sense of humour. He was also a skilled negotiator who protected the well-being of the miners. In addition, as an MP he faithfully reflected the political traditions of the North East. He entered Parliament as a Radical, devoted to the workers and to the quest for democracy, a critic of the privileged in society, an advocate of state support for education, and an early proponent of Home Rule for Ireland. His ideas, as well as his moderation and self-effacing attitude towards his own role, helped gain him support not only within the working class, but also from the varied sectors of society involved in trade and industry. His acceptance among the middle and upper classes, in industry as well as governing circles, was to a great extent based on his policies of conciliation and arbitration. In labour–management relations, in politics and in international affairs, Burt was always a staunch advocate of conciliation. He supported a strike only after all other avenues to settlement failed. Compromise and practicality were for him the norms in politics, and he became one of the great advocates of using arbitration to settle disputes between nations. He served as president of the International Arbitration League, a working-class organization, for some forty years. The policy of conciliation is the one theme that runs through all facets of Burt's life.

Public testimonials to Burt's contributions to society were bestowed on him during his own lifetime. The Northumberland Miners' Association office, built in the 1890s, was named Burt Hall. In 1906 he was made a Privy Councillor. Durham University awarded him a Doctorate of Civil Law in 1911. At about the same time, he was made a freeman of Morpeth and of Newcastle upon Tyne. In 1913 labour honoured him with a huge banquet in London, and in June 1914, shortly before the Great War broke out, the International Arbitration League paid their respects to him for his long service to the cause of international peace.

Yet there is another side to this most honoured and most public of men. He was subject to much criticism, sometimes exceptionally pointed, throughout his long career. Some coal miners found his conciliatory stance unacceptable and regarded him as little more than a tool of the mine owners. His adherence to the theory of political economists – theory that the market system, through the law of supply and demand, determined prices as well as wages – angered supporters of a minimum wage for miners. Burt's opposition to the restriction of supply upset critics who advocated a curtailment of production to help drive up wages, while his devotion to his county union offended miners who wished to create a national organization. Criticism mounted against him in the 1880s with the emergence of the aggressive New Unionism and accelerated at the turn of the century when Socialists attacked his adherence to Liberalism. Burt's greatest political crisis occurred towards the end of his career when, in the general election of 1909, he lost the formal support of his own union because he refused to join the Labour Party. While a life-long supporter of Irish Home Rule, his refusal to countenance Irish obstructionist tactics in the House of Commons in the early 1880s brought rebuke from some of his traditional supporters. His anti-war activities, particularly during the South African War, earned him public scorn and near-defeat in the 'khaki' election of 1900.

Burt survived all of these attacks, defending his actions with grace and holding little rancour towards his critics. His life-long devotion to his union and to miners everywhere always earned for him, even in the most tumultuous of times, a large reservoir of support from his mining constituency. His character, honesty and openness blunted much of the criticism and gained him widespread public support outside the mining community. Indeed, his career was followed with interest throughout the nation.

Labour and political historians have tended to concentrate their attention on individuals such as Keir Hardie and Ramsay MacDonald who were instrumental in the formation of the New Unionism and the Labour Party. We would do well, however, not to ignore those members of the working class who, like Burt, remained within the older political parties and labour traditions. The Labour Party and most labour unions even in the twentieth century have never completely adopted Socialist ideology. The elements of Radical, Liberal, and class cooperation as advocated by Burt have survived in the Party and the unions, and are deserving of consideration.

This is a biography of the public life of this influential, honoured, yet controversial labour leader. Relatively little is known of Burt's private life. With the exception of his *Autobiography*, which ends with his election to Parliament in 1874 (supplementary chapters were added by Aaron Watson), Burt seldom wrote about himself. No private papers have survived. Letters he wrote to friends and political colleagues are available, but they are few in number. Fortunately, Burt expressed himself in public in a variety of ways. In addition to his *Autobiography*, he wrote several articles for periodicals and newspapers. As a public figure, his addresses were often recorded in detail by the newspapers. His parliamentary speeches were, of course, recorded in *Parliamentary Debates*. The greatest source of information on his union activities are the extensive records of the Northumberland Miners' Association at the Northumberland Record Office. Studies of his life, most notably Aaron Watson's *A Great Labour Leader*, provide valuable information and record important documents, but they are not critical evaluations.

Moreover, since they were written during Burt's lifetime, they lack historical perspective.

Scattered throughout this biography are portions of articles I have written about Thomas Burt, particularly 'Thomas Burt and the Crisis of Late-Victorian Liberalism in the North-East', in *Northern History* (1987), and 'Education and Religion in the Shaping of Thomas Burt, Miners' Leader', in *North East Labour History Society Bulletin* (1992). I wish to thank the publishers for permission to include portions of these articles.

I owe thanks to many people who have helped make this book possible. Albert Hayden and Martin Berger both read the complete manuscript and offered their sage comments, while Pres Crews reviewed the first few chapters. My brother-in-law George Ohlson used his considerable editorial skills to tighten the narrative. My wife Ellen accompanied me on my stay in England, assisted with the research, made useful suggestions on the text, patiently advanced my modest computer skills, and provided constant moral support. Bill Lancaster, Robert Colls and Joan Hugman made valuable suggestions on the format of the book. Norman McCord, Raymond Challinor, Nigel Todd, Eric Wade and Owen Ashton encouraged me to write the biography and provided me with valuable references.

Librarians and archivists in Britain and the United States were invariably helpful with my many requests. I extend special thanks to the staff at the Northumberland Record Office, the Local Studies Department of Newcastle Public Central Library and the Reference Department at Maag Library, Youngstown State University. Several of my graduate assistants helped compile the bibliography.

Thomas Burt's grandson, Peter Burt Jr, and great-granddaughter, Rosemary Halsey (both of Newcastle) shared their memorabilia with me. Peter Burt and his wife Betty drove us to many of the sites in Northumberland of importance in Thomas Burt's life. Peter has also responded by correspondence to my many requests for information about his grandfather. Ian Lavery arranged for my visit to the Ellington Colliery in Northumberland, an experience I will never forget.

The secretarial staff at the History Department at Youngstown State University were always cooperative. William Jenkins, chair of the History Department, and George Beelen, past chair, were most supportive of my research and writing. The university provided me with two opportunities to undertake research in Britain.

Chapter 1

FORMATIVE YEARS

Thomas Burt was born on 12 November 1837, in Murton Row, Northumberland, a small hamlet of about fifteen single-room cottages located two miles north of the Tyne River and three miles from the North Sea. The derelict cottages were demolished some time after early 1939.[1] A large stone marker in front of the Preston Grange Primary School marks what was once Murton Row. Not only has Murton Row ceased to exist; little remains of the vast coal-mining world into which Thomas Burt was born and to which he devoted his entire life. Coal mining is an extractive industry, and when pits are exhausted or deemed too inefficient to operate, they are abandoned. The last National Coal Board deep-level mine in Northumberland ceased operations in the 1990s. Open-pit mining now predominates.

Yet evidence of the great coal-mining period of the nineteenth and early twentieth centuries still exists. Roads dip over old mines that have collapsed. Many cemeteries contain memorials to pit disasters. Burt Hall, built by the Northumberland Miners' Association as its offices in the 1890s, still stands in red-brick splendour, now owned by the University of Northumbria, while Aged Miners' Homes dot the villages of Northumberland, a testimony to the benevolence of the miners. Area museums keep the mining heritage alive: the Beamish Open Air Museum includes a pit village; the Washington 'F' Pit Museum maintains a winding engine; and the Woodhorn Colliery Museum displays banners of mining lodges and memorabilia of Thomas Burt. The Stephenson Railway Museum contains a steam engine, built in 1950, named the 'Thomas Burt'.

* * *

Burt's memories of his childhood were, on the whole, very positive, even though he enjoyed few material comforts.[2] The cottage at Murton Row was typical of the housing provided for miners, with a single ground-floor room serving as the kitchen, living area and bedroom, with an attic – reached by a ladder – for additional sleeping space.

Burt's fondest memories were of his relatives. Both sides of Burt's family were associated with coal mining. His father, Peter, was born in 1810 at Hebburn, just south of the Tyne, to Peter Burt and Margaret Davison Burt. Thomas Burt's father came from a family of three sisters and five brothers, all of whom were coal hewers. Thomas Burt's mother, Rebekah, was four years younger than her husband. She was of the Weatherburn family, most of whom were colliery enginemen.

By the time Thomas Burt was fifteen years old, his family had moved eighteen times.[3] After a short stay at Murton Row, the family moved to Whitley (now Whitley Bay), and then to the Seghill colliery, where Burt lived from about age three to seven. Burt recalled a life similar to 'that of tens of thousands of pit children of that time'.[4] He played games, including marbles and kite-flying, watched older boys bathe in a burn near the Burt home at New Row (later called Blake Town), and admired the huge standing engine, its wheels and ropes drawing the coal wagons from the Cramlington collieries.

All was not well in the coal fields, however. Burt seldom saw his father, who laboured long hours at a dangerous job for which he received meagre compensation. Hewers were paid by their productivity, and masters refused to pay for tubs that included too much 'small' coal. One day at Seghill the inspector struck off seven of Peter Burt's eight tubs of coal, to which Burt responded to his companion:

> Aw's sure, Tommy Niel, this day has me sair hurt,
> He's laid seven out of eight for poor Peter Burt.[5]

Grievances such as these helped lead to major strikes in the North East in the 1830s and 1840s.

The North East had long played an important role in England's coal trade. In 1830 the area produced over 22 per cent of the nation's coal, the greatest of any single region, and provided most of the coal for the London market. The Newcastle and Durham coalfields dominated the coastal trade and generated over two-thirds of Britain's coal exports.[6] Coal producers in the Tyne and Wear area regulated output for the London market by a rather complicated system, the Limitation of the Vend, which allocated the output of participating coal producers. The Vend, which operated with some interruptions from 1771 to 1844, ended when production and competition increased.[7]

Disagreements and competition among the coal producers were paralleled by confrontations between miners and masters (owners) in the 1830s and 1840s. Beginning in 1825 Tommy Hepburn's union worked to alter the yearly bond, which regulated working conditions and pay rates and provided continuous employment over the year. The union also attempted to curtail the long work days of the boys; to stop the truck system requiring miners to purchase goods at the company shop; and to restrict output to protect the health of the workers against the increasingly competitive capitalistic mining industry. While the strike in 1831 gained the miners concessions on wages and days of work, the owners broke the strike and the union in 1832 by importing 'blacklegs' (workers brought in to replace those on strike) and by utilizing the services of magistrates and militia to intimidate the miners.[8]

These encounters between masters and workers, between the politically privileged and the unfranchised, played an important role in shaping the mining world in which Burt grew up. Burt vaguely recalled that as a very young boy he watched cavalry ride through the streets of Whitley during the days of Chartist agitation.[9] More memorable to him was the seventeen-week miners' strike of 1844, which involved over 20,000 miners in the Durham and Northumberland coalfields. The strike revolved around the owners' strict enforcement of the yearly bond and the miners' demand for a higher guaranteed wage. The union, the Miners' Association of Great Britain and Ireland, was led by Martin Jude, a self-effacing man who had initially regarded strike action as premature. The owners broke the strike and the union by importing blacklegs to hew the coal, by encouraging tradesmen to deny credit to the strikers, and by evicting the mining families from the colliery-owned housing.[10]

Burt was six years old at the time of the strike, and his family was among those evicted from housing. Mine owners employed 'candymen' (unkempt local traders who collected rags and paid for goods with candy) to remove contents from the cottages. While many of the Seghill miners were forced to live in temporary outdoor shelters, Burt's family was provided with a cottage by a friendly farming family, the Duxfields. In addition to the four members of Peter Burt's family, several Weatherburn relatives, including the infant Mary whom Thomas Burt would later marry, were crammed into the small cottage. The family survived the ordeal, aided by credit from a merchant in Blyth named Hodgson. Burt himself could not recall suffering personal hardship; indeed, he rather enjoyed the novelty and freedom of living on a farm. The strike of 1844, however, was an important formative event in Burt's life. His father had actively supported the strike,[11] and in the winter of 1844–45 (a few months after the great strike) the family moved to the coalfields of County Durham, where they lived a semi-nomadic existence for six years before returning to Northumberland.

The bitter strike of 1844, as well as the earlier activities of 1831–32, became important and memorable hallmarks in labour's struggle in the North East to gain union recognition and economic justice. Two historians contend that the suffering occasioned by the 1844 strike helped to shape Burt and other labour leaders as proponents of conciliation.[12] As a union official, Burt often paid homage to the efforts of the early mining leaders. In November 1875, he spoke at the ceremonies when memorial markers were placed on the gravesites of Martin Jude at Elswick Cemetery and Thomas Hepburn at Heworth Churchyard. Burt remarked that his father had always taught him to 'reverence and esteem the names of Hepburn, Jude', and other early union leaders.[13]

Burt's formal education totalled no more than two years. While at Seghill in Northumberland and at Elemore and Haswell collieries in County Durham, he picked up some reading and writing skills. He was dismissed from the Haswell school after he refused to help the ill-tempered and violent teacher who had fallen while on a school ice-skating expedition. Burt's educational experience was by no means exceptional, either in its brevity or lack of substance. There were few schools in the coalfields, and their scope was limited.[14]

Many observers commented on the positive contributions that Methodists made towards the improvement of morals in the mining communities.[15] Burt grew up in a Primitive Methodist family, and his views on education, morals and labour unions were heavily shaped by this vibrant Methodist sect. Methodism had entered the North East early – John Wesley had preached in area villages in the 1740s. Primitive Methodism broke from Wesleyan Methodism in 1811, as the Primitives desired more tent meetings and revivals, advocated a greater amount of lay leadership, and were critical of the high level of monetary contributions expected of members. After 1821 Primitive Methodism became the sect in the North East that provided religious growth and aided and harboured political reformers.[16]

Burt recognized that Primitive Methodism moulded his character and shaped the mining community. His parents were Primitive Methodists, and his father and his uncle Andrew Burt were lay preachers. As a child Burt willingly attended religious services at the chapel and as a young man he taught Sunday school. He knew and admired the travelling preachers who would stay at their home. Burt respected Primitive Methodists because they showed 'practical sympathy with the aspirations and the efforts of the working people to achieve political and civil equality and to ameliorate their hard material condition'. Moreover, Primitive Methodists supported the temperance and trades union movements, both of which were 'democratic in spirit and in origin'.[17]

Primitive Methodists played a leading role in the miners' union activities in the North East. Burt identified several activitists in the 1831–32 and 1844 strikes as local Primitive Methodist preachers, and stressed that government reports heaped great blame on the Primitive Methodists for these labour problems.[18] Hugh Tremenheere, Commissioner of Mining, reported that the miners' unrest in the Earsdon parish in 1844 was fomented by Chartist leaders, union delegates and 'their local preachers, chiefly of the Primitive Methodists'. Charles Carr, an owner of the Seghill colliery, where Thomas Burt's father was working at the time, charged that the 'Primitive Methodists were the worst of the people at the time of the strike'.[19]

While mine owners and government authorities blamed Primitive Methodists for at least some of the violence, many scholars believe otherwise. Wearmouth, for example, maintains that Methodist miners often counselled against violence, even when they and their families were turned out of their homes and replaced by blacklegs.[20] Burt argued that Tremenheere's charges that the preachers 'encouraged violence and lawlessness' was a 'gross libel', but did reflect the 'ordinary conventional view of the situation during these turbulent times'.[21] There is no doubt, however, that the Primitive Methodists played an important leadership role in the mining communities and in union activities. In an age when illiteracy was still common the Primitive Methodists, skilled in reading and writing, were often pressed into positions of responsibility.[22] Moreover, the lack of centralized structure and formality within the mining communities and the Primitive Methodist chapels helped make it possible for individuals to work for the betterment of society.[23]

On 13 November 1847, the day after his tenth birthday, Thomas Burt began working underground at Haswell. Pits in the North East were mined by the bord and stall, or bord and pillar method. Tunnels, or bords, were driven parallel to each other through the coal, then cut through the remaining coal, leaving large pillars of coal to support the ceiling. Working as a team of two per shift, hewers mined their own bord and pillar area. Putters moved the coal in tubs on rails from the coal face to a station where the tubs were loaded on wagons, or rolleys, and then taken to the shaft. Traditionally, access to the mine was via a rope, from which miners hung with one leg in a sling. Coal was removed from the mine by baskets, or corves, attached to the ropes. Just before Burt began working at Haswell the mine introduced the cage for access to the mine and for removal of the coal. Coal tubs were loaded into the cages and taken to the surface where the coal was screened and separated by surface workers.

Mines in the North East were deep, and access to the pit was normally limited to a single shaft. Movement of air through the tunnels was essential to remove dangerous gases. A furnace at the bottom of the shaft created an air current by forcing the hot air up one side of the shaft while drawing cold air down the other. An intricate set of trap doors circulated this cold air through the tunnels and working stations.[24] Explosions remained a real danger, however, throughout the nineteenth century. On 28 September 1844, just three years before Burt entered the mine, an explosion ripped through the Haswell pit, killing ninety-five people by fire and choke-damp, a resulting gas.[25]

Burt graphically describes his life as a pit-boy in his *Autobiography*.

As in most North East mines, coal dust at Haswell was everywhere, created by hewing, shovelling and constant movement. Coal dust (which contributed to the explosion at Haswell) remained an unregulated condition and danger for much of the century. Darkness pervaded the pit, broken only by the dim light of lamps. Burt began work in the pit as a trapper-boy, a common task for newcomers. Trapper-boys opened and closed the ventilation doors. The work day was exceptionally long – about thirteen hours including the time entering and exiting the mine – and pay was only 10d. a day. While the work was not physically demanding, it was carried out in darkness and could be boring, especially when mining activity ceased due to a stoppage. Burt remarked that 'the dulness and loneliness were then oppressive'. He fell asleep on one occasion causing a putter to drive his tub through the closed door.

After a short term as a trapper, Burt became a donkey-driver at double the pay. At a steep incline, where the putter needed to move the loaded tub, Burt hitched the donkey, a fine old specimen by the name of Spanker, to the front of the tub. He later became a pony driver on the night shift, guiding an obedient and energetic pony named Lady. Danger lurked everywhere in the dimly lit mines, especially for youngsters, who tended to be careless. Shortly before leaving the Haswell pit, Burt was nearly crushed by the cage, his closest brush with death. He had unwittingly tried to enter the cage before it descended completely and he tumbled to the bottom of the shaft. A miner jumped in and removed him only moments before the heavy cage dropped into place at the bottom.

In 1848 the Burts moved to the Sherburn House pit owned by the Earl of Durham. While at this pit, Burt often engaged successfully in fist-fights with the exceptionally physical and quarrelsome boys. Burt was injured when his foot was run over by an empty tub, and again when he stepped into scalding water which had been emptied from a boiler. Burt was also exposed to labour disputes. The biggest issue at Sherburn – which festered throughout the North East for many years – was over the weighing of tubs, which determined the pay for the hewers. Managers all too often shorted or discounted tubs that were regarded as underweight. Burt often attended miners' meetings to hear the lively debates. These were held out of doors, as no halls or shelters were available to them. Much to his pride, his father and uncle, who often spoke, were highly regarded for their ideas.

South Hetton was the next stop for the Burts, where Burt 'spent some of the worst days' of his life, working at Murton (also known as Dalton or Datton) colliery. As a pony-putter, his work day stretched to fifteen hours. Though he was large and strong for his thirteen years, the hard work overtaxed him, and he believed it caused him health problems for the rest of his life. Accidents were common in the poorly-run pit: 'Never had I seen so many crutches, so many empty jacket sleeves, so many wooden legs.' His trials and tribulations in this terrible pit led him temporarily to excessive swearing.[26]

The Burt family left the Durham coalfields in about 1850, glad to return to Northumberland where their closest relatives still lived. After brief stops at the New Hartley and Cramlington collieries, they settled at Seaton Delaval for eight years. Burt became an expert putter (mover of the coal tubs), thus gaining the respect of hewers and earning decent money. At about eighteen he became a full-time hewer (miner) of coal. As a putter Burt had often worked as many as thirteen hours a day, but as a hewer he laboured eight hours bank-to-bank (from the time he entered the mine until he came out). As a hewer he earned about 5s. per day and worked on average nine days per fortnight or (two-week) pay period. Taking into account the various deductions for items such as tools and candles, and the occasional short work times, he estimated that he earned on average 21s. to 23s. a week, which he regarded as an acceptable wage for the family. (By this time, Burt was providing most of the income for the family, since poor health had forced his father to quit mining.) Hewers worked as a 'marrow', or a group of four, with two miners per shift cutting the coal and filling the tubs. Earnings for the fortnight were divided equally among the four. Every quarter the team would cavil, or ballot, for a work-place in the mine. Since work-places varied considerably in the thickness of the seam and the difficulty of removing the coal, a good cavil went a long way towards determining the earnings of a hewer. Cooperation in the marrow was also important in determining the output of the group. This form of mining was common in the bord and pillar system of the North East.[27]

While at Seaton Delaval, Burt began to educate himself through extensive reading. His father had a decent library, although it was heavily oriented towards religion. *Uncle Tom's Cabin*, which had a considerable vogue in England during the 1850s, was read aloud to the family and whetted Burt's interest in the abolition movement. He also read the autobiography of Frederick Douglass, as well as *Pilgrim's Progress*. Burt found in his father's library a book of essays by the American Unitarian leader William Ellery Channing. These essays introduced him to John Milton, and may also have planted in him seeds of interest in Unitarianism. (Later in life he occasionally attended the Church of Divine Unity in Newcastle.) With the increase in his free time as a hewer, Burt devoted much of this extra time to reading, and spent some of his money on acquiring a library. Usually he bought books in Newcastle – walking the nearly twenty-mile round trip in order to save money. Burt read relatively little 'light literature' throughout his life. He bought and read at this time, for example, Edward Gibbon's *Decline and Fall of the Roman Empire*. His self-education, however, did not simply involve voracious reading of the standard literature. He purchased education serials and used them as guides. He particularly utilized Cassell's *Popular Educator* to learn, with varied results, French, Latin and Greek.[28]

Miners at Seaton Delaval grew increasingly discontented because of several grievances, none of which the employers would acknowledge. When filling a tub, miners were required to separate the valuable large chunks of coal, called the round coal, from the smaller pieces. In 1859, employers not only struck tubs containing small coal from the total but began fining the hewers, seemingly at random, for sending it up. Though not formally organized, the miners called a work stoppage. The owners had nine miners tried for breach of contract. Eight miners, including Thomas Burt's uncle Robert Burt, were found guilty and sentenced to two months' hard labour at the Morpeth jail. Ironically, the eight selected had opposed the strike. They were excellent miners and well-educated leaders in the mining community, in addition to being teetotallers. Six were active Primitive Methodists. Thomas Burt was particularly disturbed by this deliberate abuse of authority against specifically selected, morally upright men. Shortly after this episode Burt, who had not participated in the strike, and his uncles were given notice to leave the mine. On 1 January 1860, they began work at the nearby Choppington colliery.[29]

Burt's personal responsibilities grew while at Choppington. On 27 February 1860, two months after arriving there, Burt married his cousin, Mary Weatherburn, in a quiet ceremony in nearby Bedlington. Burt was accompanied by his father, now listed in the records as a tea dealer. Burt was twenty-two years old, his wife eighteen. In his autobiography, Burt emphasized that the marriage was exceptionally successful, an ideal marriage of mutual help and admiration. Burt mentioned that his wife's education was less than his own. (A letter written by her on display at the Woodhorn Colliery Museum is quite crude in its penmanship and spelling.)[30] By 1861, Burt was the head of a large family that included his wife Mary and their infant daughter Rebekah; his father, age fifty and listed as a grocer; his forty-six-year-old mother Rebekah; and his brother Peter, a nineteen-year-old miner.[31] Burt's cottage was one of about one hundred situated next to the pit, which had opened in the late 1850s. According to an 1873 report, these cottages were of a 'very good class' with one room downstairs and one up. The upstairs room had a finished ceiling. There was also a pantry and 'other conveniences'. No roads were paved or flagged, however, so mud and dirt were constant problems, and sanitary conditions were exceptionally poor.[32] A Primitive Methodist church stood almost in the shadow of the colliery, and the Morpeth branch of the Blyth and Tyne railway ran nearby. Included in Burt's marrow was his brother Peter.[33] The work was steady and management reasonably good.

Joy was often mixed with sorrow. Burt was a compassionate man, as was exhibited by an incident in late 1860. A young friend of his died at Christmas time, apparently from a mining accident. In a letter to a newspaper editor, Burt displayed compassion and thoughtfulness, as well as a literary style that would become characteristic. The letter, excerpts of which follow, is the earliest example of his writing:

> Our rejoicings and our sorrowings are strangely intermixed. There is no season of the year when everybody can be happy ... It was my sad lot to attend the house of mourning. William Robinson (aged 17) of Seaton Delaval, a young man of great promise, died at Cramlington on Sunday Dec. 23rd 1860, and was interred at Seghill burial-ground on the 25th. His kindness of disposition, and his uniform courtesy to all with whom he came in to contact, made him a general favourite ... He was a youth of a very studious, inquisitive turn of mind, and at his early age had acquired an amount of information, seldom gained by any in his sphere of life ... His life of faith, his uniform consistency, and his ardent unpretending piety, justify the hope that he has realised a home beyond the grave where, all fare well ...

Burt admired and loved those like William Robinson who were interested, inquisitive, hard-working and polite. To a great extent, these characteristics describe Burt himself. He also exhibited a deference towards others that would be evident throughout his life – too much so, according to his critics. In his cover letter to the editor, he wrote:

> I have written the foregoing in hopes that you will insert it in your valuable paper. If you can conveniently do so, I believe you will. If you cannot insert it there is no harm done. Should you insert it, I hope you will 'right it up a bit.' I am but a young man, and quite a novice in the art of writing, so that there will likely be a few blunders in it.[34]

At Choppington, Burt became involved in several ventures. Having taken the temperance pledge at the age of fifteen, he was active in related organizations, serving as secretary of the Northern Federation of Temperance Societies and as a speaker at Band of Hope meetings. He was also the secretary of the joint committee of miners and employers that ran the colliery school.[35] Choppington gained a reputation as a centre of Radicalism. Miners questioned the value of the House of Lords and the Church of England, and became strong labour union supporters and local government activists, pushing authorities to improve the sanitary and water facilities. Religious dissent also became common: a Unitarian Chapel, located between the Sleek Burn and the railway station, was built in 1868.[36]

Burt remained an avid reader, and perhaps no author was so influential in shaping his life as John Ruskin. While Ruskin was not a political economist, his *Unto this Last* had an enormous impact on the study of political economy. Ruskin published this treatise in the new *Cornhill Magazine* in 1860, the year of Burt's arrival at Choppington. While Ruskin was not well read in the area of political economy, he offered two elements absent from the work of political economists: a literary style and a stress on the role of justice in political economy. Ruskin's concept of justice included not only a just wage, but the labourer's need for a constant wage and regular employment.[37] Burt was attracted to Ruskin for precisely these reasons – his literary style and his concept of justice. Burt stated that 'the style – so simple, so beautiful, so telling – captivated me'. He mentioned that while Ruskin did not deny the role of supply and demand as an economic element, he stressed that other factors were vital:

> Morality, justice, emotion, social affection, the temper – in a word, the soul – of the worker come into effective play as well as the laws of supply and demand. In the very first sentence of *Unto this Last* Ruskin strikes this keynote, and his booklet is a landmark in the history of the Labour movement.[38]

Burt's years at Choppington were important to his development. He was by this time responsible for a large extended family. He had become active in community affairs and his intellectual horizons expanded. On the whole, however, he lived a quiet life. From all evidence, he was content with his work, his family, his books and conversations, and his relatively limited involvement in public life. By 1865, however, a series of events in the coalfields of Northumberland and Durham would thrust him into the public limelight, where he would remain for the rest of his life.

Chapter 2

UNION LEADER

A series of events brought change to the coalfields of the North East in the 1860s and led to the formation of the Northumberland Miners' Mutual Confidence Association (hereafter referred to as the Northumberland Miners' Association, or the NMA). Burt was elected general secretary of the NMA two years after its establishment and found himself suddenly thrust into the limelight, where he remained for the rest of his life. He worked diligently from 1865 to the early 1870s to ensure the survival of the infant labour organization. In spite of public scorn heaped on him and the union by mine owners and coal miners alike, Burt finally convinced critics that he and the union were valuable assets to the mining community. His efforts reached fruition in 1872 when the union and the mine owners agreed to their first negotiated wage contract.

Three pit disasters shook the North East mining community in the early 1860s. On 2 March 1860, an explosion caused by a buildup of gas rocked the Burradon colliery in Northumberland, taking a total of seventy-four lives. Later that year on 20 December in Hetton colliery, County Durham, a blast took the lives of twenty-two men and boys. The greatest, and one of the most unusual tragedies, occurred on 16 January 1862, at New Hartley, Northumberland, when a huge beam from the pumping engine broke and fell into the mine shaft. Escape for those in the mine was impossible, since the mine had but one shaft. In spite of heroic efforts to reopen the shaft, all 204 men and boys trapped in the mine died from the buildup of gas.[1] Nine days after the New Hartley disaster, a group consisting mainly of miners met in Newcastle to discuss mining conditions. In addition to criticizing the government for its inadequate inspection system, the men passed a resolution urging the government to improve the safety of mines, specifically requiring that each colliery have at least two shafts.[2] Meetings held to arrange relief for the families suffering losses in the catastrophe led to the establishment of the Northumberland and Durham Miners' Permanent Relief Fund.[3]

While the disasters of the early 1860s promoted a degree of unity among the miners, it was the mine owners' attempt to impose new working conditions which prompted the movement to unionize. On 11 November 1862, the Steam Colliery Association,[4] which included owners in the Blyth area, agreed to reduce the wages of the hewers and the majority of other mine labourers, and to require that miners sign a yearly bond. Miners wishing to sign a monthly bond rather than the proposed yearly contract would be required to pay cottage rent and buy fire coal at the rate of 2s. per week.[5] Cottage and house coal had traditionally been provided by employers and were an important part of a hewer's family support.[6] Miners' opposition materialized immediately. By 23 December, officials of eight collieries reported that almost all hewers had refused to sign a yearly bond.[7] On 25 December two to three thousand miners from collieries in the vicinity of Blyth held a meeting on land owned by a Mrs Hardman at Horton. The miners voted enthusiastically to resist imposition of the yearly bond; addressed the issues of wage reductions and the need to decrease the hours of the boys; and approved a resolution to form a union. Following the outdoor meeting, several delegates went to 'The Folly', or 'Polly's Folly', a public house at Shankhouse (this pub, renamed the Albion Inn, was still standing in 1995, though abandoned), to plan the formation of the union.[8] Although Burt attended the meeting at Horton, he was not directly involved in this dispute. Since the Choppington colliery was not part of the Steam Collieries' Association, miners there had not received notices over the bond and wages.[9] The miners' resistance worked. Two days after the Horton rally, colliery owners reported that they had had no success in achieving the yearly bond and voted to rescind the resolution of 11 November 1862, 'in consequence of the want of unanimity in the Trade on the question of Hiring'.[10]

The new union held several meetings after the initial Horton rally, drawing up the rules of the Association and setting up a fund for those dismissed from their work for involvement in union activities. Durham miners became involved, and when the rules were approved at a mass meeting at Horton on 3 April 1863, it was for the 'Northumberland & Durham Miners' Mutual Confidence Association'. The purpose of the union was to protect the interests of the miner. Charter language emphasized moderation and avoidance of strikes.[11]

The fledgling union was immediately beset by problems, with violence or strikes at the Ashington, Newsham and Seghill collieries in Northumberland.[12] Durham miners, dissatisfied with the yearly bond and the method of counting coal tubs, engaged in a wave of futile strikes.[13] Miners at the Choppington colliery, where Burt worked, were slow to join the union, as they were quite satisfied with their employer. After a branch formed at Choppington, Burt attended meetings and participated in discussions. In early 1864 he was elected as a delegate to the union's council meetings and was shortly thereafter selected for the Executive Committee. The union often asked him to write letters to the newspapers defending the association, and to speak at rallies. In his *Autobiography*, Burt contended that Northumberland miners believed that the readiness with which the Durham miners struck 'without counting the cost' could lead to the demise of the union.[14] The miners also feared that the area of Durham and Northumberland was simply too large to govern effectively. In a meeting at Plessy, Northumberland miners determined to go their own way. Burt was selected to call for the separation of the Association into two unions, which he did at the annual meeting on 3 June 1864. The parting of the ways was apparently amicable. Each union retained one of the two agents, William Crawford remaining with Northumberland.[15] The Durham association languished and died. A new organization, the Durham Miners' Association, was formed in 1869 and quickly surpassed the Northumberland union in size and power.[16]

Burt obviously enjoyed the support of the miners, for they elected him to important positions in the young union. In June 1865, he and Crawford were selected to present evidence to a government committee in London examining conditions in the mines. This was Burt's first visit to the great metropolis; he found it fascinating, as he would for the rest of his life. He also met Alexander McDonald, the miners' leader from Scotland who had helped set up the committee and had encouraged Burt and Crawford to testify. Burt admired McDonald for his ability and devotion to the miners' cause,[17] and would later become a close collaborator with him in both union and parliamentary affairs.

In 1865 Crawford resigned his position as secretary of the Northumberland union to take more secure employment as manager of the cooperative store in Blyth. When the Choppington miners proposed Burt as Crawford's successor, the twenty-seven-year-old Burt was reluctant to seek the post, as he had little ambition for public office, and he feared that he would lose his treasured privacy. Moreover, his salary would be cut to 27s. 6d. per week, and from this he had to pay house rent and buy fire coal. In addition, the union was weak, as membership was small and funds minimal. Choppington miners continued to press him, however, and at a delegate meeting at the Astley Arms, Seaton Delaval, on 15 July 1865, Burt was unexpectedly elected over three other nominees. He took up the position almost immediately, and moved to Cowpen Quay, Blyth, a town centrally located for union affairs. His home there also served as the union's headquarters. After one year as secretary, his salary was increased from 27s. 6d. to 30s. a week.[18]

Even as the union struggled to survive, the miners paused to celebrate their labour and their organization. In 1864 the NMA held its first picnic at Polly's Folly in Shankhouse, just north of the Cramlington Colliery's Amelia Pit. The second picnic was held on 12 June 1865, at a field at the Blyth Links House.[19] This Northumberland picnic, or gala, predated by several years the celebrated Durham miners' gala, which began in the early 1870s.[20]

When Burt assumed the position of secretary in August, 1865, the union had twenty lodges with 4,000 members, and a total of £23 in the treasury. In his *Autobiography*, written some fifty years later, Burt remembered having taken personal stock of his strengths and weaknesses upon assuming office. He was, he recorded, 'almost entirely inexperienced and untrained ... shy, retiring, unaggressive ... inclined more towards quiet meditation than to an active public life'. He was also 'strongly and whole-heartedly democratic', an 'ardent trade-unionist', and 'more of an organizer than an agitator'. He personally carried out most of the work of the union, since the president and the treasurer both worked full-time at their occupations. As secretary, he maintained the financial records, conducted correspondence and worked to expand membership.[21]

A few days after the annual picnic and shortly before Burt became secretary, one of the most bitter and memorable strikes in Northumberland history erupted. On 17 June 1865, six to seven hundred miners at Cramlington struck after the employer, Mr Potter, refused to concede a modest wage increase, which the miners argued they deserved due to the difficulty of gaining some of the coal. The strike began at the West Cramlington pit, where miners 'had struck twenty-three times in twenty-two years'.[22] The union offered its services to help negotiate a settlement, but management refused. The difference over wages was minimal, but the strike quickly became a contest of wills between the coal owners' association and the miners' union. The union supported the strikers financially, while the Steam Colliery Association subsidized the Cramlington mine owner.[23] During the long strike, Burt wrote letters to various newspapers and spoke at rallies, explaining the position of the strikers and the association. In August, he defended the strikers' wage demands, contending that a particularly thin coal seam made mining difficult.[24] He also criticized the owner and the coal owners' association for refusing the miners' offer of arbitration and for attempting to break the union.[25]

The affair became ugly when the company, following a directive of the owners' association, took steps to eject the miners and their families from colliery-owned cottages in bitter October weather.[26] Miners, angered by heavy-handed measures and the careless conduct of the candymen brought in to remove belongings, verbally harassed them, threw stones, tore off their clothes, and banged loudly on large metal sheets to disturb the horses. Police and soldiers restored order, and six people were arrested for participating in the disturbance.[27] While Burt pleaded with the miners to avoid additional violence, he laid heavy blame for the disturbance on the owner, who had brutally turned people out of their homes in terrible weather. Moreover, miners could not leave and find work elsewhere, since they had been prohibited by other mine owners from gaining employment.[28] By November the owner, encouraged by the coal owners' association, began to recruit replacement miners from other districts, including Cornwall and Staffordshire. Burt and other officials worked hard to dissuade these miners from accepting employment at Cramlington. Evictions continued, with forty more cottages cleared on 16 and 17 November.[29]

From 21 to 24 November, the Miners' National Conference met in Newcastle. Alexander McDonald presided over the meeting of representatives from many coal districts. Delegates discussed the Cramlington strike, and raised the question of forming a larger union from the several districts. Northumberland delegates spoke strongly against such a development. Burt maintained that Northumberland miners wanted power to remain within their local society and not with a larger body. While a national miners' organization could discuss general matters, it should not be responsible for settling strikes. He argued that effectiveness would only come from the strength of local unions. To become part of a larger union at this time would simply weaken the local association. Burt summed up his argument by citing Alexander Pope:

> Like Kings we lose the conquests gained before
> By vain ambitions still to make them more.[30]

This reluctance on the part of the NMA to join a larger union was present from the very beginning of the organization, and might have stemmed from the unfortunate experience of the union with Durham.

In the midst of this conference a series of letters about the Cramlington strike and the role of the union and its leader, Thomas Burt, appeared in Newcastle area newspapers. On 11 November, a long letter from Burt about the actions of the coal owners had been printed in the *Morpeth Herald*. He charged, in particularly biting phrases, that they were

> turning to the door their old servants who have served them all their lives, and contributed to their immense wealth, preventing these men from procuring employment in other parts of the county, and trying by means the most artful and despicable to force the men to submit to their hard and unjust terms.[31]

On 24 November a long anonymous letter by a mine owner appeared in the *Newcastle Daily Chronicle* in response to Burt's letter. The reply was so disparaging that it likely gained Burt and other leaders additional support. The core of the argument was that as the union had attempted to dissuade miners from working the pit, so the owner was entitled to take the steps necessary to have his coal mine worked. The writer argued that the poor unsuspecting miners had 'put themselves in the hands of demagogues' or 'Jackalls' to bargain with the owners.[32]

The miners at the Newcastle meeting engaged in a long discussion about the contents of the owner's letter. McDonald and John Nixon, the NMA president, were particularly disturbed with the tone of the letter, which was directed at Burt, the miners and the conference itself. Burt, who had preferred to ignore the issue, finally agreed to respond.[33] He opened his letter by charging that the *Chronicle* would not have published the letter had it been written by a poor person rather than a wealthy mine owner. He was glad to see it in print, however, since such an ' "able" piece of literary composition' should not be hidden. He had not been disturbed by the attack on him personally, for the coalowner did not have the 'skill to wound'. Citing Macaulay's comment on an opponent, Burt said the coal owner was like a 'juggler's snake. The bags of poison are full, but the fang is wanting'.[34]

The *Newcastle Daily Chronicle* devoted a long editorial to the owner's initial letter and Burt's response. The purpose in publishing the letters, the *Chronicle* contended, was to present both sides of the story. Of the two letters, the newspaper stressed, the coal owner's seemed the more unreasonable, Burt's the more calm and measured.[35]

Burt's numerous letters to the press and his controversy with the mine owner brought him to the attention of Joseph Cowen, the owner of the daily and weekly *Newcastle Chronicle*. Cowen, a Radical and a supporter of the right of labourers to organize, used his newspapers in the great pit disasters of the early 1860s to push for effective government safety rules. During this period, Cowen's *Daily Chronicle* developed into a powerful provincial paper which enjoyed respect nationwide. The *Chronicle* newspapers normally lent Burt and the miners excellent coverage as well as editorial support. A remarkable platform orator, Cowen was the most popular and powerful speaker in the Newcastle area, and would later serve with Burt in Parliament.[36] After the two met, Cowen introduced Burt to the *Chronicle* writers as the 'young pitman who had so effectively answered and silenced the coalowner'.[37] Among the staff Burt met was W. E. Adams, a Chartist and Radical who had been recruited by Cowen in 1863 to run the *Weekly Chronicle*, to which Adams also contributed a weekly political column under the pseudonym 'Ironside'. Adams, a powerful and respected writer and a consistent defender of workers' rights, became Burt's friend.[38] The columns of the *Chronicle* newspapers were almost always open to Burt.

The miners had selected a secretary who was certainly the match of any opponent when it came to the pen. But this remarkable facility with words did not lead to success in the Cramlington strike. In December 1865, the owner brought in labourers from Cornwall to work the mine.[39] The trial for the six charged with rioting at Cramlington in October took place on 5 January 1866. All were found guilty and received sentences ranging from six to nine months in jail with heavy labour. Bail arrangement, trial expenses and support of the dependents of miners who served time in jail were costly for the association.[40]

Burt always contended that the strike strengthened the young union. Although the strike cost the union dearly, with estimates running from four to ten thousand pounds, the special levy paid weekly by union members to maintain the strikers and their families resulted in long-lasting unity and loyalty. Moreover, while the union began the strike with virtually no funds, it had about £700 at the end. Burt stressed that while it had been the practice before the strike to leave funds with the local colliery branches, it subsequently became policy for the central association to control the funds. The most important lesson of the strike for Burt, however, was that extremists in both the miners' and owners' camps took positions that failed and should not be repeated. Burt the arbitrator often referred to this strike as an example of how labour relations should not be conducted. He saw it as the 'last strike of the old pattern'.[41]

For the next five or six years, Burt devoted much of his time to consolidating the NMA, working to expand its membership, building up its funds, making it respectable and trying to get the coal owners' association to the negotiating table. The union developed comprehensive rules throughout the 1860s and early 1870s. After September 1873, the size of a lodge determined the number of votes it could cast at a delegate assembly. Until June 1870, approval to call a strike required a simple majority of those voting. After 1870, rules called for a two-thirds majority to begin or continue a strike. The NMA had to hold mass meetings of the miners to explain the issues before a general county-wide strike could commence. When a strike in a single colliery began, control of the strike moved to the central executive committee, although the colliery could continue to negotiate and settle, providing the offer was acceptable to the association.[42]

Mine owners constantly tested the young union. For example, in the late 1860s, Thomas Forster, owner of the Seaton Delaval colliery, refused to pay miners for tubs of coal that contained an excessive amount of small coal. Burt, reluctant to call a strike, instead held a meeting of 5,000 miners. At the huge rally of 5 October 1868, Burt criticized the owner, charging that both men and boys were overworked in a mine which required a long walk to the face.[43] In a letter shortly thereafter, Burt complained that several of the oldest and longest-serving miners at Seaton Delaval had been dismissed at a time when business was very brisk and owners were short of hands. Cause of dismissal, according to Burt, was for engaging in union activities, including one miner who spoke at the October rally. 'His offence', Burt said, 'was that he dared to exercise the right of free speech in a free country.'[44] While the conflict at Seaton Delaval did not lead to a strike, it did illustrate a major problem for the union. Commenting many years later, Burt said that in the first ten years employers often fired miners who were active in the union: 'scarcely a Committee meeting was held but they had to deal with victimized members'.[45]

Meaningful negotiations between the miners' and the owners' associations began in the early 1870s. That the owners would agree to come to the negotiating table appears logical, at least in hindsight. The coal trade was expanding and healthy, and owners wanted to avoid difficulties with their labour force. The union was by all indications well-organized and led by a secretary and other officials who were pledged to seek amicable settlements. The recent long, bitter, but successful engineers' strike in the Newcastle area, waged especially over the length of the workday, may also have encouraged the owners to negotiate.[46] The first formal meeting between a deputation from the union and members of the coal owners' association occurred on 2 December 1871.[47] The main issue was the length of the boys' work-day. At the annual picnic on 17 July 1871, Burt spoke about the need to reduce the hours that boys worked in the mines – this was commonly thirteen hours bank-to-bank. Although he accepted the owners' argument that reduced hours would mean less productivity, and that the hewers would earn less, he believed that one should not

> live and thrive on the ruin and degradations of others, and especially of the young. These boys are the men of the next generation, and is it not worth considering whether, as a matter of economy, it is not wise to risk getting less coal now for the sake of having a stronger, a more intelligent, and better developed class of workmen in the future?[48]

The goal of the miners' union was to reduce the boys' hours to ten, but negotiations with the owners on 2 December 1871, which Fynes said involved 'some friendly and good-tempered discussion', ended with a compromise of eleven. The owners argued that a bill winding its way through Parliament would likely lead to a reduction to ten hours, thus satisfying the miners.[49] Ironically, this argument was accepted by NMA leaders.[50] While the union's delegate assembly approved the proposal, not every miner was satisfied. Ralph Young, a strong union man, thought that the NMA officials had shown ineffective leadership and should have held out for a negotiated ten hours, which could easily have been won.[51] Why did Burt and others accept this compromise with the owners? Burt was probably of a mind that the miners be perceived as reasonable men, agreeable to discussing problems and settling them through compromise. He was still building a union that needed the respect of the public as well as the mine owners.[52] As it was, the Mines' Act passed Parliament in 1872, reducing boys' hours to ten.

Two months after the meeting about boys' hours, the two sides met again, this time over wages. The steam coal trade was thriving in the early 1870s, substantially increasing the price of coal. On 27 January 1872, union delegates met at Seaton Delaval, and after extensive discussion – including some remarks critical of the executive committee – agreed to ask for an advance in wages of 15 per cent. Three officials, including Burt, then drew up a circular, or memorial, which they sent to the owners, calling for the advance and requesting a meeting to discuss the proposal. Seven union officials, including Burt, Nixon and Young, met with owners at the latter's offices on 3 February. Burt explained the basis of the miners' request for an advance of 15 per cent. The owners countered with an offer of 10 per cent, saying that 15 per cent was too much, since they had not reduced wages in 1868 when many other owners had. The union negotiators accepted the 10 per cent offer. A delegate assembly approved the offer with twenty-four delegates voting for 10 per cent, thirteen still calling for 15 per cent.[53]

Thus the pattern for negotiations was set for many years: memorials, meetings, counter-proposals and delegate assembly approval, often with some opposition to the settlement in the assembly. Burt was always the chief spokesperson for the Association. Why had the coalowners agreed to these negotiations over wages, something they had steadfastly refused? Roy Church presents a convincing argument that the 'employers probably regarded the executive as more amenable to persuasion and argument than the rank and file'. Indeed, after the initial agreement on wages, the miners' negotiating team, according to the minutes of the coal owners' association, promised 'to use its influence with the Boys to keep them steady in their work'.[54] Burt believed that the miners had to honour a signed contract and regularly report to work. He would not apologize for such a stance; indeed, he always pointed with pride to the fact that, with rare exceptions, the Northumberland miners respected a signed agreement.

Not everyone in the Association was satisfied with this state of affairs, and the leaders came under intense and apparently vicious criticism. In early 1872, a proposal was made to increase Burt's pay, which had been relatively low, and to appoint an assistant-secretary to help conduct the business of the organization. Until this time, Burt had been the only paid official. Some miners bitterly opposed this proposal. The cause of much of the criticism stemmed from the willingness on the part of Burt and the other negotiators to accept and support the 10 per cent pay increase instead of 15 per cent.[55]

Burt defended himself in a letter dated 3 April 1872, which was distributed to all the miners and printed in the newspapers.[56] In this letter, Burt complained about the personal, often anonymous, attacks on him that used 'the most coarse, the most vulgar and abusive' language. He also charged that while the Northumberland miners were well paid, some were unwilling to provide just compensation to the agent, who received less than agents in comparable positions. He also stressed that the proposed position of assistant-secretary was for the Association's benefit, not his. He had considered resigning, but had decided that such an act 'would be unfair to the Association, and to the great mass of the men, against whom, I repeat, I have no complaint'. If he was to continue as the agent, he requested that 'Something must be done to protect me and other leading men against the personal attacks, in meetings at any rate, of the evil-disposed and ignorant.' He also claimed the right to live a private life and to enjoy leisure as he wished. He claimed the right to speak on issues as he saw fit:

> I will never consent to become the mere tool and mouth-piece for any man, or any body of men. What I am convinced is right, I shall ever advocate to the best of my ability; and what I am convinced is wrong, I shall ever oppose, whether popular or unpopular. To act otherwise would be to degrade myself, and ultimately to become useless to you.

As for the pay question, he said that the Association would have to decide. He did not expect a lot, but he did want 'sufficient to maintain my family'.

At the 13 May delegate meeting Burt gained support for all his requests: members passed a vote of confidence in his leadership, and approved a resolution providing that charges lodged against officers be brought to a delegate assembly so that the accused could defend themselves. A final motion assured that 'our Agent [is] entitled to the same privileges as to leisure time as we ourselves possess'. The delegates also voted to increase Burt's pay to £2 10s. a week.[57] The whole process strengthened Burt's position within the Association. Fynes wrote that 'a powerful reaction set in in his favour; and he became more popular and influential than ever he had been'.[58] The issues of Burt's leadership and pay never entirely disappeared, however. They resurfaced, especially in 1887 and 1909.

Demand for coal in the early 1870s was high, and its price increased dramatically. Arguing on the basis of these price increases, the NMA demanded and received several advances in wages in 1872 and early 1873.[59] The miners came under criticism for having driven up the price of coal. Some economists and journalists, however, stressed that the miners' wages, which were a relatively small part of the total cost, had not been the cause of the price increase. Rather, the owners were taking advantage of a marked increase in the demand for their product in the iron trade and in foreign markets.[60]

Such arguments among economists over the movements of prices and wages were common in the 1870s and Burt understood these arguments. After he became union secretary in 1865, Burt felt he had to know 'how far the doctrines of political economy had a direct bearing upon the interests of labour and upon the basis of workmen's unions'. We have seen that he was influenced earlier by Ruskin's views on political economy; he now examined the ideas of Adam Smith, John Stuart Mill and William Thornton.[61] While Smith and Mill are familiar figures, Thornton is relatively unknown. Thornton worked at India House, where he was secretary for public works and a colleague and close friend of Mill. He spent much of his leisure time in literary pursuits; his *On Labour* appeared in 1869.[62]

Burt carefully examined Smith's *The Wealth of Nations*, Mill's *Principles of Political Economy*, and Thornton's *On Labour*. All three writers stressed the need for unions. Thornton was the most forceful in advancing the cause of workers' associations.[63] Given the environment in which he was raised, Burt did not need political economists to tell him the necessity or justification for unions, but he appreciated the intellectual reinforcement of his viewpoint. The wage issue was the primary item involved in collective bargaining, and political economists hotly debated how high wages could go. Mill argued that while the supply and demand for labour helped determine wages, wages were also tied specifically to the capital available and could never be greater than the total wages fund.[64] If one accepted this wages theory, Burt argued, then 'trade unions were, indeed, powerless, or almost powerless, to influence wages'. According to Burt, Thornton demolished the wages fund theory by pointing out that each employer was free to set his own level of wages; indeed, Mill accepted Thornton's arguments.[65] There is some question, however, of how quickly Thornton's viewpoint was adopted. Eugenio Biagini indicates that while Thornton's book was published in 1869, neither Burt nor other labour leaders recognized its significance until at least 1875,[66] after the first several wage settlements between the NMA and the Northumberland coal owners.

Burt vigorously defended the ability of unions to affect wages, but he also believed that such power was limited. To him, wages were closely tied to the price of coal, and therefore a reflection of supply and demand. He was wedded to the classical economists' concept of a market economy. He intensely disliked union efforts to restrict output in order to increase wages, and preferred to use negotiation to bring wages in line with coal prices. He believed that cooperation between the two parties would result in a common end – winning the coal and earning a living. Throughout his long career he generally counselled against strikes, and to a great extent reflected Thornton's assessment of union leaders:

They [union leaders] take a natural pride in the wealth of their society, and do not like to see it wasted, and experience has taught them that, even when there is an object worth striking for, a strike is a very wasteful mode of attaining it. The consequence is, that the executory of any one of the larger trades' unions, instead of being the most bellicose, is commonly the most pacific section of the whole community. Instead of originating strikes, it sanctions them only as a last resource.[67]

Burt's advocacy of conciliation and arbitration, while supported by many Northumberland miners, was often opposed by an element who wanted Burt and other leaders to be far more vigorous in pushing for better wages and working conditions.

The year 1872, which saw significant contacts between the union and owners, also brought changes in union leadership. John Nixon, who had long served as president while working full-time as a checkweighman, was elected to the salaried position of assistant-secretary, giving some relief to Burt. Burt got along well with Nixon, describing him as 'a man of high character, of exceptional intelligence, of sound judgement, of moderate views, and of a most conciliatory disposition'.[68] Ralph Young, who became treasurer and eventually served as a paid official, was particularly valuable in understanding financial information. Like Burt, he was self-educated and had broad intellectual interests.[69] The union headquarters moved in 1872 from Blyth to Newcastle, that city being more centrally located to serve the union's membership, which had come to include collieries to the west of Newcastle. Moreover, the coal owners' association was located in Newcastle. In 1873, the NMA purchased houses in Lovaine Crescent (which bordered on the Blyth and Tyne Railway), turning one into an office and committee room for the Association. Two adjoining houses provided accommodation for Nixon and for Burt and his family. Burt lived at that site for fifteen years.[70]

Burt and other union officials were exceptionally busy. For the first ten years of the union, Burt normally spoke at colliery meetings four nights a week, 'besides acting as a sort of missionary in visiting non-union collieries, to bring them into the Union fold'.[71] Union officials were involved in any pit closure, wage dispute, or accident. While Burt did not mind criticism of union officials, he very much preferred that such discontent be aired in the proper setting. He always wanted the miners and their leaders to appear reasonable and capable of solving their own problems.[72] Moreover, once the owners' association agreed to meet with the union, preparing for those sessions involved considerable time.

The healthy coal trade led to the establishment of the Joint Committee in February 1873. Burt always regarded this as one of the great breakthroughs in collective bargaining. The wage increases which the miners' union and the owners' association negotiated provided the base wages for all the member collieries. Conditions varied considerably from one mine to another, however, and miners demanded that local circumstances be considered in determining their wages.

According to Church, the constant demand by local collieries for wage increases weighed heavily on the union officials and may have been partly responsible for the formation of the Joint Committee.[73] The committee consisted of six representatives from each side who met regularly to settle local disputes or disagreements not covered under the general county-wide agreement. These disputes often involved wages and working conditions. Burt was among the original six elected to the Joint Committee by the NMA delegate assembly.[74] In an article written for *Shipping World* in 1908, Burt proudly noted that the Joint Committee was still in existence, having helped to bring peace to the individual collieries.[75]

Burt and the union were also active in the early 1870s in many other areas of the miners' lives, including housing and pit safety. While Burt's concern over safety was often expressed in local meetings, he also pursued this issue through his involvement in the Miners' National Association (MNA), which was founded in 1863 under the leadership of Alexander McDonald. The purpose of the MNA was to improve the lot of miners, primarily through legislative action. The MNA was organized around county unions (such as Durham, Northumberland and South Yorkshire), and encouraged conciliation and arbitration rather than industrial action. Another organization, the Amalgamated Association of Miners (AAM), was formed in 1869, with its base in Wales, Lancashire and the West Midlands. The AAM was a national rather than a county-based organization, and was more strike-oriented than the MNA. The MNA found the aggressive attitude of the AAM unacceptable, and the two eventually emerged as rivals.[76] While both associations thrived during the period of expanding demand for coal in the early 1870s, the downturn of the mid-seventies forced the MNA to reorganize and caused the AAM to fail altogether.

Historians interested in the development of coalfield unionism have extensively debated the roles played by McDonald and Burt. Critics see them as directed more towards conciliatory practices and county associations.[77] Burt would certainly have agreed with this description. He saw the MNA primarily as a way to educate miners on the importance of developing strong local unions, the public and owners on the benefits of strong unions, and Parliament on its duty to provide necessary protection for miners. He had little interest in devoting time and effort towards a centralized national association. The MNA did play an important role in encouraging the establishment of unions. Burt personally appeared countless times throughout Britain extolling the benefits of unionization. At the same time, the MNA and Burt fought for the passage of better safety measures. Burt worked hard, locally and nationally, for the passage of the Mines' Regulation Bill, which was finally passed in 1872.[78] He regarded the act as a 'triumph' of the miners themselves, who through their unions had intimately shaped the bill to reflect their needs. The act provided for a strengthened inspectorate, protection of the checkweighmen from arbitrary dismissal, and an increase in the minimum age for boy workers to twelve.[79]

Burt was also concerned over the state of the miners' housing. Traditionally, mine owners in the North East provided cottages for the miners at no cost. At the annual picnic in June 1872, Burt stated that while the NMA had thus far concentrated on improving wages and working conditions, it was now expanding its objectives to include better housing and political enfranchisement. He specifically thanked the owners for having recently built cottages that were adequate, but emphasized that too many were 'old, ricketty, dilapidated, tumble-down hovels, which were not fit for human beings to live in'.[80] From October 1872 to early 1874, the *Newcastle Weekly Chronicle* carried a major series on miners' villages describing the generally deplorable living accommodations in pit villages. Also in 1872, the London *Daily News* sent a reporter to investigate colliery life in the North East. Burt accompanied the reporter, Archibald Forbes, to one of the villages. Forbes was impressed by how neat and friendly the housewives were in such generally appalling conditions.[81] In spite of the efforts of the union, housing conditions seem to have changed slowly, although new housing was better laid out and constructed. Housing remained a contentious issue, however, as owners often attempted to charge miners for what were normally free accommodations.

Burt's life had changed dramatically after 1865, when he became the executive secretary of the NMA. By 1873 the NMA was an established labour union and Burt played a key role in its success. His life would be altered again in 1874, upon his election to Parliament.

Chapter 3

ELECTION TO PARLIAMENT

When Burt declared at the miners' picnic of 10 June 1872 that the miners were going to work to gain political enfranchisement, efforts towards that end were already well underway. The franchise reform movement of the miners in the early 1870s not only affected their lives, but had a pivotal impact on Burt's career, culminating in his election to Parliament in 1874.

The miners and other workers in the North East were involved in franchise reform during the Chartist era of the 1830s and 1840s. Although the working class was frustrated in this early effort to gain the vote, the movement gained momentum in the 1860s.[1] The Northern Reform League, a product of the broad reform movement, was founded in November 1866, in order to gain universal manhood suffrage and a secret ballot. While the League's council consisted predominantly of members of labour unions, other prominent council leaders included Cowen and Adams of Newcastle's *Chronicles*, and Newcastle Unitarian minister Rev. J. C. Street. An old Chartist and long-time advocate of universal suffrage, Adams handled much of the League's publicity.[2] Reform meetings were held in the Newcastle area 10–12 December 1866, with Burt on the platform on the last day.[3] The League sponsored a great Reform demonstration at the Newcastle town hall and on the moor on 28 January 1867. An estimated 25,000 marched in the parade, with the NMA contributing bands and banners from fourteen collieries. At each of the six platforms set up on the moor, resolutions were introduced and subjected to a vote. Speaking at the No. 2 platform, Burt introduced the first resolution, which protested Parliament's portrayal of workers as immoral and indifferent to reform. Burt emphasized that the working class, simply by participating in the demonstration, displayed its interest in reform. He argued that it was wrong that workers should serve in the army and pay taxes, yet not be able to vote.[4]

While the Reform Act of 1867 enfranchised a substantial number of urban workers, its application was at best irregular. Although there were a few exceptions, it did not provide the vote for coal miners in the North East. A concerted attempt to enfranchise miners began in the borough of Morpeth in the early 1870s. The borough had long been under the control of the Howard family, headed by the Earl of Carlisle.[5] The act of 1867 had expanded the borough to include the mining villages of Bedlington, Choppington, Bebside, Newsham, Cambois and Cowpen, and the coal port of Blyth.

The franchise movement in the borough of Morpeth began over a local government issue.[6] In 1871 Thomas Glassey, a miner at Choppington Guide Post, led a successful movement to elect Dr James Trotter, a pit doctor, to the local board of health in order to gain better sanitary facilities. During the campaign, Glassey realized that few miners could vote. The miners had not been enfranchised after the 1867 Reform Act. Since they were regarded as inhabiting their colliery houses as a prerequisite of their employment, the miners were viewed essentially as servants, and not as occupiers paying rates or taxes for the Poor Law, a basis for enfranchisement. Glassey believed that miners should possess the right to vote in local and parliamentary elections, and began the drive to extend the vote to them in the borough.

While Burt's personal involvement in the franchise movement was limited, he became the focal point of what was ultimately a crusade. The leaders of the movement decided early that the quest to gain the vote would be tied directly to electing the popular Burt to Parliament. These leaders would play an important part in Burt's political and personal life. Robert Trotter, Choppington, and James Trotter, Bedlington, were from a family of several brothers, all of whom practised medicine in the Northumberland area. James Trotter was a close friend of Burt, and would serve as his political adviser especially on constituency matters when Burt sat in Parliament. Trotter was such a popular figure in Bedlington that in 1900, shortly after his death, a memorial drinking fountain was erected in his honour in the village. At the unveiling of the fountain (which still stands near the centre of the village), Burt said Trotter possessed 'great intellectual' gifts and had 'sympathy for men of all classes, of all complexions, . . . for humanity everywhere'.[7] Glassey was born in Ireland in 1844 and spent much of his early life in Scotland where he was active in union affairs. He arrived in Northumberland in 1867 and worked as a miner. Though fervent and sometimes hotheaded, he was a good organizer; later in the 1870s he carried out constituency business for Burt. Moving to Australia in 1884, he became involved in politics and founded the Labour Party. Other miners active in the franchise movement were Robert Elliott and A. Fairbairn. Elliott, well-known for his poetry, would later move from Choppington to Gateshead and become active in local government. Fairbairn was from Bedlington and would later serve on the District Council and the Northumberland County

Council.[8] W. E. Adams aided the movement immeasurably through his columns in the *Newcastle Weekly Chronicle*, where he praised the activities, intelligence and hard work of the miners. Owen Ashton convincingly maintains that Adams was 'the campaign's best image-builder'.[9]

Elliott, Glassey and James Trotter were elected officers of the Franchise Association, which held its initial meeting on 20 May 1872. The Association's task was a difficult one, since local election officials had either little knowledge of the law or were not interested in examining the issue. The leaders visited many mining communities to gain support for the vote. These meetings, especially in July and August 1872, often ended with a resolution in favour of selecting Burt as a candidate to represent the borough of Morpeth in Parliament.[10] Burt did not participate in these meetings, and he later claimed that he had advised the leaders of the movement that they should concentrate on gaining the vote before selecting a candidate.[11] Nevertheless, a delegate assembly of the NMA voted in September 1872 to support Burt as a candidate for the House of Commons.[12]

The most notorious incidents of the franchise movement occurred in Morpeth, where the efforts of the franchise committee were not always well received. Residents of Morpeth recognized that they would be outvoted should the miners be enfranchised. They were suspicious of the miners and loyal to their long-time MP, Sir George Grey. At the initial meeting in Morpeth on 6 August 1872, the Trotters and Glassey were particularly critical of Grey's failure to represent the needs of the miners and the gathering ended in a shouting match between contending sides. The following day Burt issued a letter stating that he had always found Grey cooperative over mining legislation.[13]

Even more celebrated was a poem, 'The Morpeth Hubbubboo', that appeared shortly thereafter. One of the many verses read:

> Nine groans for Burt the Howky [colloquial for miner];
>   And if he ventures here,
> His dry teetotal carcase
>   We'll soak in Robberts' beer.
> We'll put him in the stocks, too,
>   And pelt him well with eggs;
> We'll black his Howky eyes, boys,
>   And kick his bandy legs.
> He would unseat Sir Georgy,
>   He would be member, too;
> We'll hunt him out of Morpeth,
>   And spoil his Hubbubboo.

The long poem, which attacked Burt and other miners, was unsigned.

People assumed that someone from Morpeth had penned the verses, and it led to a miners' boycott of public houses that served Roberts' beer, and a refusal by their wives to purchase goods from Morpeth merchants. In fact, the verse was written by Robert Trotter, and was designed to restore interest in a flagging campaign.[14]

Poetry played an important part in the culture of the Northumberland miner. One of the greatest of these pitman poets was Robert Elliott, the president of the Franchise Association. Describing the meeting at Morpeth on 28 September 1872, Archibald Forbes of the London *Daily News* remarked that Elliott spoke with 'a Northumbrian burr that made the leaves tremble on the trees across the river', and delivered a long verse that praised the franchise movement and Thomas Burt. One part read:

> Yes, we have found a Miner, a man of sense and worth,
> A one to nobly represent the Miners of the North.
> Possessed of high intelligence, with culture much refined,
> Whose labours in the past have been to elevate mankind;
> To banish strikes for ever from every form of trade,
> Where they on peace and happiness have often havoc made.
> Then let us pledge ourselves to-night to do what'er we can,
> To send to famed St. Stephen's this true-hearted working man.[15]

The Morpeth franchise movement had early on been applicable only to those residing in a borough. Since most miners in Northumberland and Durham and elsewhere in Britain lived outside boroughs, the movement would not have benefited them. Hence, the reformers attempted to broaden the base of support by calling for equalization of the voting requirements in the boroughs and counties as well as for universal manhood suffrage.[16] Other activities in the North East helped focus attention on franchise reform. Cowen organized a remarkably successful mass rally for universal manhood suffrage. Held on 12 April 1873, an estimated 80,000 union members marched slowly and in orderly fashion through the streets of Newcastle to the town moor, where six platforms were set up for the speakers, including Cowen, Burt and Glassey.[17] Franchise reform was the common theme of the speakers at the annual picnics of the Durham and Northumberland miners' associations in 1873.[18] The revitalized Northern Reform League held a series of meetings throughout the North East in the summer and autumn of 1873 supporting universal manhood suffrage, payment of MPs and other parliamentary reforms.[19]

Northumberland miners in the borough of Morpeth were finally placed on ratebooks as occupiers in the spring of 1873. On 27 September 1873, a revising barrister certified the names on a new franchise list that included the claims by the miners. The township of

Morpeth had 804 listed voters, while the mining communities of Bedlington numbered 2,244 and Cowpen 1,377. The total number of voters increased from 2,661 to 4,916, most of the newly enfranchised being miners.[20]

Following the certification of the new voters, Burt's supporters moved quickly to solidify his candidacy for Parliament. The NMA voted to increase his salary to £500 per year should he be elected to Parliament.[21] This raise was necessary since MPs were not paid, and the expenses of a legislator (including travel, as well as food and lodging in London) were significant. For the miners of Northumberland and, indeed, for all members of the unenfranchised British working class 18 October 1873 was a day of celebration and significance. On that day, at the market cross in the mining town of Bedlington, the people of the district revealed a petition stretching some sixteen yards and containing about 3,500 signatures requesting that Burt be their candidate at the next election. Collieries were well represented with banners and bands.[22] Certainty of Burt's election had been strengthened the day before when George Grey, the sitting MP, gave notice that he was retiring from political life. In effect, Grey had been forced into retirement by the enfranchisement of a large number of well-organized miners determined to elect one of their own to Parliament.[23] Cowen, who presided, stressed that Burt would be a representative of all the people, not just the working class, having all of the characteristics of a good MP: 'natural capability, knowledge, practical experience, and an untarnished character'.[24] Burt addressed the crowd, suggesting that he identified with their needs and desires:

because you want the exclusive barriers which have hitherto kept poor men outside the House of Commons, and made that House a 'rich man's club', broken down and swept away; it is because you want labour, which has so long been trodden down and scorned, even by those who owe everything to it; it is because you want it exalted to its proper position, and recognised even in the highest places of the nation – it is chiefly because of these considerations that you have asked me to come forward as representative on your behalf. Here I am in entire sympathy with you; and, after mature reflection, I have resolved to place myself at your disposal.

The candidate, he added,

ought to be a man of clear and cultured intellect, of broad and generous sympathies, able to speak bold manly words in defence of liberty and human rights before any assembly in the world. I feel painfully how short I come of my own ideal.[25]

This address was vintage Burt – self-deprecating in style, but willing to give it his best effort.

Gladstone's Liberal government had held office since 1868 and with its mandate wearing thin, an election loomed in the near future. Parliament was suddenly dissolved on 26 January 1874, and the date for balloting in the Morpeth constituency was set for 5 February. Elliott, Glassey and James Trotter led an election committee that included Cowen, Adams, George Howard (later the Earl of Carlisle) and Ralph Young. The NMA agreed to contribute up to £400 for the campaign and relieved Burt temporarily of his union duties. Cowen had given £100 at the celebrated Bedlington meeting, and mine owner Hugh Taylor sent £50 and a letter of support. Even George Howard, whose family had long enjoyed political control of the borough of Morpeth, contributed financially and served on Burt's committee.[26] As were the Greys, Howard was a member of one of the great aristocratic Whig families. While many of Burt's Radical friends did not respect these aristocrats and wanted nothing to do with them, Burt felt otherwise. He viewed the Whigs as past reformers who had fought for the rights of individuals, including the extension of the franchise. Yet he recognized that many of his own Radical views were at odds with those of the Whigs.[27] Burt carefully spelled out his convictions in speeches beginning at the Bedlington meeting of 18 October 1873 and continuing until polling day on 5 February 1874.

Burt offered a traditional Radical platform calling for political reform and criticizing privileged elements within society. He believed that extending the franchise would lead to the election of reform-minded MPs who would support the revision of laws restricting labour unions.[28] On 11 November 1873, Burt called for universal suffrage, reapportionment of districts to provide for roughly the same number of voters in each constituency, shorter duration of Parliament, and payment of MPs. 'Will any one', Burt remarked, 'say that a country, which pays nearly a million a year for royalty, cannot afford a few thousands of pounds to its parliamentary representatives?'[29] Burt's call for manhood suffrage included the extension of the vote to women. In a speech at Choppington Scotland Gate on 27 January he reiterated that 'manhood' embraced women: 'The arguments upon which they based their claim for manhood suffrage were equally applicable and forcible to woman suffrage.'[30]

Burt attacked privilege within Britain, calling for the abolition of the land and game laws which protected the landed aristocracy at the expense of small farmers and agricultural labourers. He also promised to work for the disestablishment of the state churches of England and Scotland. Burt was opposed to the principle of state churches, explaining that 'religion belongs to the individual conscience and the Creator; it is in its very essence free and voluntary'. He argued that the Church of England had not taken care of the spiritual needs of the people and did not deserve protection by the state. Moreover, all churches should stand on their own merits, separate from the state.[31]

Only briefly did Burt's religious viewpoint become a matter of concern during the campaign. His biographer and acquaintance, the newspaperman Aaron Watson, reported that during a meeting at Blyth Burt was asked if he believed in the Bible. To this query he responded:

> As I am not a candidate for a professorship of theology or the occupancy of a pulpit, I decline to say whether I do or do not believe in the authenticity of the Bible. The question is entirely foreign to the business before us. The contest in which we are engaged is a political and not a religious contest. I maintain that the constituency has no right whatever to institute an inquisition into the faith or creed of any candidate who may solicit its suffrages. For this reason I refuse to answer all and every question of a theological nature that may here or elsewhere be put to me.

Watson concludes that Burt's reply 'is probably the finest that has ever been made under similar circumstances'.[32]

Burt's views about religion had evolved considerably over the years. As much as Burt respected Primitive Methodism and appreciated its importance in the life of the miners, he never formally became a member of the denomination, with which he had certain 'intellectual difficulties'.[33] What exactly his difficulties were we do not know, although according to Watson, Burt inclined towards a 'rather detached interest in Unitarianism'. Burt may have had difficulty accepting the doctrine of the Trinity, hence his interest in Unitarianism with its denial of the Trinity and its toleration of diverse religious values and concepts. Long penalized for their beliefs, Unitarians had traditionally worked for civil rights, which would have attracted Burt. As we have seen, Burt became acquainted early with the writings of the American Unitarian leader William Ellery Channing. On Burt's twenty-first birthday his father had given him a copy of Barker's biography of Channing. Burt and Cowen occasionally attended the Church of the Divine Unity on New Bridge Street in Newcastle, where an outstanding preacher named J. C. Street was minister until 1870.[34] Unitarianism was a known religious element within the Northumberland mining community. The Rev. Street spoke twice in Choppington in 1867 before large numbers.[35] By 1873 the Unitarians were 'rather strongly represented' in Choppington Scotland Gate and had a 'neat little brick chapel' near the railway station.[36]

Burt's disposition to Radical thought was evident in his other campaign proposals. He championed a national system of free, compulsory and non-sectarian education, and promoted a permissive bill that would give local residents control over the sale of intoxicating beverages from public houses. He also called for Home Rule for Ireland, and advocated the freeing of Irish political prisoners.[37]

The campaign between Burt and his Conservative opponent, Capt. F. Duncan, was memorably cordial, perhaps because there was never any doubt as to the outcome. Duncan, from Woolwich, was in his late thirties, with degrees from Aberdeen University. He had been in the artillery for nineteen years and had written several books on the colonies and the Royal Artillery. While admitting that his late entry into the campaign would probably hurt his chances of success, Capt. Duncan defended the traditional Tory Party institutions of the established Church, the monarchy and the army. He charged that Burt, if elected, would not be his own man, but 'would be tied by five hundred strings', meaning the £500 salary promised Burt by his union. Burt claimed that there was nothing wrong with being paid for one's services. Besides, he added, being paid put him in the good company of the royal family, bishops and clergy, all of whom Duncan so readily defended.[38]

Election day – Thursday, 5 February 1874 – was a great and, for most voters, unique event. Most of the electors in the borough of Morpeth had never cast a vote in a parliamentary election, since the seat had been uncontested for many years. Burt's colours, green and white, were evident everywhere, even on dogs. Pits were idled for the day so that the miners could cast their vote. In many instances, miners marched together from their pit to the polling-booths, which were few and far between.[39] The poll results were declared on the following day, with Burt receiving 3,332 votes to 585 for Duncan.[40] Elliott marked the victory with a memorable poem, 'A Pitman Gan Te Parliemint'.[41]

A banquet celebrating Burt's election to Parliament was held at Morpeth on 28 February 1874. Over three hundred people were present at the non-alcoholic event. In his remarks, Burt emphasized that while he would work very hard for his constituents and take their views into consideration, his votes would ultimately reflect his own beliefs:

> when I go to the House of Commons, you may depend upon it I shall always speak and act in accordance with my own honest convictions. They may be mistaken, but, so long as they are mine, I shall assert them.[42]

In an unusual twist, Burt's opponent in the election was present at the banquet. Burt would retain contact with Duncan, who served as MP for the Holborn division of Finsbury from 1885 until 1888.[43]

The election of 1874 was an historic event. Two representatives of the labouring class, Burt and Alexander McDonald, had been elected to Parliament. Both of them had worked in coal mines as children. McDonald, elected for Stafford, had received a university education and was middle class in his orientation, although he remained a great spokesman for the labouring classes, especially the miners.

Several newspapers commented on Burt's election. The *Newcastle Critic* viewed Burt's election as:

a distinct embodiment of the highest triumph which the working classes have up to the present time achieved ... he owes his present position neither to ambition nor to agitation, but to the esteem which his abilities, his manliness, and his honesty have awakened amongst his fellow-workmen.

This was a fair evaluation of Burt's popularity. He had helped to develop a well-organized, effective and financially secure union, and was regarded as honest even by his severest critics. Moreover, he had exhibited no ambitions for either his union position or the parliamentary seat. The *Critic* also rightly identified Burt's command of poetry as a source of his strength:

He seldom speaks in public at this time without quoting the words of some poet whom he has read, to lend a grace and a charm to his oratory. Perhaps no man of his educational advantages has committed more poetry to memory, or can more readily embellish his speech with a poetical quotation. His studies and acquirements lent him considerable weight amongst his fellow-workmen [early in his life].[44]

The Miners' Advocate, published in Middlesborough, stressed that Burt was respected not only by the miners and other members of the working class, but also by the mine owners and the industrialists of the North.[45]

In this adulation by his contemporaries, we can find some key ingredients to Burt's success. Coal miners regarded him as one of their own, one who had but eight years earlier toiled in the mines with them. The miners were proud of his ability to address all of the issues facing Britain, not just those affecting miners. As Burt always reiterated, the Northumbrian miners were worldly-wise, in spite of their reputation as provincial creatures of the restrictive pit villages. Burt also commanded the respect of the more privileged classes in society. His control over a large and generally cooperative work force, as well as his espousal of a market-oriented economy, made him acceptable to mine owners and many of the great industrialists. Finally, his lack of class hostility, his humility and honesty, and especially his command of poetry (though remarkable, still in the tradition of the miners) won him immediate respect from other MPs, who were from the middle or upper classes.

Some people anticipated that the election of Burt and McDonald would lead quickly to an improvement in the life of the labouring class. Burt, on the other hand, was not only a patient man, but also a realist, and never expected any dramatic change in life or politics because of his election. He did expect gradual improvement, however, and believed that the working class and its representatives could facilitate change. The opportunity for Burt and other Radicals to bring about change in the near future was dramatically reduced because Gladstone's Liberal Party lost its majority to the Conservatives, headed by Benjamin

Disraeli. Burt was joined in Parliament by his friend Cowen, who was re-elected to represent Newcastle. Cowen had been elected to Parliament in January 1874, following the death of his father, who had held the seat for Newcastle. The quick dissolution of Parliament in late January 1874, meant that Cowen did not take his seat until after his second election.[46]

Three weeks after the banquet in Morpeth, Burt and McDonald were honoured by the Labour Representation League as 'the first direct and fully recognized representatives of labour in the British Parliament'. In his brief remarks at the dinner in London on 18 March, Burt stated that simply by being elected he 'felt that something had been done to break through the exclusiveness which had hitherto kept the poor man outside the House of Commons'. He stressed, though, that he did not regard himself as representing a class, for 'as the working classes had for generations complained of the exclusive class representation in the House of Commons, it would be a mistake and worse to continue class representation and legislation'.[47]

Burt's maiden speech to the House of Commons came on 13 May 1874, in support of G. O. Trevelyan's private member's bill to equalize franchise requirements by extending the borough franchise to the counties. It was appropriate that Burt speak on this subject, as he had promised action on the issue to his constituents. In his brief remarks, he declared that the unfairness of the present law was evident to the miners of Northumberland. Of workers at the same colliery, miners residing in the borough could cast a ballot, while those living in the county could not. Also, because miners often moved from one colliery to another, they could easily lose the vote previously enjoyed. This inequality among the workers was particularly disturbing to Burt.[48]

An object of curiosity in Westminster, Burt was listened to with interest by the MPs. The speech was very well received.[49] What apparently intrigued many was Burt's Northumbrian burr, which delighted a correspondent for the *Liverpool Weekly Post*:

> His dialect was pure English, far purer than some of our pretentious speakers use. One of the charms, indeed, of this speech was the singularly well-chosen, pure English words. Nor was there throughout his short speech a single fault in his grammar. In short, this was an exceedingly good speech, delivered in a quiet, unassuming manner ... Mr. Burt spoke not more than a quarter of an hour, but into that quarter of an hour he packed more sound argument than many of our speakers would in twice the time.[50]

Burt had obviously passed the test for the reporter, who must have expected that Burt's English would not be up to the normal standards of parliamentary speakers. Burt's maiden speech set the pattern for his parliamentary career: he spoke only on subjects to which he believed he could meaningfully contribute, he was well informed, and he kept his remarks brief. He did not speak often, but when he did he commanded the interest and respect of his colleagues, who viewed him as a wise representative of the labouring classes.

Chapter 4

THE GREAT CONCILIATOR IN A PERIOD OF ECONOMIC RECESSION

After 1874, Burt split his time between London and Newcastle. He was a conscientious MP, regularly attending debates and casting his vote. In the 1870s he normally spent the period from February to August in London, often returning to Newcastle on the weekends, where he saw to union duties. While everyday union affairs were carried out by other officials, Burt was usually listed as present at important meetings, and he always participated in negotiations with the owners.

The union was extremely busy after 1874 with a variety of major issues. Euphoria in the mining community over franchise reform and Burt's election was quickly dampened by economic problems caused by a downturn in the coal trade. During the nineteenth century the short-term earnings of miners fluctuated in all regions of Britain. The miners of the North East were normally some of the better paid in the country, especially during the boom period of the early 1870s.[1] Wage increases of the early 1870s in Northumberland, however, were followed by several reductions after 1874. A long and costly form of arbitration employed by the NMA and the coal mine owners to settle outstanding issues – including wage rates – provided little solace to miners, who saw their wages continue to tumble. The depression also directly affected the union's financial health, bankrupting three cooperative ventures in which the union had invested. One group of mine workers broke from the NMA to form its own union. Frustration and bitterness led to several local colliery strikes and culminated in two county-wide strikes in 1877. Union leaders, including Burt, faced extensive criticism throughout the period, as union members charged them with failing to protect the interests of miners. While earlier Northumberland coal mining unions had often crumbled when faced with complications in a depressed economy, the NMA managed to survive, even though miners' wages remained low until the late 1880s.

Beginning in March 1874, mine owners frequently demanded and gained reductions in wages. A typical negotiating session occurred in October 1874, when the owners called for a 20 per cent reduction, the union offered 8 per cent, and the two sides settled at 14 per cent.[2] In January 1875, when the owners called once again for a substantial wage reduction, the union requested that the issue be settled by arbitration. After a good deal of bargaining, the two sides agreed to present their cases to two arbitrators for each side. Should these four individuals be unable to agree on a recommendation, the matter would be submitted to an umpire for resolution.[3] After hearing all the evidence, the four arbitrators could not agree, so the umpire rendered a decision.[4] The following year a similar issue went to arbitration.[5] In both hearings, the award was a compromise between the owners' demands and the union's claims. Burt and McDonald served as arbitrators for the miners in both of these arbitration hearings.

While wages were reduced through negotiations and arbitration hearings, miners were also confronted with a series of pit closings and operating-time reductions. The NMA paid the laid-off miners stoppage allowances, a substantial burden on the union treasury.[6] Northumberland miners feared that the large influx of labourers into the collieries contributed to an oversupply of coal.[7] At a national meeting in April 1875, miners discussed possible measures to arrest the downward trend in wages, which was national in scope. They also took steps to support the miners on strike in South Wales,[8] where owners had forced miners to take a wage reduction and refused all pleas for arbitration. Burt felt strongly that the well-organized Welsh miners should be supported by all miners in order to overcome the actions of the owners, whom he labelled 'feudal tyrants'. For Burt, the issue was not simply wages, but 'whether the miners of Wales shall be treated as serfs and imbeciles, who are to be coerced into abject submission to their employers' terms without even the right of asking the reason why'. The NMA supported the strikers financially, but the futility and cost of the strike reinforced the view of a moderate leader like Burt that there should be no strikes.[9]

Northumberland miners also resorted to strikes in an attempt to maintain their hard-earned wages. From 1874 through 1876 there were twelve strikes in Northumberland lasting from nine days to eighteen weeks.[10] All of these strikes were approved by the union and supported by union funds. Unauthorized strikes, including those at Elswick, Ashington, Seghill, Cleator Moor and North Wylam, posed a more serious problem for the union.[11] NMA officers, fearing that they were losing control over members, were upset that local collieries would not abide by negotiated agreements. Miners, who openly criticized union officials at delegate meetings,[12] were particularly aggravated by the owners' attempt to pay hewers on the basis of the Billy Fairplay, the Welsh system. Billy Fairplay required that the miners discard small pieces of coal and send up only larger pieces. While the miners were unable to muster the two-thirds vote required to call a county-wide strike over the issue, they held several unsanctioned protest meetings. Miners were angry that their agents, including Burt, supported the introduction of Billy Fairplay even after they knew that the majority of miners opposed it.[13] The NMA lost over 500 members in 1875 when the mechanics (a broad term applied to a variety of skilled workers including blacksmiths, bricklayers and plumbers) left the Association to form their own union.[14]

In the expanding and vibrant economy of the early 1870s, cooperative ventures had blossomed. Cooperative stores sprouted in mining communities throughout the North East. Successful and long-lasting, these stores provided the workers with good, unadulterated and inexpensive food, and equipment including picks and lamps. Burt always encouraged communities to support their local cooperative as a means of self-help.[15] By 1875, however, the NMA suffered financial losses from three bankruptcies. In 1872, Burt and other NMA officers were instrumental in helping to form the Co-operative Mining Society, which intended to purchase and run coal mines on the cooperative principle. Speaking at a meeting held on 21 December 1872 to promote the sale of its shares to miners, Burt indicated that one of the ways to overcome industrial strife was for miners to own their own mine.[16] In 1873 and 1874 the NMA invested £6,000 in the society, which purchased the Monkwood Colliery in Derbyshire in March 1874. By 25 September 1875, the venture had failed and investments by mining associations and individual miners were lost.[17]

The Industrial Bank of Newcastle, which opened in 1872, did business primarily with cooperatives and unions. Burt promoted the Bank as willing to do business with unions in a more efficient manner than other financial institutions. The Bank, which handled some accounts for the NMA, became insolvent in 1876. In addition, the Ouseburn Engine Works, a cooperative venture in Newcastle that had been set up in the early 1870s, went bankrupt in 1875. The NMA apparently lost the £1,000 worth of shares it had invested in each of these ventures, and had difficulty in gaining access to its deposits in the Industrial Bank. Burt helped to close down both the Bank and the Ouseburn Works.[18]

Although Burt spent a substantial amount of time on parliamentary duties, he was an influential presence in Northumberland during these troubled times. He urged members to stick by the union during periods of economic distress. He believed that the union played an important role by paying an allowance to those thrown out of work. He also justified the several authorized strikes, since he felt action should be taken against employers who arbitrarily demanded reductions greater than those negotiated county-wide with the owners. Burt, however, had mixed feelings about the use of arbitration. He admitted that arbitration was not yet trusted by miners, partly because it had been used only during wage reductions. He also believed that the entire process, which involved 'experts' with 'prejudice' for each side, was far too costly and time-consuming. He called instead for a permanent arbitration board composed of members acquainted with the trade but truly impartial.[19]

The uneasy peace in the Northumberland coalfields came to an end in 1877. In April the owners called for a substantial reduction in wages and for an end to free cottages and fire coal. The owners eventually offered to arbitrate the last two matters, but the miners refused the offer. The owners then issued notices of the end of contract to the miners, after which the union balloted the miners as to whether they wished to strike over the issue. Before the miners cast their ballots, Burt issued a letter encouraging them not to vote in favour of a strike. He agreed that the owners had made a major error in calling for both a wage reduction and an end to the free cottage and house coal. The owners had, however, agreed to reconsider the cottage and coal issue, and would arbitrate the wage reduction. The miners had made a mistake, he argued, when they turned down arbitration, as the Association had long promoted its use. Burt feared a strike because the union's financial resources were low and the state of the coal trade was poor.[20] In spite of pleas by Burt and other officers, miners voted overwhelmingly to strike: 11,310 to 946.[21]

The miners, who began the strike on 28 May 1877, did not enjoy substantial public backing, mainly because they refused arbitration. Moreover, they rejected what appeared to many the wise counsel of their own leaders.[22] Within five days after the strike began, an increasing number of miners favoured wage arbitration as long as the house coal and rent issues were dropped.[23] The union's executive committee held three mass meetings to let miners air their differences. NMA President Bryson, who had been adamantly opposed to the strike, was unable to preside at the meetings – he was howled down and pelted with stones. Burt on two occasions admonished the crowd for their ill treatment of Bryson and other officers. He added that the agents (Burt, Young and Nixon) were willing, if the miners so decided, to give up their positions, as once they had lost support they had effectively lost their power and authority. Burt understood why arbitration was unpopular, as all three arbitrations had led to reductions. One problem with arbitration as presently structured, he added, was that the umpires knew little about miners or mining and were of the same social class as the owners. He called again for a permanent and impartial board of arbitration. Even better than arbitration, Burt contended, was a sliding scale to determine wages, but the owners had thus far rejected it. Joseph Hilton of Ashington argued that arbitration had reduced wages too much, taking them below the basic cost of living. He called for a 'national suspension of labour' by the miners to show people the economic power of the miners and to convince 'pig-headed political economists that labour was superior to capital'.[24] The Portuguese consul in Newcastle, who reported on these meetings to his foreign minister, said that the miners regarded arbitration as a 'hypocritical way of legalizing robbery. Against this firm opinion on the part of the men, all the logic and reason of the leaders was of course impotent.' The meetings, he added, degenerated into shouting matches, with heightened passions, and 'Communist views were heard, as in the worst of revolutionary times'.[25]

Northumberland miners were clearly and rightly distressed over declining wages and the unsatisfactory outcome of arbitration. They also believed that their officials cooperated too much with mine owners. Apparently not all of the opposition was substantive. Some of those who created disturbances were quite young or had recently arrived in the area. One observer charged that they had no arguments, but just made noise, jammed in around the platform, and refused to let many of the people speak.[26]

The strike lasted two weeks. The miners garnered little public support, and the union possessed few financial resources to support a long strike. The miners agreed to wage arbitration, as long as the issues of house coal and rent were dropped. The owners concurred, although they expressed their displeasure that miners had resorted to a two-week strike instead of using arbitration.[27]

Burt appears to have retained the support of the miners throughout the dispute. While there were sharp comments and even stones thrown at some of the officers, Burt was apparently immune from such personal rebukes, even though he had criticized strike advocates. At the union's annual meeting in June 1877, all officers and agents were re-elected, although all but Burt faced opposition.[28] Since no annual picnic was held in 1877, critics of the union officials were unable to use that occasion to express their displeasure. In lieu of a picnic, the NMA decided to participate in a celebratory procession in Newcastle for the former president of the United States, Ulysses S. Grant, who was touring England. Grant was exceptionally popular in England, and the miners of both Durham and Northumberland joined in the festivities at the Newcastle town moor. In his welcoming address at the rally, Burt stressed that the English workers had closely followed the American Civil War, as they believed the conflict had 'involved the great questions of freedom, of the rights of man, and the dignity and honour of labour'.[29]

The end of the strike, in June 1877, brought a fragile truce to the Northumberland battlefield. Union officials found it difficult to get miners to fulfil parts of the arbitrator's award. While delegates quickly approved working eleven days in the fortnight instead of ten, it was not until late October that miners agreed to throw out the small coal and retain only the more valuable large coal. They refused to extend their work-day in order to hew six hours per day at the coal face.[30]

Some observers considered the coal trade to be at its most depressed level in thirty years.[31] As we have seen, when the prosperity of the mining industry disappeared, cordial relations between owners and the union waned. The breakdown in collective bargaining was most noticeable during the lock-out of 1877–78. On 1 December owners informed the NMA that trade was so poor that they had no choice but to demand a 12.5 per cent wage reduction. The miners requested arbitration, but the owners refused to consider it. Following the owners' rejection of arbitration, the miners voted overwhelmingly to strike rather than accept the reduction.[32]

On 22 December Burt wrote a long masterful letter explaining the causes of the strike; it was published in many newspapers. He began by stressing that for many years owners and miners in Northumberland had been remarkably successful at settling issues without recourse to strikes or lock-outs. During the early 1870s, when demand for coal was great, the miners had 'worked vigorously and constantly, the pits were kept going, and the coalowners thus gained the full advantage of the brisk trade and high prices which then prevailed'. Workers' wages had also benefited handsomely from the healthy trade. When the first arbitration case was heard, owners emphasized how pleased they were with productivity and the character of the miners. In the ensuing period, when the price of coal dropped and the owners demanded wage reductions, arbitration had helped to determine the final rate. Miners, employers and the public as a whole had all benefited from this 'wise and conciliatory policy'. 'The district', he continued, 'has won a high reputation, and has been pointed to as a model for the imitation of the other trades throughout the country.' All this, however, was about to change. Not only would many people suffer, but 'conflict and contention' and 'secrecy and suspicion' would replace 'frankness and cordiality' in labour–management relations. The cause of this? The owners had decided on a non-negotiable wage reduction, and had immediately issued notices ending the contracts. Burt admitted that the miners had struck recently and had refused arbitration. Leaders of the union, however, had opposed the strike, and the miners had quickly agreed to arbitration. 'If the men committed a mistake', Burt added, 'they soon put themselves right; and it will be well if the coalowners see their error with equal readiness, and retrace their false step with the same promptitude.'[33]

Burt's letter gained substantial support in both the local and national press. Newspapers praised Burt for his leadership and criticized the mine owners for refusing to utilize arbitration.[34] On the other side, *Capital and Labour*, a weekly paper which supported the industrial owners, contended that Burt and the union failed to recognize reality: the trade was depressed, the labour supply was great, many pits were closed, and prices were down everywhere in England, with Northumberland's still too high to be competitive. The article not only questioned the use of arbitration, but also doubted the very value of the union itself.[35] Theo Bunning, the secretary of the Northumberland Steam Collieries' Defence Association, responded to Burt's letter on 1 January. Bunning contended that the miners' association had broken the coalfield's peace by striking earlier in 1877 and failing to live up to the arbitration award requiring a longer work-day and dispensing small coal.[36]

Meanwhile, Burt and the other officers attempted to raise funds to support the miners and their families. The NMA's financial resources were limited. Before the strike, the union had paid benefits to laid-off miners. The number of union members decreased by late 1877, so total income would have been significantly reduced. Most of the £17,000 deposited in the defunct Industrial Bank was still unavailable to the Association.[37] On 25 December 1877, Burt appealed to the labour unions and other interested parties for financial support. He spoke directly to the unions, including a council in West Yorkshire and the Newcastle and Gateshead Trades Council.[38] Because of poor economic conditions and high unemployment, few contributions came from outside the coal industry. On the whole, strike payments to members were minimal. Economic distress was common in the mining communities – soup kitchens opened and people resorted to begging.[39]

Disunity among the miners set the NMA at a distinct disadvantage during the lock-out. There were several collieries in Northumberland where miners did not belong to the NMA.[40] Moreover, a new miners' union had formed in June 1877 to protest the NMA's acceptance of arbitration to settle the earlier strike. With 300 to 400 members, this new union was centred in collieries at Bebside and West Sleekburn, areas which had long harboured critics of the NMA. The break-away union, however, lacked funds and was unable to bargain effectively.[41]

Union officials wanted to end the lock-out. Miners and their families were suffering and the union lacked the unity needed to negotiate effectively. NMA miners returned to work at some collieries.[42] Besides, the owners remained united and gave no indication that they would offer anything less than the full 12.5 per cent wage reduction. In a February ballot, when miners failed to gain a two-thirds majority for continuing the strike, the NMA executive committee declared that the lock-out was over, that the 12.5 per cent reduction had been accepted, and that the miners should return to work.[43]

The end of the lock-out did not bring immediate peace within the union or end concessions borne by the miners. Some miners remained opposed to the decision and encouraged fellow workers to resist, while a few owners demanded more than the 12.5 per cent reduction.[44] In a long letter published shortly after the end of the lock-out, Burt defended the actions of the union while attempting to mend fences with the owners. He praised both parties for their good conduct during the dispute, and admitted that 'the owners, beyond having been unusually stiff and exacting in enforcing their demand without mitigation, have done nothing to embitter the conflict'. He stressed, however, that the miners believed that the owners had misused their power and had extracted unfair concessions. The miners would have more readily accepted a reduction gained through arbitration. Burt suggested that some miners wanted to retaliate against the owners as soon as the opportunity arose, but he very much opposed such action because it would simply cause additional suffering and do harm to the coal trade. He closed his letter by emphasizing that 'confidence, harmony, and co-operation' were needed in the coal trade, and by calling for a sliding-scale agreement, which 'is just in principle' and 'gives some guarantee against the repetition of industrial conflicts such as that through which we have just passed'.[45]

Dissatisfaction persisted. At a union delegate meeting in June, miners from some collieries submitted motions to censure leaders associated with conciliation. These critical motions called for with-drawal from the Miners' National Union and abolition of the Joint Committee. All motions failed.[46] In November 1878, owners called for an additional wage reduction of 12.5 per cent. Burt worked hard to avoid another strike, visiting collieries to urge miners to permit the union leaders to negotiate a settlement. By the end of November, these negotiations resulted in another round of wage reductions and other concessions.[47] Several collieries struck in 1879.[48]

Negotiations over a sliding-scale wage rate began in May 1879 and were successfully concluded on 15 November. A union report optimistically concluded:

> we earnestly trust that the arrangement will prove a real and permanent benefit to the district, and that it will inaugurate a new era when strife and turmoil will give place to peace and harmony between employers and workmen in the Northumberland Coal-Trade.[49]

Burt had finally gained the agreement that he had so long sought.[50] A sliding scale did not by itself, however, guarantee industrial peace. The Durham Miners' Association had negotiated a sliding scale based on the selling price of coal to determine wages in 1877. The scale had unfortunately become inapplicable by 1878, when the coal price dropped so low that the scale could not be used to calculate wages. In the midst of the depression and growing unemployment, many Durham lodges ignored the county contract and negotiated their own wages with owners. This led to a particularly bitter strike in the Durham coal fields in 1879.[51]

Several developments caused the nation-wide coal trade crisis of the late 1870s. Industries had become more efficient in their use of coal after enduring high prices in the early 1870s. Moreover, trade cycles were common throughout the nineteenth century; 1873, one of the peak years, was followed by leaner years, with trade eventually reaching bottom in 1879. Also, the North East faced stiff competition with South Wales coalfields for the steam-coal market, as the latter's production increased in the 1870s.[52] Miners from the period believed that overproduction was a cause of the depressed market price. While Yorkshire miners summoned national meetings in 1879 to consider reducing production and demanding a wage increase, nothing came of the discussions – unions were still too regional and fragmented to undertake such a nation-wide stratagem.[53]

Burt and other officials worked hard in the depression of the 1870s to save the NMA and to establish a collective bargaining process that would avoid costly and painful stoppages. While Burt enjoyed the support of the majority of the miners, resistance to his conciliatory approach would persist throughout his long reign as secretary of the NMA. In spite of the many difficulties he faced as a union official, he enjoyed his job. There is no hint in his speeches or in what little correspondence survives that he ever felt discouraged. He had faith that the cause of the union and the working man was just, and that labourers' lives were improving. His contribution to this progress was not only as a labour leader but also as an MP in London, where he focused much of his time and energy.

Chapter 5

PARLIAMENT AND THE WORKING CLASS

Thomas Burt's power and prestige were initially based on his leadership of Northumberland's mining community. His calm demeanour and quiet but firm leadership guided the Northumberland Miners' Association through its formative years and helped the union survive the troubled economic period of the late 1870s. While he worked as a union leader in Northumberland and throughout Britain, Burt also sat as a Member of Parliament from 1874. National recognition as a labour leader came as much through his parliamentary career as his union activities.

Burt loved the House of Commons. This is clearly evident in his *Autobiography* and in his article 'Forty Years in the House', as well as in his correspondence with friends and comments to constituents. The rational deliberation which he found in Parliament was the basis for personal decision-making throughout his life. Burt also found companionship in the House, moving among men who appreciated both his thoughtful speeches and his command of poetry. He admired Gladstone, as a 'noble orator and a past-master in the art of the impromptu', and respected him for his 'loftiness of ideals and for depth of passion'.[1] Burt and Cowen frequently attended Parliament together and remained on close terms, even while disagreeing on issues. By 1876 the two had participated in meetings with other Radicals including Joseph Chamberlain, Charles Dilke and the journalist John Morley. In August 1876, the Radicals acted as a single body in submitting several motions to the House of Commons. While some observers discussed the possible emergence of a separate Radical Party, differences in personalities and political agendas served to break up this small group.[2] Cowen was often discouraged with the legislative process and by 1878 regarded his entry into Parliament a mistake.[3] On the other hand, Burt enjoyed the congenial atmosphere of Westminster and tolerated even the most ineffective political opponents.

Burt and Alexander McDonald were the only two MPs directly representing the working class between 1874 and 1880. They were joined by Henry Broadhurst in 1880. After McDonald died in 1881, Burt and Broadhurst were the only two labour representatives until 1885. As the only working-class MP serving continuously from 1874 to 1885, Burt played an important role in defining the issues of importance to his class. He toiled not only for the interests of the miners, but for all members of the working class, advocating legislative items such as the legal status of labour unions, employers' liability, safety for merchant seamen, extension of the franchise and free public education.

Burt is correctly regarded as having been a Liberal-Labour MP. Generally abbreviated 'Lib-Lab', the term refers to those labour representatives who also supported the Liberal Party and its principles.[4] While the term Lib-Lab was originally a derogatory one used by Socialist critics in the 1890s, Burt and others branded with the appellation were proud of their position within the political spectrum.[5] The term should not be applied to Burt's first ten years in Parliament, however, since there were too few labour representatives in the House of Commons to be regarded as a separate group. The number of working-class MPs increased dramatically when ten were elected in 1885, including six connected with the coal miners' unions.[6]

Matthew White Ridley, a Northumberland landowner and MP for North Northumberland, charged that Burt was not a true representative of all the citizens in his constituency, but simply a 'delegate ... of one particular class'. Speaking before the Morpeth Conservative Association in 1879, Ridley, who had doubts about the push for a broader franchise, contended that Burt was in Parliament 'by accident ... As far as he could see he was likely to be a perpetual accident.'[7] Burt countered that 'a great number of that kind of accidents would happen up and down the country', if the franchise were extended. As it was, many MPs were in the Commons because they were accidentally born 'the heirs to great landed estates'. Burt emphasized that he was not a delegate but an MP whose constituents expected him to make his best independent judgement on a variety of issues and not just those applicable to labour.[8] Regarding himself as free to engage in debate on any items before Parliament, Burt attacked the methods used to grant money to the royal family, supported Charles Bradlaugh in his quest to be seated in the House of Commons, and criticized the government's aggressive foreign and imperial policies.

Burt's political philosophy was based on core principles shared with many members of the working class of the North East: Nonconformity, temperance and Radicalism. The Nonconformity of his home and village life helped make him a critic of the Church of England and a champion of public education. His support of the temperance movement led him to advocate control of public houses and to push for members of the working class to extend jurisdiction over their environment as far as possible. Finally, under the influence of the Radicalism of the North East, he became an adversary of the privileged and a proponent of the democratization of politics.[9]

Burt's parliamentary interests during the period from 1874 to about 1892 can be divided arbitrarily into two areas. In domestic affairs, Burt strived to enhance the quality of working-class life through improved employment conditions and educational opportunities, and by the extension of workers' political power. These legislative efforts will be the focus of the remainder of this chapter. The next chapter will concentrate on Burt's views on Britain's foreign and imperial roles.

During Burt's first eighteen years in Parliament, leadership of the government lay in the hands of three great politicians. Benjamin Disraeli guided the Tory government from 1874 to 1880. William Gladstone, who retired from his leadership position following the general election of 1874, returned to lead the Liberal governments from 1880 to 1885, and for about six months in 1886. Lord Salisbury headed the Tory government from 1885 to 1886, and again from 1886 to 1892.

* * *

The first legislative issue confronting Burt concerned the legal status of the labour unions. Labour unions in nineteenth-century Britain often operated under severe handicaps. Those not regarded as outrightly illegal enjoyed no protection under the law. While the Trade Union Act of 1871 had legalized unions and offered them some degree of protection, Parliament had also passed the Criminal Law Amendment Act, which substantially restricted union activity by holding individuals responsible for actions taken in support of union activities. During the parliamentary election campaign of 1874, union members pressured candidates to make substantial changes in these laws.[10]

In 1875, Disraeli's government introduced and passed the Employers and Workmen Act and the Conspiracy and Protection Act. With the support of various MPs, especially A. J. Mundella (the Liberal MP and manufacturer from Sheffield), labour organizations were able to offer numerous amendments to the bills, so that the final acts substantially reflected labour's wishes. Under these new laws, unions were freed from the conspiracy law in labour disputes, and the right of peaceful picketing was protected.[11] Burt spoke occasionally on these bills, offering a labourer's perspective on the functioning of the proposed law and facilitating useful amendments.[12]

The passage of these two bills made it possible for unions and labour leaders to turn their attention to other pressing matters. Burt focused much of his parliamentary effort in the 1870s and 1880s on developing an effective law requiring employers to compensate workers for job-related injuries. While efforts by labour leaders resulted in the landmark Employers' Liability Act of 1880, Burt's endeavours throughout the 1880s to amend this act were constantly frustrated and led to division within the coal miners' community.

Employers often avoided compensating employees for injuries by applying the doctrine of 'common employment'. Based primarily on a judgment rendered by the court in the 1830s and on subsequent interpretations, this doctrine held that an employer could not be held liable for injuries caused by the negligence of *other* employees, including foremen. The unfairness of this doctrine, which caused enormous suffering among the labouring class, was readily apparent to many sectors of society.[13] In 1876, McDonald co-sponsored a bill framed by the Trades Union Congress (TUC) to require employer liability. Speaking for the government, the Attorney-General argued that because owners already suffered enormously in a disaster, it was unfair to hold them liable for the actions of a negligent servant. He contended that miners were aware of the danger of their profession and were well paid for their work: 'We have heard of miners who enjoyed all the luxuries of life, and whose favourite daily beverage was champagne.' Responding to the Attorney-General's remarks, Burt insisted that even at the height of coal prosperity in the early 1870s, there were few miners who averaged more than £2 10s. a week. He referred to the allegations that miners 'lived extravagantly and drank champagne' as 'claptrap'.[14] When discussing a similar bill in 1878, Burt pointed out that miners did not know or effectively share a 'common employment' in a mine, except for the four miners who made up a team. He added that 'any responsibility for an accident caused by the act of one of those four men could not justly apply to the other 400 or 500 men who might be in the mine'.[15] Passage of an employers' liability bill was difficult, not only due to the legal complexity of the issue, but because so many interested parties were reluctant to agree to its principle.[16]

In the general election of 1880, labour organizations gave high priority to a strong employers' liability bill. The new Liberal government, under pressure, agreed to introduce such a bill. Throughout the summer of 1880, an interested public watched while both labour and management lobbied heavily to influence the direction of the bill. Coal mine owners feared that the bill would seriously cripple their industry. While the bill did not abolish the doctrine of common employment, it held employers responsible in several areas previously exempted. Employers were appeased, at least in part, because the law did not specifically prohibit companies from contracting out of the law. In general, most labour leaders and sympathizers in Parliament kept a deliberately low profile, letting the government handle the bill.[17] Burt spoke on several occasions, arguing that the bill would not have a negative impact on trade and supporting an amendment to end the doctrine of common employment. The working class, he emphasized, wanted nothing less than a law holding employers liable.[18]

Though the new liability act made it easier for employees to sue employers to collect compensation for injuries suffered on the job, it was not welcomed by all coal miners. John Bryson, long-time president of the NMA, thought that the Miners' Permanent Relief Fund provided sufficient protection for the miners. He was also concerned that Northumberland miners would lose their 'smart money', a five-shilling-a-week compensation paid to injured miners by employers in Northumberland.[19] Burt responded directly to Bryson's criticism. Burt thought that Parliament in this instance had done good work. He agreed with Bryson that Northumberland's Miners' Permanent Relief Fund was excellent, but miners in other parts of the country did not have such a benefit and thus needed protection by law. Besides, he did not expect local owners to drop their aid to injured miners.[20] Shortly before final passage of the bill, Burt wrote an article on the bill concentrating on the absurdities of the doctrine of common employment. While the bill was not perfect, he stressed that it was a great advance. Although it did not entirely abolish the doctrine of common employment, it required owners to take greater care in providing protection in the work-place, and was particularly beneficial for the railway employees.[21]

Employers were able legally to contract out of provisions of the 1880 Act, sometimes by agreeing to a form of mutual insurance with the employees. Under such a plan, an employer could contribute a given amount and hence have a set cost. There was generally a limit to the amount of compensation that an employee could collect. Many labour leaders, including Burt and McDonald, opposed contracting out.[22] Northumberland miners were deeply divided over the issue, and the NMA narrowly voted down an insurance plan favoured by the coal owners.[23]

After McDonald's death in 1881, Burt took over the task of introducing a bill drawn up by the TUC prohibiting the practice of contracting out, which had become common for certain employers, including the railways.[24] While coal mine owners in the North East did not contract out, owners in other regions did so.[25] On several occasions during the 1880s and early 1890s, Burt introduced bills to restrict contracting out. These private member bills usually failed to gain sufficient parliamentary time to be seriously considered.

Powerful opposition to Burt's bills came from the Liberty and Property Defence League, an organization founded in 1882 to protect private property and individual freedom. It included among its members several peers and representatives of trade associations (including the Mining Association).[26] The League hired spokesmen to travel to the coalfields and rally opposition to the amendment. The most notorious of these was John Pringle, a former miner at the Barrington Colliery in Northumberland. He and other paid representatives spoke before at least twelve large gatherings in the North East, where they gained signatures on a petition calling for the defeat of Burt's measure.[27]

For all of Burt's hard work in attempting to amend the liability law, he was never optimistic about its success. Addressing the TUC's annual meeting in 1884, Burt stressed that while the cause for amendment was absolutely just, he had recognized from the beginning that the forces opposed to the measure were exceptionally powerful. More important, he asserted, was the difficulty in getting Parliament to reopen debate on a recently enacted law.[28] Burt continued throughout the 1880s and into the 1890s to lead labour's efforts to revise the Act. His pessimism, however, was fully justified. Even government-sponsored bills to amend the Employers' Liability Act foundered before powerful opposition forces until the passage of Joseph Chamberlain's Workmen's Compensation Bill in 1897.[29]

Disraeli's Tory government of 1874–80 is often credited with enacting reforms benefiting the working class.[30] As we have seen, this government, under the pressure of labour and labour sympathizers, passed two laws in 1875 that gave legal protection to labour unions. However, labour's efforts for an employers' liability law did not reach fruition until Gladstone's Liberal government of 1880. The same was true for two primary issues affecting merchant seamen: safety and civil rights. Labour, especially through the Parliamentary Committee of the TUC, was interested in these issues, as was Burt, who represented the seamen at Blyth. Shortly after entering Parliament, Burt, who introduced several bills on seamen, addressed the issue of the civil rights of seamen while in port. A ship's captain had the right to control and imprison without warrant a sailor who left the ship while in harbour. Burt contended that a seaman who broke contract, e.g. did not report to work or refused to go to sea, while in a harbour should be charged with a civil offence, not a criminal one. Burt wished to provide sailors with protection from seizure or imprisonment without just cause, and the right to be tried, if necessary, in a civil court. These efforts by private members got nowhere in the Tory-controlled Parliament.[31]

After the Liberal victory in 1880, Burt, Cowen, McDonald and others introduced a private bill for the protection of seamen, withdrawing it when Chamberlain, speaking for the government, promised to study the issue.[32] Their efforts were rewarded later in the year with the passage of the Merchant Shipping Act. Burt explained in an article in the *Newcastle Weekly Chronicle* that the Act not only protected seamen from arbitrary actions by employers, but permitted sailors to allot a portion of their pay to their families or to a bank. He was delighted with this provision, which he thought would encourage thrift on the part of the sailors.[33]

While Burt attended to the needs of all workers, his greatest attention in Parliament was directed to the miners. He spent an inordinate amount of time questioning Home Secretaries about mining accidents and safety measures. Mining disasters, especially the spectacular explosions which took so many lives, kept the issue regularly before the mining community and the public at large. Burt was always outspoken when criticizing those responsible for these disasters. He wanted to strip incompetent managers of their certification, 'and in cases where gross mismanagement occurred, . . . those who were guilty . . . should be tried for manslaughter'.[34] While public attention focused on disasters, these large tragedies were not responsible for most mining deaths. Burt was always quick to emphasize that daily accidents, such as the fall of the roof, cumulatively brought the greatest death toll.[35] Burt put constant pressure on the Home Secretaries throughout the 1870s and 1880s to improve mine inspection in order to minimize accidents. Burt found an especially receptive ally in William Harcourt, who served as Home Secretary in Gladstone's administration from 1880–85. Burt clearly admired Harcourt both as a public servant and as a learned friend who loved to talk about literature.[36] In 1884, Burt and Henry Broadhurst, secretary of the TUC's Parliamentary Committee, led a deputation of miners to meet with Harcourt, asking for his support of a resolution calling for an increase in the number of inspectors. Harcourt responded favourably, indicating that he appreciated the importance of the coal industry in providing energy for the nation, and the dangers of working in the trade.[37] Two days later, in one of his longest speeches in the House of Commons, Burt called on the government to provide additional inspectors for the coal mines. He argued that the coal trade, which lay at the very heart of the prosperity of the nation, was a dangerous trade, annually accounting for a huge loss of life and limb. Inspectors, he stressed, had reduced the number of accidents over the previous three decades. The recent rapid expansion of the mining industry, however, outstripped the resources of the inspectors, making it 'physically impossible' for them to make 'any real and thorough inspection of mines'. An increased staff with adequate time to inspect 'narrow and intricate passages' was necessary for the good of miners and the industry. Burt hoped that some of the new inspectors would be selected from the ranks of the working miners, as their increased 'education and mental improvement' would qualify them for the position. The added cost would be well worth the lives saved, and Burt thought that the Home Secretary recognized that 'the salaries of these extra Inspectors for all time' was less than the cost of sending out 'the smallest military expedition'.[38]

The address was vintage Burt. He carefully spelled out the issue, describing coal mining and all of its attendant dangers as only someone who had been there could, and praised virtually everyone in the government and the coal trade for their efforts to improve mining. Harcourt and others responded quickly and positively to the resolution.[39] The following year, the Home Secretary carried out his pledge by adding seven inspectors, although none was from the working class.[40]

Burt's concern with mining safety was most evident during the debates over the Coal Mines Regulation Bill of 1887, the first major piece of safety legislation since the 1872 Act. The bill consolidated existing mining legislation with recommendations suggested by the Royal Commission on Accidents in Mines in 1886.[41] As a member of this commission on mining accidents and as the president of the Miners' National Union,[42] Burt was the leading spokesman for miners during these debates. He stressed that all necessary safety measures be taken to protect the 'lives of the wealth creators in the mines ... all that money, skill, and care could accomplish should be done to protect those who pursued this dangerous occupation'.[43] Burt was heavily involved in the debates and successfully introduced several amendments for certifying mine managers and for the timely inspection of mines before the commencement of a shift.[44] He also gained passage of an amendment prohibiting the employment underground of boys under the age of twelve.[45]

While Burt was reluctant to extend to the State the power to restrict the length of the work-day for adult male workers, he was normally willing to use the power of the State to provide care for the poor, and to correct what he deemed unnecessary social evils.[46] Such was the case with his unsuccessful attempt to introduce an amendment to the 1887 Coal Mines Regulation Bill prohibiting the employment of women at the coal pit-head. This is an important and complex issue, involving not only Burt's attitude to the role of women in society, but also many of the social, economic and political forces shaping late Victorian society.

On the whole, Burt held progressive and enlightened ideas about the role and ability of women. He believed that all educational facilities should be open to them, including endowments at colleges and universities.[47] He also favoured suffrage for women, although he was reluctant to support an amendment to that end in the 1884 debate to extend the franchise to more males, fearing that the amendment might endanger the entire bill.[48] Burt also defended the right of women to organize into unions. Speaking to the annual meeting of the TUC in 1891, Burt argued that 'wherever women [sic] does the same work, in quality and in quantity as men, she ought to ask for the same pay as the man. And we ought to support her, not only on the grounds of justice and humanity, but on grounds of self-defence in asserting that claim.'[49]

At the same time, Burt reflected the prevailing trade union attitude towards the pit-brow women. The term 'pit-brow lasses' originally referred to those working at the pit opening, but had come to include all women working in the coal mine area.[50] In the early 1860s Alexander McDonald had opposed the employment of women at coal mines altogether. His attitude partly reflected a desire to protect the jobs of miners from the competition of women. There were no women employed in the North East mines during the 1870s and 1880s, so Burt was not attempting to protect jobs in his union. About 6,000 pit-brow women were employed in other parts of Britain, including a substantial number in Lancashire.

The issue regarding women's labour at the mines peaked in 1886 and 1887. On 22 January 1886, in a meeting of the Miners' National Conference in Birmingham at which Burt presided, Thomas Ashton of Lancashire moved 'that women be not allowed to work about mines'. The motion passed unanimously.[51] Two months later at a meeting with the Liberal Home Secretary Hugh Childers, Burt testified that he believed that almost all miners wanted to prohibit the employment of women in and about the mines.[52] In 1887, Burt led a delegation to meet with Henry Matthews, the Tory Home Secretary. Burt argued for the abolition of female employment on the 'ground of morality, social order, and harmony with female life and place'.[53] Shortly after this meeting, the pit-brow women held their own conference with the Home Secretary, who was opposed to the abolition of female labour, to present their views in favour of their continued employment.

In the opening debate over the Coal Mines Regulation bill on 20 June 1887, Burt called for an end of 'this relic of barbarism [women's employment at the mine]'. He especially hoped that the Home Secretary had not been unduly swayed by the 'carefully-selected sample of the women of the pits' who had met with him. Several MPs supported Burt, including his mining colleague from Northumberland, Charles Fenwick, who described the heavy tubs that women had to push, and charged that employers hired women in an effort to keep 'down the wages of the labourer'. Benjamin Pickard, a miners' MP from Yorkshire, charged that the pit labour 'unsexes the women – we say that we want our pit women and girls to feel that they are women, and we do not want them to feel that they are exactly like the men by whom they are surrounded'.[54] On the other hand, supporters of the continuation of female labour commented on the excellent moral character of the pit-brow women, their robust health and their usefulness to society. Charles Bradlaugh, a free-thinker and individualist, and a close colleague of Burt, feared the tendency to 'interfere between individuals in this country ... to look to the House of Commons to redress all grievances and to make all people moral, as well as taking care of how they live and what they do'.[55]

On 23 June Burt again commented on the pit-brow women. He admitted that the women's labour was useful and not in itself degrading, and some of it not particularly 'arduous'. Nevertheless, the work as a whole was detrimental to women and needed to be abolished. Women had no basic private facilities at the collieries. He implied that women could not remain morally pure while working at the pits. Burt supported his argument by referring to a particularly impulsive pit-brow woman who had testified at the recent meeting with the Home Secretary:

> She declared that she had left pit work and gone into domestic service, and that as she could not stand the monotony of that kind of service she had gone back to the pit-head. This is a typical instance of the effect of the work in spoiling women for domestic life. If that woman should marry, she will find it very difficult to adapt herself to the restraints which it imposes and become a model wife.[56]

For Burt and his supporters, the mere presence of a woman at the mine made her unfit for her more important role as a wife. Women would not be able to measure up to the moral standards of the period.

The forces marshalled against Burt's arguments were considerable. The *Englishwoman's Review* defended the right of the pit women to their employment. The *Review* argued that the hard work and the dirty conditions, the exposure to coarse language, the need to dress like men, and the charge that the hiring of women led to a decrease in the wages of men, were not unique to pit-brow women. Besides, a woman had the right to earn a living.[57] Protest meetings against the abolition were held at several pits.[58] In addition, the Liberty and Property Defence League, the Personal Rights Association and the Society for the Employment of Women backed the pit-brow women.[59]

The employment of pit lasses was not abolished in the 1880s. The debate over their employment illustrates some of the complex issues facing English society in the late nineteenth century. Coal miners and their leaders were still struggling to improve their standard of living. The presence of the pit-brow women at the collieries was symbolic of the competition encouraged by mine owners to drive down wages. The miners believed that they should be able to earn a wage sufficient to maintain a family by themselves, without 'the wife' working. Moreover, Burt and many other northern union officials of good Methodist background, knew the coarse language and immoral behaviour practised by some of the miners. After all, Burt had been working throughout his career for the moral and educational improvement of the miners. At the same time, Burt must have sympathized with his opponents, who asserted that an individual should be responsible for his or her own actions, free of the constraints of the State. As a good Radical and Liberal, Burt held many of those ideals.

Burt worked hard in Parliament for the labouring class, not only to improve working conditions but also to extend the franchise. He regarded the franchise as a fundamental right as well as a necessary tool to bring about reform.[60] When Burt was elected to Parliament in 1874 by the *borough* of Morpeth, relatively few miners or other workers living in the *counties* were eligible to vote. He regularly backed G. O. Trevelyan's annual motion calling for the equalization of the borough and county franchise requirements. This would extend suffrage to most people living in the rural areas. In supporting Trevelyan's motion in 1876, Burt pointed out the injustice of the present franchise:

> The broad line of distinction between the voters and the non-voters in a country village was this. The voters lived in big houses and never soiled their hands by manual labour; whereas the non-voters lived in the small houses, and were people who tilled the fields and performed the manual labour of the country ... The working classes did not desire patronage or favouritism, but they wanted fair play, and they did not believe they were fairly treated at the present moment.[61]

Over the years, Burt urged workers to indicate clearly their desire for the vote by participating in meetings, demonstrations and petition drives. This pressure was needed, he claimed, to convince political leaders of the necessity of reform.[62] Two huge reform rallies – dominated by the miners – were held in Newcastle in 1883 and 1884, when the movement reached its height.[63]

When it appeared late in the 1884 session that the Liberal franchise bill would be defeated in the House of Lords, Burt almost welcomed the possibility, thinking it would bring to the forefront the entire issue of democracy.[64] Following private negotiations between Gladstone and Salisbury, the franchise bill and a bill to redraw the electoral districts were enacted, thus avoiding a major crisis over the actions of the House of Lords. Burt hoped that the new voting laws would bring more working men into Parliament, although he wanted new members elected for their overall ability, not just because they were of the working class.[65] The miners and their unions made particularly good use of the new franchise laws, and Burt was shortly joined at Westminster by Charles Fenwick, another member of the NMA.

Burt believed that citizens had the right to elect whomever they wanted to Parliament, and that Parliament should respect the wishes of the electorate. As much as Burt loved the House of Commons, he recognized that the institution sometimes failed to operate in an equitable manner, as in the case of Charles Bradlaugh, a well-known atheist and promoter of birth control. When Bradlaugh was elected to Parliament in 1880 by the voters of Northampton, the House of Commons refused to permit him to take the oath of office. Five long years of political struggle ensued before Bradlaugh, who was re-elected after every rejection by the House, was permitted to take his seat. As Walter Arnstein explains, this case reflects the complex political and religious issues dividing Britain.[66]

Burt had known Bradlaugh long before either of them entered Parliament. Bradlaugh was an exceptionally popular speaker in the North East, probably more for his republicanism and Radicalism than for his atheism. He spoke in the small mining community of Seghill as early as 1869, and on one occasion Burt opened his house to Bradlaugh when other places in Blyth were closed to him.[67] He was the most popular speaker at the Northumberland miners' picnic, where he was elected year after year by the miners to address their gala.[68]

Following the initial parliamentary attacks on Bradlaugh in May 1880, Burt reported to his friend, the editor W. T. Stead, that 'the proceedings relative to Mr. Bradlaugh have been discreditable to the House of Commons. I never saw such a manifestation of bigotry & intolerance'.[69] Reminiscent of remarks in his first parliamentary campaign, Burt explained to his constituents on 15 December 1880 that he believed 'theological opinions and such matters should be considered as entirely apart from politics'. He admitted, however, that 'it was quite legitimate in a contested election for people to object to be represented by a man who might hold opinions theological or social of which they entirely disapproved'. He maintained that the 'House of Commons was not the fit tribunal to decide a question of that sort', – that should be decided by the electors of Northampton.[70] At the Northumberland picnic in July 1881, Burt asked the miners to pass a resolution criticizing the actions of Parliament and calling for the Government to 'vindicate the rights for constituencies of free elections'.[71] Shortly thereafter, Burt stressed in Parliament that even though the citizens of the North disagreed with Bradlaugh's religious views, they strongly believed that members of a constituency 'have a right to elect the man they think proper'.[72] Burt was one of seven MPs who voted against the speaker, who had ordered Bradlaugh to be physically removed for entering the lobby of the House.[73]

On 11 February 1884, Bradlaugh once again attempted to take his seat. He was presented to the House of Commons by Burt and Henry Labouchere. During the ensuing debate, Burt remarked briefly that Bradlaugh was 'quite prepared to come to the Bar of the House and enter into an engagement not to disturb its proceedings', when he was interrupted with the shout, 'No, no!' to which Burt responded, 'I do not know, Sir, whether the right hon. Gentleman, who has just addressed the House would wish to bind himself by oath to such engagement.'[74] Following the debate, Burt served as a teller for the division. He reported on the day's events to James Trotter:

Bradlaugh, Labby [Labouchere], and I certainly broke through all the usual forms of the House in marching up the floor without being called upon by the Speaker. I expected to be 'hauled over the coals,' but I suppose Bradlaugh himself afforded material enough for the wild spirits to work upon without importing others into the business. It was a great treat to see the stately Tories including Irish landlords marching through the Lobby, respectfully lifting their hats, & profoundly bowing while they were being counted by Mr. Healey & 'yours truly'.[75]

Bradlaugh was finally seated in 1886 and served in Parliament until his death in 1891. While in the House of Commons, he gained passage of an act permitting MPs to make an affirmation of office rather than take an oath.[76] Burt regarded Bradlaugh as a good man who did much for humanity during his brief term in Parliament. Reminiscing in 1901, Burt thought 'there was something almost tragical in the way that brave, noble, and capable man was treated'. Late in his life, Bradlaugh told Burt, 'My only regret is that I am getting old, and there is so much to be done.'[77]

For Burt, the moral and social development of the working class was as important as the franchise. The key to improving the character of the workers and to their operating successfully in the political arena was better education, although Burt also valued education as an end in itself. Shortly after entering Parliament in 1874, he described the miners' use of shorter hours and higher wages to improve their educational level to make themselves better people, not simply to earn a better living or to enhance their political power: 'we say educate a man, not simply because he has got political power, and simply to make him a good workman; but educate him because he is a man. Educate him because he has an intellect – an intellect of almost boundless power and capacity.'[78]

The Education Act of 1870, which was guided through a Liberal-controlled Parliament by William Forster, provided basic state aid to education. It retained the Anglican schools, while authorizing the creation of school boards to construct and provide for secular schools where needed. For the next two decades, the government continued to define and extend its role in elementary education. Attendance was made compulsory in 1880. School fees were dropped in 1891.[79]

Shortly after he entered Parliament, Burt was appalled at the Disraeli government's apparent reduction in the educational requirements for pauper children. He stressed that the only way to help those in poverty was to give them 'the tools [education] to cut their way to a higher position'. He thought 'the worst economy was to be stingy in paying money for the moral and intellectual improvement of the people in a country'.[80] At the end of each year, Burt addressed his constituents in a series of speeches reviewing the legislative activities of the past session.

In 1876, he concentrated his remarks on education. On 25 November at Shankhouse, he complained of critics who attacked the school boards over money spent on education. He charged that many of these same critics did not complain about the money spent on drink or on the military, which was for 'destructive purposes', nor were they upset over the high cost of ignorance as seen in 'its attendant evils of pauperism and crime'.[81] In December he gave a major address at Blyth on the anniversary of the town's Mechanics' Institute. He praised the nation for having recently recognized the importance of education, and for taking steps to make school attendance compulsory. There had been, and still were, he admitted, certain people in society, especially from the more privileged classes, who believed that education was inappropriate for poor people, as it might make them less willing to do mindless but necessary tasks. He told of a person who had protested to Burt: 'What is the use of so much education? Things will be brought to such a pass soon that we shall have nobody to clean our boots.' To that complaint, he had responded that even if education meant people would no longer agree to perform such tasks, 'the world would not necessarily be brought to a standstill, since those who dirtied their boots would perhaps have courage and manhood enough to set to work and clean them themselves, or, at the worst, they would manage somehow to get on with them uncleaned'. Burt was at his noblest when he described the benefits of education to the whole of humankind:

> Education is no longer the luxury of the few – it belongs exclusively to no one class, to no special period of life. It belongs to all men, and to all time. It is broad as humanity and, rightly considered, it is the great business of life ... The future of the working classes, the future of England, and of the human race depends on the spread of education ... Let us uproot and cast from us for ever everything false, mean, narrow, and implant whatever is true, noble, beautiful, and good – unfold, develope, and cultivate all that is highest and best in man – the heart, the affections, the moral nature, not less than the intellectual faculties with which we are so richly gifted.[82]

The audience loved Burt's speech. In the *Newcastle Weekly Chronicle*, the writer of 'Gossip's Bowl' was amazed with the 'breadth of thought and observation'. He added that Burt was 'a man of whom the entire North of England ought to be proud'.[83]

The speech closely reflected Burt's background and education. He had probably not written it down, as he rarely had time to prepare his remarks to that extent. He provided very few specific examples with regard to education. As always, he was optimistic. He did not concentrate on the forces of the past, which had retarded the growth of education, but rather encouraged people to take advantage of all opportunities: formal elementary education, enlightenment through continual study, and use of the Mechanics' Institutes. More than anything, the speech reflected the many writers and poets whom Burt had lovingly read and admired over the years. He used two brief sets of verses for illustration. The speech was more a literary essay than a formal political address.

While Burt supported the expansion of education to facilitate the intellectual and moral improvement of the people,[84] he also favoured opening public institutions like museums and galleries on Sundays. Throughout the nineteenth century, Sabbatarian and Sunday observance societies fought to keep such institutions closed on Sundays. When Burt and McDonald were elected to Parliament in 1874, Charles Hill of the Working Men's Lord's Day Rest Association requested their support for continued Sunday closings. They declined, due to their support of Sunday afternoon openings of museums.[85] Burt, who was occasionally criticized for his stand, told his constituents that the openings were needed to help raise community moral and educational standards. He was especially distressed that some who wanted to keep museums closed were the same people who demanded that pubs be kept open. He realized that there were some churchgoers who wanted museums closed so as not to lure people away from church. He argued, however, that no one could require people to attend church.[86] In 1882, Burt seconded a resolution in favour of the Sunday opening of institutions including the National Gallery and the British Museum. He argued that the exhibits would be most beneficial for the working classes, who often had no other days available to visit such places. Workers, he emphasized, regularly sought wholesome recreation.[87] It was not until 1896, however, that Parliament passed a law enabling several national institutions in London to open on Sunday afternoons.[88] Burt had little tolerance for the inordinate amount of time that Parliament spent on religious affairs, particularly those involving the Church of England. He opposed a state church, and on first entering Parliament he complained to his electors that the House devoted 'some of the best weeks and months of the session in deciding a question as to whether a clergyman should stand with his face to the east or to the west, or whether they should have lighted candles upon their altars'.[89]

To improve their lifestyle, members of the working class also needed to exercise political power on both local and national levels. Burt wished to do away with all property qualifications as a requirement for serving in local offices. In 1879, he emphasized that local authorities had many important problems to deal with, including sanitation and housing. In smaller communities the choice of candidates was often so limited that voters could not find someone in whom they had confidence. He cited an example of a small mining community of 2,000 in Northumberland in which only twelve to fifteen people were eligible to serve on the local governing board, and those were all under the control of the colliery owner. Burt pointed out that he had lived in his present borough for fourteen years, but he had not yet occupied a house that would qualify him as a member of a local board. It was, he maintained, 'an anomaly that ought to be remedied that a man could not be a member of a Local Board, and yet he might be sent to take part in legislation affecting the whole Empire'.[90] When a local government bill was finally passed in 1888, Burt supported an amendment providing officials with compensation for reasonable travel expenses to attend meetings. Otherwise, he stressed, only the middle class could afford to serve.[91]

No area of local political control was more important to Burt than the licensing of public houses. The temperance movement, closely related to licensing, played a central role in Burt's personal and public life. According to Aaron Watson, this was a 'topic which had been close to his heart from his early days. He never pleaded on any subject more earnestly than in the cause of temperance.'[92] Temperance was common among the Primitive Methodists in the northern coalfields. His father signed the pledge to abstain from alcoholic drinks in 1836, and Burt decided to abstain at the age of fifteen. While a hewer at Choppington in the early 1860s, he became the unpaid secretary of the Northern Federation of Temperance Societies and spoke at several temperance meetings. He was a long-time member of the Order of Good Templars, a member and vice-president of the North of England Temperance League, and was associated with the United Kingdom Alliance, the National Temperance Federation and the Newcastle Band of Hope.[93] In an address to the Northern Light Lodge of Good Templars in 1874, Burt referred to drink as a 'great evil', and a waste of 'good nutritious grain'. Drink, he charged, created social problems, 'filled our gaols, workhouses, lunatic asylums, and sent to a premature grave thousands upon thousands of victims every year'. Two years later, at a temperance rally of 50,000 working men and women, Burt asserted that the public house was often a detriment to other workers' institutions, such as chapels and schools. Daniel Defoe, he said, once wrote,

> Wherever God erects a house of prayer,
> The devil always builds a chapel there;
> And 'twill be found upon examination,
> The latter hath the largest congregation.

Burt realized that early temperance reformers had not considered the social needs of people, and had failed to 'provide a healthy, pure, and harmless substitute for the public-house'. By the 1870s, he was encouraged by increased emphasis on education and better housing to overcome the drink problem.[94]

In the 1850s, the United Kingdom Alliance, a leading temperance organization, promoted a permissive bill giving local ratepayers the right to prohibit the sale of drink in their area with a two-thirds majority vote. Beginning in the 1860s, Sir Wilfrid Lawson led the Alliance effort in the House of Commons by regularly introducing the Permissive Bill, which was consistently defeated.[95] Burt always supported the Bill, as he believed that the working class should have the right to make decisions with regard to the sale of drink in their own localities. He seems to have been more concerned about who made the ultimate licensing decision than over drink itself: 'It is a question', he argued, 'of whether or not the inhabitants of a locality should have a voice in deciding if they will have public-houses, or that magistrates and landowners should decide that for them.' There were, he said, some 2,000 districts in the United Kingdom where landlords declared that there would be no public houses.[96] Burt wanted the workers to have political authority in these matters.[97]

Burt was a very popular speaker at temperance meetings in the Newcastle area. He called for local power for the people, encouraged young people to abstain from drink, and stressed that while temperance would not *end* poverty, it would help to alleviate it.[98] Controlling drink was for him an all-encompassing issue, as it involved political rights, social issues and moral rectitude. While his efforts in Parliament were unsuccessful, he believed that the efforts of the temperance reformers did educate the public on the evils of drink. Burt's finest parliamentary effort on licensing would not come until 1904, during the debate over the Balfour government's Licensing Bill.

Chapter 6

THE MONARCHY, THE EMPIRE AND FOREIGN AFFAIRS

Before examining Burt's views on the monarchy and Britain's foreign relations, let us glance at some personal aspects of his public and private life. Involved locally and nationally in both politics and labour relations, as well as raising a large family, Burt was an exceptionally busy person. Though he spent several months of each year in London, as a conscientious politician he also paid careful attention to his local constituency.

Burt maintained close ties with his borough. He attempted to address his constituents at the end of every session, usually giving speeches at Morpeth, Bedlington and Blyth. His friends, as well as an agent, coordinated and scheduled these engagements. While Burt faced no electoral opposition in the 1880s, he still found it necessary to raise funds should he be faced with an opponent at the last moment.[1] James Trotter, the Radical doctor in Bedlington and Burt's close friend, served as an informal political advisor, as did Thomas Glassey, a miner who also worked as his agent. Both had played leading roles in Burt's election to Parliament in 1874.

The largest collection of Burt's personal letters are found in the Trotter Papers at the Northumberland Record Office. Trotter was always willing and eager to make the necessary arrangements for Burt's talks.[2] Burt enjoyed receiving Trotter's letters and original election ballads, apparently full of wit and wisdom about happenings in Northumberland.[3] In one delightful letter written on 16 March 1880, from the House of Commons, Burt thanked him: 'Your letters do me a power of good. They raise my spirits, stir my sluggish liver into activity, and digestion and renovate the whole physical, moral & spiritual system. Send me another packet.' Burt could also share with Trotter his criticism of those whose judgement was shaped by a warped view of Christianity: 'I cannot stomach those loud-mouthed champions of orthodoxy who go whoring and fuddling about, & professed to be shocked at the slightest departure from the narrow shibboleth they set up to worship.'[4]

Among his many duties, Thomas Glassey regularly updated the parliamentary register of electors, a time-consuming but necessary task in a district where movement of voters was common.[5] Burt participated in a testimonial to Glassey in 1884, when he moved to Queensland, Australia. There Glassey became involved in politics, was elected to the Queensland legislature and served in the first parliament of the Commonwealth of Australia.[6]

Burt found time to do some writing. During the parliamentary session of 1877, he wrote a series of articles on social, industrial and political issues for the *Newcastle Weekly Chronicle*. While the articles are not profound, they do illustrate Burt's broad interests, including reform rather than simple punishment of convicts, the propensity of the French peasant to save more than the English urban worker, the need for more effective local government, and the dangers of working on the railways.[7] In January 1878, however, Burt turned down a request by W. T. Stead to write a London letter for the *Northern Echo*, citing that he was much too busy.[8] In the early 1880s, Burt wrote short articles on Methodism, trade unions, Ireland and war.

We know very little about Burt's family life during this period. His father, Peter, having lived with his son's family for many years, died on 27 September 1882.[9] The growing Burt family resided at 35, Lovaine Crescent, in Newcastle. In late April 1881, Burt was summoned to the Newcastle police court to answer for non-compliance of the Vaccination Acts in regard to his son, Wilfrid, who was born on 21 August 1879. Thomas Burt did not appear, but his wife, Wilfrid and NMA official John Nixon did. The court ordered that the child receive a vaccination shot within thirty days. On 14 June, however, the Burts (only Mrs Burt was present at court) were fined 20s. and costs for failing to obey the order. Apparently the Burts refused to comply as a matter of principle.[10] Two years later Burt asked in Parliament if the government intended to revise or repeal the compulsory clauses of the Vaccination Acts.[11] In his actions Burt reflected a common working-class suspicion of a central government which was perceived as violating one's privacy.[12] Earlier, Burt opposed a private bill which would have restrained or regulated those who were not formally trained in medicine, such as herbalists.[13] In 1878, Burt testified in an advertisement in the *Newcastle Weekly Chronicle* that he and his family used 'DR. WHITE'S COMPOSITION ESSENCE' to treat a variety of ailments.[14] In fact, Burt was often ill and complained about a lingering cold and not feeling 'first-class for some time'.[15] In October 1879, he told Stead: 'I have been laid up a fortnight – unable even to write a letter. An attack of inflammation of Liver – complicated with touch of inflammation of the bowels, & intermittant fevers. I am mending fast, but still so feeble that I can just walk out for ten minutes.' On at least two occasions he went to the Hexham Hydropathic establishment for a water cure.[16]

In spite of his less than robust health – respiratory ailments would always plague him – Burt did some travelling. In late 1883, he spent ten weeks touring the United States and Canada, visiting friends who had emigrated from the North of England, inspecting coal mines in Ohio, Illinois and Pennsylvania, as well as other industrial centres, studying American labour unions, and examining educational facilities. Burt wrote two articles on his tour for the *Pall Mall Gazette*, edited by W. T. Stead. Also present at the *Gazette* was Aaron Watson, who had served as assistant editor of the *Newcastle Weekly Chronicle* and would later write Burt's biography.[17]

Burt visited Ireland in 1886 and Switzerland in 1887 with his friend, James Annand, who served as editor of the *Newcastle Daily Chronicle* from 1873 to 1878, finally breaking with Cowen over policy on the Eastern Question and Russia. Of working-class origins and self-educated like Burt, Annand became, in 1885, editor of the *Newcastle Daily Leader*, a Liberal newspaper established by the wealthy colliery owner James Joicey to counter Cowen's *Chronicle*. The Radical Cowen and the Liberal political leaders of Newcastle were in bitter disagreement over the direction of local and national politics throughout much of the late 1870s and the 1880s.[18]

Burt's parliamentary efforts were devoted extensively to gaining greater social and political equality for members of the working class. Equality and fairness would also be the basis for Burt's observations on the monarchy, as well as the government's conduct of foreign and imperial affairs.

By the early 1870s the royal family had fallen into disfavour and a republican movement calling for the end of the monarchy emerged. The unpopularity of the Crown was due partly to Queen Victoria's long seclusion from public ceremonies after the death of her husband, as well as to the embarrassing activities of her son, the Prince of Wales.[19] The Queen's constant requests to Parliament for financial support for members of the royal family caused public outrage. While Burt did not oppose the monarchy as an institution, he openly criticized the royal family for its constant demands for public funds. On 30 July 1874, shortly after taking his seat, Burt commented on a bill providing a £15,000 annuity for Queen Victoria's son, Prince Leopold, upon his coming of age: 'these repeated applications to the public purse for the maintenance of the Royal Family should by some means be put an end to'.[20] The issue of royal subsidy emerged again in 1875 when the Prince of Wales requested substantial government funds to help pay for his personal visit to India.[21] Burt opposed the bill because the visit was essentially a private affair and the funds requested were substantial. The Conservative-dominated Parliament, however, approved the sum of £112,000; the government of India was expected to contribute £30,000.[22] Burt was also disturbed over the £250,000 spent in India in 1876 on 'pageantry and pomp' to celebrate Victoria's new title, 'Empress of India'.[23] In 1878, Burt refused to support an additional annuity of £10,000 on the marriage of the Duke of Connaught, another of the Queen's sons. Burt did not believe that the Chancellor of the Exchequer's remark as to the 'amiability and accomplishments' of the royal couple was sufficient justification for the requested annuity:

> If the Royal Duke and his intended bride had been less accomplished and less amiable than they were, he presumed that this demand would still have been made; and even in these degenerate days, and with all the vices that abounded, he should incline to think there was a very large number of amiable and accomplished people who would like very well to be married and have £10,000 a-year added to their incomes.

Burt reminded the MPs that they should 'not be surprised if a man who worked hard for 15s. or £1 a-week should look at a subject of this sort from a somewhat different standpoint from that of the man who enjoyed an income of £15,000 to £25,000 a-year'.[24] Burt often mixed the light-hearted with the serious, and he was especially successful at spelling out the incongruities between the wealthy and the poor. He was polite to an extreme. According to observers over the years, he was always carefully listened to and respected by members on both sides of the House.

On 29 July 1889, fifteen years after Burt first questioned the process of voting subsidies for the royal family, he again returned to the attack, this time over a grant for the children of the Prince of Wales. The working class, he said, resented these subsidies for they disliked the 'artificial distinctions, the social inequalities, and the extravagance prevailing in high places'. He concluded his remarks with sage advice that serves the late twentieth century as well as it did the late nineteenth:

> The Crown, I believe, has a firm hold on the people of this country; but its future must depend on its securing the confidence, the affection, and the good-will of the masses of the community. We have a right to look to the Court, we have a right to look to the Crown not only for an example of pure living and domestic virtue, which I dare say it gives, but also for a model of sensible housekeeping and of wise expenditure of money.[25]

Greater notoriety came to Burt, however, over Prince Louis Napoleon, the son of Napoleon III. After the Franco-Prussian War and the overthrow of Napoleon III, Prince Louis Napoleon lived in England, where he was educated at the military academy at Woolwich.

He yearned to regain control of the French government for his family. In the late 1870s, he requested assignment to South Africa, but the British government turned him down. He went out, nevertheless, in an unofficial capacity, and was killed by the Zulus in 1879. Queen Victoria was distraught over his death, and the royal court requested that a statue be placed in Westminster Abbey to honour the fallen prince. Many people in Britain, however, vocally opposed the statue and staged major protests.[26] On 8 August 1879, the House of Commons debated the proposed monument. Burt spoke out strongly against it, arguing that the prince had gone to South Africa 'to win a name and a reputation, in order to strengthen his position as a claimant to the Throne of a neighbouring and friendly nation'. The prince, Burt added, did not qualify for such an honour. Besides, if this man was to be honoured, should not those English soldiers who had died at the same time also be recognized?[27] At the NMA picnic the following summer, Burt described the absurdity of erecting a statue to Louis Napoleon, whose family had caused so much suffering in the world.[28] On 16 July 1880, Parliament passed a resolution urging that the statue not be placed in Westminster Abbey.[29] As a result, the statue came to rest in St George's Chapel at Windsor.

Both Liberal and Tory governments conducted aggressive imperial and foreign policies in the last quarter of the nineteenth century. On several occasions – in Afghanistan, South Africa and Egypt – these governments chose to wage war. Great Britain and Russia were often on the verge of conflict as they vied for influence in central Asia and in the Ottoman Empire. The affairs of Ireland, particularly the issue of Home Rule, came to preoccupy the British government. As an MP and a citizen, Burt was deeply concerned with these issues. When he addressed these problems, other political leaders were attentive, since he was perceived to reflect the views of the large labouring element. Burt himself was always careful to emphasize that he did not speak for the working class. No single person, he said, could speak for such a large portion of society whose opinions and ideas were as diverse as those of the other classes.

In 1876 the 'Eastern Question' again exploded onto the scene. A revolt by subjects in Bosnia sparked several wars in the eastern part of the Ottoman Empire, and reports emerged of a Turkish massacre of Christian subjects in Bulgaria. Gladstone, who had retired as the Liberal Party leader, returned to the public platform, angry that Disraeli refused to take action to control the brutal Turkish government. Russia launched a war against Turkey after Turkey refused to initiate reforms for its Balkan subjects. Disraeli – by this time Lord Beaconsfield – considered Russia's presence in the Ottoman Empire a threat to Britain's interests in the area and sent the fleet to the Dardanelles. War fever swept Britain. The Treaty of San Stefano ended the war between Russia and Turkey in 1878, but Britain regarded the pact as too advantageous to Russia. The Congress of Berlin of 1878, attended by Disraeli and Foreign Secretary Lord Salisbury, substantially reduced Russia's influence in the Balkans and gave Austria administrative rights over Bosnia and Herzegovina.

Having been in Parliament for two years when the crisis erupted, Burt helped to dampen enthusiasm in the North East for war against Russia.[30] Though usually a non-interventionist, he felt that steps had to be taken to protect the lives of Christian women, children, and unarmed men.[31] At Blyth he spoke of Britain's obligation to help solve the tragedy, short of becoming the world's policeman. Because it had long defended the Ottoman Empire and made its survival possible, Britain was compelled to pressure the Turkish government to change its ways.[32]

Burt led or addressed several London rallies in opposition to Tory policy. On 2 May 1877, he chaired a meeting in London sponsored by the Labour Representation League at which 150 delegates of labour organizations criticized Disraeli's support of a corrupt Turkish government. William Morris, the Socialist and founder of the Eastern Question Association, was in attendance. He thought that the meeting, which included some people from the middle class, had gone very well, and that Burt 'spoke excellently though shortly, with a strong Northumberland tongue: he seemed a capital fellow'.[33] On 10 April 1878, Burt addressed a large peace meeting sponsored by the Workmen's Peace Association. He blamed the possibility of war on 'mismanagement of the Government', and emphasized that British workers and their leaders, contrary to many reports, were not advocates of war.[34]

Burt's efforts for international peace reflected his working class ethic. The Workmen's Peace Association (WPA) was central to his endeavours. William Cremer founded the WPA in 1870 in an effort to keep Britain neutral during the Franco-Prussian War.[35] This was one of many peace organizations formed after 1870. Those interested in peace, including Quakers, liberals and nationalists, agreed on the use of arbitration as a useful tool.[36] By August 1872, the WPA had held sixty-five public meetings promoting international arbitration, and had circulated petitions encouraging the government to 'take the initiative in establishing a permanent system of international arbitration'.[37] Burt represented the NMA at a WPA meeting in Newcastle in April 1873. Shortly after the meeting, the NMA voted to send £3 3s. to the peace society.[38]

Burt was appalled that three European nations supported standing armies totalling 5.5 million soldiers. This was, he told his constituents in 1875, a great waste of men and resources. During the nineteenth century, he added, Britain had devoted the majority of its national expenditures for war. He thought that the time had come when 'working classes throughout Europe should speak out on this subject, and declare that we should refer all these international disputes to the tribunal of law and reason rather than the bloody arbitrament of the sword'.[39] Burt's outlook fitted the philosophy of the WPA. Not only did he wish to use arbitration in international disputes, but he regarded arbitration as an integral aspect of union bargaining. Moreover, he viewed his role in Parliament as one of mediation and arbitration. Burt became the president of the WPA (later renamed the International Arbitration League) in about 1880, and remained in that position into World War I.[40]

Burt took every opportunity to express his opinion that members of the working class were not champions of war. He was convinced, he told W. T. Stead, that 'any attempt to involve this country in war to assist Turkey would meet with the unanimous & determined opposition of the working people'.[41] While Burt enjoyed the support of the NMA in his criticism of the government's Russian policy,[42] he was castigated by many Newcastle newspapers. On 18 May 1878, Burt presided at an anti-war rally on the Newcastle town moor. Though critical of Turkey, he condemned as warlike the actions of his own government, such as voting additional funds for the military, calling up reserves and bringing soldiers from India. Moreover, he did not believe that Russia's operations posed as great a threat as the British government claimed.[43] Burt disagreed with the *Newcastle Daily Chronicle* and Cowen, who had been exceptionally critical of Gladstone's defence of Russia and had defended the performance of the Tory government.[44] Burt continued to censure the British government for having done 'nothing for the purpose of protecting the oppressed' and then intervening 'as soon as anyone else had attempted to make the attack upon the cruel oppressor'.[45] Meanwhile, the Tory government engaged Britain in a war with Afghanistan.

The government feared that an aggressive Russia would endanger both the crumbling Ottoman Empire and India, centrepiece of the British Empire. Since the end of the Crimean War, the Russians had been expanding into Central Asia, and British officials considered the Russian advance a threat to British India. When Lord Lytton, the aggressive Viceroy in India, feared that the Afghan Amir had fallen under Russian control, he sent a military force under General Frederick Sleigh Roberts to Afghanistan. War began late in 1878.

Burt told his constituents on 3 December 1878, that the war in Afghanistan was 'unjust' and 'uncalled for'.[46] Two weeks later, in his first parliamentary speech on foreign affairs, Burt declared the war 'indefensible'. British officials had not dealt openly and honestly with the Amir, and the government had not deliberated sufficiently before resorting to war. Parliament had not been consulted and the public had not been properly informed. He particularly hoped that the government would not dump the cost of this fiasco on the 'patient, dumb, and famine-stricken millions of India, who had no articulate voice, and who were now groaning under the military despotism of our Empire'.[47] While General Roberts quickly won a victory and laurels, the peace did not hold. In September 1879, members of the British mission at Kabul were murdered and Roberts led a second invasion of Afghanistan. Ultimately, Britain would exercise influence in Afghanistan through the new amir, Abdur Rahman. Historians have agreed with Burt's charges that the war was 'unnecessary'.[48]

Disraeli's government became embroiled in another unpopular imperial war in the late 1870s, this one in South Africa. The war against the Zulus, caused in part by Britain's representative Bartle Frere, involved embarrassing and deadly reverses for British forces and led to the untimely death of Prince Louis Napoleon. Speaking to his constituents in January 1880, Burt remarked that he 'knew of nothing more unjust, more unprovoked, more utterly infamous, than our wars in Afghanistan and in Zululand'. He contended that the Zulus had

never done us any harm, nor interfered with us in the slightest degree. With our Gatling guns and other machines of destruction we killed or murdered – aye, murdered was the proper word – thousands of those brave, but poorly-armed and half-naked savages.

Burt contended that people were often critical of those daring to question government foreign policy. He, for one, refused to accept restrictions which meant: 'Back up your own country, right or wrong, and misrepresent other countries as much as possible.'[49] Disraeli's government was eventually turned out of office by the election of 1880, partly because of the blunders in Afghanistan and South Africa.

Burt was a staunch Liberal-Radical, and whenever the opportunity arose, he criticized foreign ventures of the Tory government. He was, on the whole, a 'Little Englander'. This label placed him comfortably within the influential Radical wing of the Liberal Party, as well as within the labour tradition, which was critical of Britain's ambitious imperial commitments.[50] Burt did not call for the dismantling of the Empire. He did not object to Britain's continued presence in India, although he often pressed the government to reduce taxes on the Indian people.[51] At the same time, he adamantly disputed Britain's expansion into Burma in 1886, an aggression that occurred under successive Liberal and Tory governments. He argued that it was wrong for several reasons. Parliament had had no opportunity to debate the annexation. He could find no justification for the government's actions. He argued that France, contrary to initial reports, had not been secretly meddling in the affairs of Burma thereby posing a threat to British Indian interests. Moreover, the cost of occupation would fall on the shoulders of the poor Indians or Britons who did not support such aggression.[52]

Burt was willing to censure a Liberal government when its actions extended Britain's obligations overseas. The most notable example was the entanglement of Gladstone's government in Egypt in 1882 to protect Britain's financial and strategic interests. Following the British naval shelling of Alexandria on 11 July 1882, the British government sent in a military force under Garnet Wolseley to restore order, all ostensibly to aid the Egyptian government.

Muriel Chamberlain argues that Gladstone's government failed to recognize that unrest in Egypt was, to a great extent, similar to nationalist movements elsewhere in Europe. Chamberlain also contends that the occupation

> attracted remarkably little criticism at home at the time. Only later were the arguments marshalled that it had been an intervention, not even to protect the Suez Canal, but to protect the British bondholders, who had been battening on Egypt. The very fact that Gladstone was Prime Minister silenced many of the groups who would have denounced such an action by Disraeli.[53]

While Chamberlain's evaluation may be true for most critics, Burt and his associates were certainly the exceptions.

On 20 June 1882, three weeks before the British bombardment of Alexandria, Burt presided over a London conference of MPs and working men to protest British involvement in Egypt. As president of the Workmen's Peace Association, Burt remarked to the assembly that 'it could not be imagined that the people would allow a war to be undertaken for the protection of the interests of Egyptian bondholders, or to bolster up a Government which was clearly against the wishes of the population of that country'.[54] In 1882, shortly after the invasion of Egypt, Burt wrote 'Working Men and War' for the *Fortnightly Review*. Penned two years before the Reform Bill of 1884 significantly broadened the franchise, the article claimed that the larger presence of the working class in the political process would have a beneficial impact on Britain's foreign policy. The workers would not be 'brawling Jingoes or aggressive Imperialists', and would demand greater moral justification for armed involvement than had normally been the case. He believed that working men were prone to encourage the use of arbitration to solve international problems. They had shown their careful prognosis of the Egyptian affair by speaking against involvement and later urging the government to withdraw as quickly as possible.[55]

In February 1883, Burt told his constituents that he still believed that the invasion had been unjust. While he admitted that Britain had a right to keep open its lines to India, he saw no evidence that these had been threatened in this instance. Over the next two years, Burt regularly called on the government to leave Egypt as quickly as possible.[56] He opposed the annuity to Lord Wolseley for his services in Egypt,[57] and was critical of the military force sent to the Sudan under General Charles Gordon.[58] In a peace meeting in London sponsored by the WPA on 24 February 1885, Burt attacked those who said Britain must assert itself in the area of Egypt in order to retain control over India. If, he said, India was attached to Britain with 'so frail a thread ... the sooner the thread was snapped the better'.[59]

The day before the London meeting, Burt spoke in Paris before a standing-room-only crowd of four to five thousand, as part of a WPA delegation meeting with French workers. Burt charged that wars occurred because people permitted 'scheming politicians and financiers to excite international jealousies and unreal fears of invasion'. Moreover, journalists contributed to the warlike atmosphere surrounding Egypt and other recent crises. Though the noisy meeting was crowded, warm, and even interrupted by anarchists, Burt was pleased with the conference. That evening he met with Georges Clemenceau, then editor of *La Justice*, to thank him for his critical speech in the Chamber of Deputies on the Egyptian imbroglio.[60]

Irish affairs were central to British politics in the 1870s and 1880s. Burt had been a strong supporter of Irish Home Rule even before he entered Parliament. In 1874 Burt and Cowen consistently voted with Irish members against the government's coercion bill, and they were two of ten English MPs who voted in favour of Isaac Butt's Home Rule motion.[61] However, Burt had difficulty reconciling his stance with the violence and crime in Ireland and with the aggressive behaviour of the Irish MPs, whose actions came to hinder the normal conduct of business in the House of Commons. Burt was eventually forced to defend himself against denunciation from Newcastle area critics.

In 1869 and 1870, Gladstone's Liberal government passed bills disestablishing the Anglican Church in Ireland and providing aid for Irish peasant farmers. Gladstone expected that these acts would reduce Irish grievances against the British government and would help to pacify Ireland. A Home Rule movement, calling for self-government in domestic affairs, gathered strength throughout Ireland in the 1870s. Michael Davitt and Charles Stewart Parnell made Home Rule a powerful political programme by the late 1870s, shortly after Burt entered Parliament. Parnell, a Protestant Irish landlord, was elected to Parliament in 1875. He and a handful of supporters began obstructing parliamentary business in 1877 by utilizing – many regarded it as abusing – their right to comment on legislation.[62] While gaining the attention of the government and the country, this tactic did little to endear Parnell to those English MPs who supported Home Rule. Meanwhile, Davitt founded the Land League in 1879 to aid Irish peasants caught in an agricultural depression. In addition to providing direct relief through funds raised especially among Irish-Americans, the

League attempted to gain land ownership for the peasants. Parnell became the President of the Land League, thus uniting Irish economic and political interests in the Home Rule movement.

The Tory government was replaced in April 1880 by Gladstone's second Liberal Cabinet. Gladstone's government took a step to alleviate tension in Ireland by not renewing the Coercion Act, which had permitted – by suspending the writ of habeas corpus – the arrest and imprisonment of Irish people suspected of committing crimes. The Liberal government then introduced the Compensation for Disturbances bill, a temporary measure to provide compensation for peasants evicted from their land. While it narrowly passed in the Commons, it failed in the Lords, where many Liberals voted against it.[63]

Like most Radicals, Burt supported the Compensation for Disturbances bill of 1880. It troubled him that some Irish Land Leaguers and Liberals voted against the government. He told his constituents that the 'Western Question', that is, Ireland, was as complicated and volatile as the Eastern Question. England, he emphasized, had served Ireland very badly for 700 years, but he believed that the English now wanted to do what was right. He was confident that the Liberal government, which had not renewed the Coercion Act, would work to improve Irish affairs and gain a comprehensive and just land bill. Speaking in January 1881, Burt expressed his hope that the government 'would pass a thorough, generous, and radical measure in support of [Ireland]'.[64] Events proved that Burt was far too optimistic about a resolution to the Irish problem. Moreover, on this contentious issue he would disagree with Cowen and many of his traditional supporters.

Following the defeat of the compensation bill by the Lords, the Land League stepped up the pressure on large Irish landowners and their agents by withholding rent. This 'land war' often turned violent, although the Land League itself did not approve the use of force. Radical pressure from inside as well as outside the Cabinet helped dissuade the Gladstone government from introducing a new coercion bill in 1880. In early 1881, however, the Cabinet decided to introduce such a bill, to be followed by a comprehensive land bill. Clearly the government had decided to put coercion at the top of its plan to address disturbances sweeping Ireland. Few events so split the Radicals as the debate over Ireland in 1881 and 1882. Virtually all Radicals recognized that the Irish had a real and great grievance. At the same time, there appeared to be a fundamental breakdown of law and order in Ireland. What was to be done? To some Radicals, freedom without order was of no value.[65]

Burt preferred that the government introduce a land bill first, to be followed, only if necessary, by a coercion bill. He and Cowen were among the relatively few Radicals who voted for Parnell's amendment opposing the introduction of a coercion bill at the opening of the legislative session in 1881.[66] When the Irish Secretary William Forster introduced the coercion bill, Parnell renewed his obstructionist tactics in Parliament. On 25 and 26 January, the government moved to take over private members' parliamentary time in order to expedite debate on the coercion bill. While Cowen vigorously opposed this, Burt supported the government, which easily carried the measure.[67] He turned down a request to speak against coercion at a public meeting in Chelsea, indicating that while he was opposed to coercion except when 'absolutely necessary', he did not wish to speak in public about it.[68] Burt was clearly uncomfortable with the course of events. He wrote to James Trotter that he disliked voting against the government, and 'I fear I shall have to do so again. Some of my anti-coercion friends are pressing me to speak against Forster's Bill. But added to my natural and constant disinclination to speech-making my attachment to the government & my confidence in them act as a barrier.'[69] Burt admired Gladstone and believed in the government. He was simply unwilling to take a strong public stand in opposition.

On 3 February 1881, Home Rulers' obstruction reached its height when thirty-six Irish MPs were suspended and ejected from the Commons.[70] Over thirty years later, when writing about his parliamentary experiences, Burt was still troubled by the incident. While he respected the Speaker's unprecedented steps to expedite parliamentary business, his recollection of the expulsion of the MPs was still 'so painful that I do not care to dwell on it in detail'.[71] Although the coercion bill passed, Burt voted against the second and third readings, and also many of its separate clauses. He had, however, voted against Parnell when the latter resorted to obstructionist measures, as Burt feared that such tactics hurt representative government.[72] Meanwhile, Cowen openly and stridently led opposition to the government's coercion policy, both within Parliament and outside.[73] Heated debate over coercion also broke out in the mining community. Burt responded to Trotter, who had written to Burt describing a turbulent meeting at Choppington Scotland Gate: 'I am sorry there are such divisory opinions & sentiment among you. I can however sympathize with both parties, for I am divided myself. I never spent a few weeks in such wretchedness since I came to the House of Commons as during this session.' Burt told Trotter that he was particularly upset with Cowen and the *Chronicle*, both seemingly determined to attack the government relentlessly and unfairly.[74]

In April 1881, Burt wrote 'Working Men and the Political Situation' to express what he understood to be the thoughts of the northern working class on events in Ireland. In spite of a favourable disposition towards Home Rule, many working-class people disapproved of actions taken by the Irish. Burt thought that workers and Radicals were alienated by the assault on the Liberal Party made by Home Rule

MPs. They had attacked an ally, ignoring the fact that the previous Conservative government turned a deaf ear to all of their proposals. Moreover, the Irish, who sent many speakers to the north of England, had made the mistake of appealing to class hostility and distrust of government, feelings which were no longer widespread. Also, trade unions did not readily accept the Irish contention that the Land League was equal to earlier labour unions, because England's unions, even under the most trying circumstances, had been almost always law-abiding. Respectability and proper use of power, Burt implied, were of utmost importance to the unions. Also, English unions were led by men of the trades, while leaders of the Land League were from outside the ranks of the peasants. The policy of obstruction particularly disturbed members of the working class, who respected the hard-earned power of the House of Commons. Burt stressed that even when land reform was granted, the political issue of independence would remain. There was no agreement, even among sympathizers, on what the final form of independence should be. Perhaps, he indicated towards the end of the article, the final form should follow the Scottish example, wherein substantial control over local affairs preserved traditions and customs.[75]

Following the passage of the Coercion Act, the Liberal government introduced, as promised, a major land bill that provided for the famous three Fs – fixity of tenure, fair rents and free sale. This bill went a long way to fulfilling the demands of the Irish peasants.[76] Many Radicals were disturbed when Parnell found it impossible, for political reasons in Ireland, to support the Land Act openly. A short time later, in October 1881, Parnell was arrested and the Land League suppressed.[77] On 14 October not long after Parnell's arrest and imprisonment, Burt addressed a Liberal meeting in Newcastle at which he praised Gladstone's effort in securing the passage of the Land Act. He had grave questions about Parnell's conduct; he thought 'the least they might have expected from patriotic Irishmen was to give the measure a fair trial'.[78]

In late 1881, critics severely attacked Burt for his support of the government's Land Act and his criticism of Parnell and the Land League. The Home Rulers and the anti-coercionists received extensive support in the North East. Over 50,000 Irish lived in the Durham and Newcastle area, and it was common for speakers for the Irish cause to appear there. Moreover, Cowen, in spite of ill health, continued his assault on coercion throughout the summer of 1881. He also sponsored a visit to Ireland by three English workers to report on events there. Among them was John Bryson, who returned an avid supporter of the Land League.[79]

Bryson, the former president of the NMA, led the assault on Burt's position on Ireland. Shortly after Burt's October address in Newcastle,

Bryson denounced Burt for indecisiveness and for failing to educate people on events in Ireland. When presiding over a large meeting of the Blyth branch of the National Land League of Great Britain, Bryson criticized Burt for his support of parts of the coercion bill. The following night, at Wallsend, he contended that the Irish had switched from violence to moral force, recognized the importance of education and organization, and developed outstanding leaders. The conditions among the Irish in the 1880s were similar, he argued, to those of English labour unionists in the North East some fifty years earlier, when they were jailed in their quest to earn a decent living wage.[80]

On 9 November 1881, Burt gave a major address[81] to his constituents at Bedlington. Taking the opportunity to explain his attitude towards the Land League and Parnell, he justified his votes in Parliament and responded to many of the charges made against him by Bryson and others. He began with a standard rebuttal to critics over the coercion bill, reminding them of his opposition to the bill except when Irish MPs 'resorted to deliberate obstruction and to perversion of the rules of the House of Commons'. Citing the actions or explications of Abraham Lincoln, John Stuart Mill, Jean-Jacques Rousseau and others, Burt went to extraordinary lengths to justify the use of coercion on certain occasions. Liberty without law and order simply could not exist. If, Burt said, 'Mr. Parnell himself were President of an Irish Republic he would have to maintain law and order, or put down sedition, or both he and his Republic would soon cease to exist'.

Burt responded specifically to Bryson's charges. In spite of great efforts by Bryson and others to persuade Northumberland miners to support the Land League, very few unions in the North East or elsewhere had done so, even though unions were ordinarily remarkably magnanimous in helping others. Expanding on arguments in his article, Burt emphasized that English unions simply did not perceive the Land League and its activities as being similar to their own experience. He charged that the Land League was actively hindering implementation of the recently passed Land Act because it believed that peasant utilization of the Act's provisions would hurt the Land League itself. Burt concluded that he would continue to work for the welfare of the Irish, no matter what incorrect charges were lodged against him.

According to an account of the speech carried in the *Shields Daily Gazette*, Burt was repeatedly supported with cheers, laughter and applause, though occasionally chided with hisses and shouts of 'No'.[82] The *Newcastle Daily Chronicle*, on the other hand, recounted Bryson's lengthy response and claimed that his resolution, 'That we strongly disapprove of the votes given by Mr. Burt in favour of coercion, or in any way countenancing coercion,' was backed by about one-third of the large audience. The *Chronicle* reported that members moved to thank Burt 'for his very able and instructive address, and begs to assure him of its continued confidence and support'.[83] The *Tyneside Daily Echo* reported that many believed that a vote of no confidence would be carried against Burt, as the pitmen 'have no liking for anything that savours the slightest degree of tampering with the liberty of the subject'. The no confidence vote failed because 'pitmen in the North love liberty much, but they love honesty and order more. It is not easy to persuade them that the man whose course they have watched from childhood with approval is false to them now. They have not lost their trust in Mr. Burt.'[84]

While Burt retained the support of his constituents, public criticism of his stand on Ireland continued for some time. In a long leader on his Bedlington speech, the *Newcastle Daily Chronicle* charged that Burt had succumbed to the attractions of Parliament instead of representing the workers. Burt's speech no longer reflected Radicalism, but showed that he had conformed to the dictates of the Liberal Party. Had a Tory government imposed coercion and made Ireland into an armed camp, Burt would have been one of its greatest critics.[85] Burt was disturbed with the attitude of Cowen and his newspaper over the Irish question. The newspaper, he wrote to his friend George Howell, 'has long been doing its utmost to discredit & to divide the liberal party in the North & to help the Tories'.[86]

Letters critical of Burt continued to be published in the *Newcastle Daily Chronicle*, though none were from miners. Irish MP Frank Hugh O'Donnell accused Burt of making a series of errors on Ireland because of his dependence on conventional and hence incorrect sources of information. J. O. Flanagan, from Houghton-le-Spring in County Durham, insisted that Burt was simply like a dog, running with all the others in the 'great Whig-Liberal-Radical Running Club', without an independent or reliable sense of his own politics.[87] Lloyd Jones, an old Radical who enjoyed substantial support in the North, launched a full-scale attack on Burt's view of the Land League, arguing that Burt absolutely failed to understand Ireland: 'In regard to this matter I have no hesitation in saying that Mr. Burt's speech at Bedlington proves him to have completely, irretrievably, hopelessly broken down.' Indeed, he regarded Burt as a failure as an MP: he has 'so utterly and so bitterly disappointed every hope I was led to entertain of the value of direct labour representation'.[88]

Were these charges against Burt valid? Had he surrendered his Radicalism in favour of the Liberal Party, forgotten his working-class background, dramatically erred in his judgement over Ireland, and failed as an MP? Burt addressed most of these issues before a full house at Morpeth on 30 November. There were those, he said, who were especially disappointed in his not making the Irish issue into a problem of the labouring class. While he counted the miners as great friends and supporters, he had informed them at the outset that he would not go to

Parliament solely as a class representative. That said, he had consistently voted in favour of the Irish worker. To the charge that he would have protested more had a Salisbury-led Tory government imposed coercion rather than Gladstone's Liberal government, he pleaded guilty. He trusted Gladstone, not Salisbury. Salisbury would have imposed coercion without attempting to solve the underlying issue, while Gladstone at least had tried to deal meaningfully with the problem. Did Burt blindly follow the dictates of the party leadership? He believed that the voting lists would show that he voted against the party more often than most Liberals. He approved of the party form of politics because it gave citizens unity and strength. Ultimately, however, his own best judgement was more important than the party position, though normally there was no contradiction between the two. He realized that there would always be constituents disagreeing with his stands, but that was as it should be, 'unless he remained neutral and took neither one side nor the other'. Burt defended Gladstone as a strong political leader. As the driving force during the past session, Gladstone still enjoyed substantial support from the Commons. Gladstone believed he had a mission to aid the Irish; he had been the one political leader willing to do so, thus exposing himself to the ensuing criticism. The Land Act of 1881 was already providing peasants with more security in their holding of land. Peasant land ownership was increasing and housing conditions improving. While he did not believe that total separation of Ireland from Britain would occur or was necessarily desirable, Burt thought that the English people would support a great deal of Irish self-government.[89]

Critics who expected Burt to support the Land League and to tolerate violence in Ireland failed to consider his labour union philosophy. He invariably encouraged unionists to obey the law. Workers were to respect a contract and fulfil it, even if it was unfair. A new contract could rectify its shortcomings. If a strike became necessary, it had to be carried out honourably and legally. One was to use moral suasion, not physical threat or abuse, to discourage blacklegs from going to work. When workers violated the law, they should expect the punishment they deserved. Certainly employers were unfair and abusive of workers, often enjoying the willing collusion of government authorities. Even these circumstances did not warrant labour violence. Just as organization and rational behaviour could ultimately gain for workers respect, rights and a decent contract from recalcitrant employers, so the Irish could gain recognition and support from a British government – especially a Liberal one.

Radicals were bitterly divided over the policy of coercion, and many continued to criticize the government for its application. Even Burt, in spite of what his critics said, had opposed it, with certain exceptions, during its legislative passage. Ultimately, the application of the

Coercion Act did not bring order to Ireland. As a result, Gladstone's government effectively abandoned the policy when it freed Parnell and other leaders in May 1882. Under the Kilmainham Treaty, which gained Parnell's release, the government agreed to help the peasants with rent payments, while Parnell would work to end crime. Conciliation had triumphed over coercion. William Forster, the leading government proponent of coercion, resigned from the Cabinet. A few days later his successor, Lord Frederick Cavendish, and a colleague were assassinated in Dublin's Phoenix Park. Even after these murders the policy of conciliation remained generally in effect. While a new coercion bill was passed, the expectation was that it would not be strictly applied.[90]

Burt struggled mightily over this new coercion bill. He explained to Trotter his ultimate decision on the bill:

> At the very outset I could not but allow that something exceptional & strong was needed in Ireland. On examining the Bill I found several things in it, wh[ich] though exceedingly distasteful, seemed to me to be necessary & justified by the circumstances. On the other hand there were clauses which I could not accept & approve without very great & essential alterations. I could not vote against the Bill, as I thought that would imply that I was opposed to any special legislation, nor could I without explaining my position, vote in favour of it. I therefore took a course which is very unusual with me – I abstained from voting altogether.

Ever the optimist, Burt deemed that 'some solid benefits will be left behind after the tumult subsides'.[91]

By 1882, criticism of Burt had subsided, and by early 1883 Burt contended that conditions in Ireland were improving. Crime had markedly decreased, not because of the coercion acts but because of the effectiveness of the Land Act by which a substantial number of land cases were settled. He continued to favour Home Rule 'as was consistent with the maintenance of the Union between the two countries'.[92] A year later Burt identified more improvement but warned that differences between the North and the South of Ireland, often fomented for political purposes, were a barrier to self-government. England should recognize that moral and economic bonds between England and Ireland must replace the military hold imposed by England. Always looking to the healthy influence of the working class on politics, he hoped that democratization would result in a better Britain.[93] Burt supported Gladstone's Home Rule bill (although he disagreed with certain parts of it) which dominated the political scene in 1886.[94] Even after its defeat in the House of Commons, the Northumberland miners continued to support Gladstone's Home Rule scheme. Burt was returned to Parliament unopposed in 1885 and again in 1886. A discouraged and tired Cowen chose not to run for re-election in 1886.

During the Conservative administration, from 1886 to 1892, Burt continued to champion Home Rule and back tenants' efforts to gain reasonable rents.[95] In the autumn of 1886, Burt and James Annand, the editor of the *Newcastle Daily Leader*, visited areas of Ireland that had seen some of the worst disturbances.[96] Burt continued to object to the use of coercion laws[97] and to support Parnell's criticism of government policy.[98]

Burt's involvement in Britain's foreign and imperial disputes took place while his mining community continued to face major economic difficulties. Although he participated fully in parliamentary affairs, Burt had to work particularly hard among the miners to address ever-mounting labour problems in the 1880s.

Chapter 7

THE NORTHUMBERLAND STRIKE OF 1887

The 1880s proved to be a critical decade for Thomas Burt, for the Northumberland Miners' Association, and for the entire British coal industry. The economic recession which hit the Northumberland mining community in the mid-1870s persisted into the 1880s. Wages remained low and labour unrest was common throughout the nation. Distraught over low pay and short work weeks, and faced with owners who seemed callous to their needs, NMA miners responded angrily in 1887 by waging a strike against the advice of their leaders. The conflict, lasting sixteen weeks and draining most of the financial resources of the NMA, ended in defeat for the union, although Burt and the other officers managed to hold the organization together.

The strike and its aftermath posed a major challenge to Burt. His political and union leadership came into question locally, and he clashed with an emerging breed of critics, including Socialists and aggressive new labour leaders. His conciliatory labour ideology, although still accepted by most miners in the North East, was rejected by many mining leaders elsewhere. In the early 1890s the great county unions of Northumberland and Durham stood separately while miners in other coalfields reached a new level of unity with the creation of the Miners' Federation of Great Britain.[1] On the whole, however, Burt defended himself and his ideology well, and his influence peaked in the 1890s.

Throughout this period, the NMA took steps to strengthen the union and alleviate the distress caused by hard times. The union supported an emigration scheme for miners and their families[2] and continued to pay benefits to miners fired for their union activities.[3] Meanwhile, the union worked to ensure that owners would continue providing cottages or supplemental rent payment for miners. During the previous decade, owners had tried to drop this provision.[4] The Joint Committee of owners and union representatives, one of Burt's proudest accomplishments, continued to function. The committee dealt efficiently with some 3,000 questions and disputes within individual collieries from 1873 to 1886.[5] Burt and other NMA leaders also participated in talks with the enginemen, deputies and mechanics concerning the creation of a federation of various Northumberland mineworkers' associations. The NMA and the deputies (the men responsible for placing supports for mine ceilings) approved the federation in 1882, and the enginemen followed in 1883. The federation met occasionally and fostered some cooperation among the unions.[6] Many miners were upset that non-union men still worked in the mines and argued that since 'moral suasion' had failed to convince such labourers to join, the union should force enrolment by striking select collieries. The executive committee was empowered in 1882 to call such strikes, but it declined to do so.[7]

A slightly improved coal economy brought a measure of relief to the northern coal fields in 1880. The new prosperity proved temporary, however, and by 1881 mining communities in the North East were again faced with a depression. The economic downturn led to a rash of strikes in Durham, while in Northumberland miners expressed their displeasure over the use of the sliding scale.[8] Various lodges called for an end to this scale,[9] which triggered a wage reduction of 2.5 per cent in early 1881.[10]

The lock-out of 1877–78 had led to the adoption of a sliding scale to determine basic wages. Put into effect in late 1879, this scale linked wages to the selling price of coal. Wages were adjusted every three months to reflect the selling price. In Northumberland, there was no minimum or maximum applied to these wages; hence, there could be considerable fluctuation.[11] Burt was convinced that the use of a sliding scale greatly benefited miners. He found it particularly meaningful that owners agreed to open their financial records to help determine the price of coal.[12] Spence Watson, who often served as an arbiter of disputes, saw the scale as 'the simplest and therefore the best method. It does not settle trade disputes, it avoids them.'[13]

Not all miners or labour leaders were as enamoured of the sliding scale as was Burt. In the 1880s, advocates like Lloyd Jones argued that coal production had outstripped demand and had driven down prices and wages. Arbitration and the sliding scale, he contended, did not deal with the impact of overproduction, but simply maintained industrial peace. He believed that both unions and owners would benefit by restricting production.[14]

Burt did not approve of reducing production, except when a local union negotiated a shorter working day. Having replaced the recently deceased Alexander McDonald as president, Burt presided at a meeting of the Miners' National Union at Birmingham on 12 December 1881. In his remarks, he stressed that districts with the best union organization normally reported higher wages and shorter working hours. He also emphasized that the sliding scale must be given a chance to function and to be improved. Burt later refused to support a general strike to force a wage hike.[15]

National efforts by miners in the early 1880s to restrict production through a general strike or output reduction were unsuccessful, and NMA officials effectively blocked support among its members for such schemes.[16] Over the next several years, Burt often proclaimed that miners needed to organize themselves more effectively on the county level in order to gain reasonable working hours, thereby controlling production and increasing wages.[17]

Meanwhile, NMA officials worked hard to retain the sliding scale. Many miners disliked this scale because they associated it with the decline in wages. On the other hand, executive committee members believed that the sliding scale had helped to restore the coal trade in Northumberland after 1879, and that an advance in wages could only be obtained under a new scale. After an NMA delegate assembly voted to drop the sliding scale in early 1883,[18] Burt visited collieries in Bedlington, New Delaval, Elswick, West Wylam, Prudhoe, North Seaton, Ann Pit and Old Cramlington to rally support for it. Clearly, Burt and other officials were determined to save the sliding scale.[19] The effort was successful. By early February miners approved a motion for the NMA to work towards a new scale.[20] On 9 March 1883, after lengthy negotiations, the union and owners agreed to a scale.[21]

Historians still debate the value of the sliding scale, used in several industries in the last quarter of the nineteenth century. H. A. Clegg and others believe that the survival of labour unions, following the collapse of prices and wages in the 1870s, depended on Burt's and other union leaders' willingness to accept the link between prices and wages. Had they not accepted the sliding scale, a series of strikes might well have destroyed the unions. J. H. Porter contends that arbitration, sliding scales and, later, conciliation boards inhibited the wage increases of workers and gave employers control over wage demands, although he admits that this is not easy to measure. V. L. Allen, a critic of conciliation techniques, concludes: 'Where conciliation and arbitration were employed and were succeeded by sliding scale agreements, trade unionism was contained and disarmed at a significant stage of its growth.' R. Page Arnot, historian of the Miners' Federation of Great Britain, stresses that Burt and others, by accepting the premise that prices determined wages, did little more than tie wages to the 'commercial speculations of the controllers of the market'.[22]

Burt was convinced that the sliding scale was a valuable learning experience for the Northumberland union from 1879 to 1887. Writing in 1908, Burt contended that he had supported the sliding scale, along with the earlier 'slow and cumbrous' arbitration system, 'not because I regarded these schemes as ideally perfect, but because they were steps towards a more rational method of adjusting wages ... They gave us a large body of facts and experience which have proved of permanent value.' In a period of depression and declining wages, 'they carried us over the crisis with less friction and with smaller reductions of wages than took place in almost any other mining district'.[23] Moreover, he was unwilling to jeopardize the success of the NMA, which had gained a productive working relationship with the owners, to untested schemes pushed by miners not nearly as well-organized locally as those of Northumberland and Durham.

Meanwhile, the passage of franchise reform in 1884–85, extending the vote to the counties, spurred political activity among Northern miners. In Northumberland, the NMA – in spite of opposition by some miners who disliked spending union funds on politics – agreed to a salary for Charles Fenwick, a miner who stood for Parliament for the Wansbeck district.[24] Not only was Fenwick elected to Parliament in 1885, but so were William Crawford and John Wilson, both members of the large and powerful Durham Miners' Association. All told, twelve labour representatives, including six miners, were elected to Parliament in 1885. Burt was delighted with the presence of so many miners in Parliament. In remarks to a miners' conference on 26 January 1886, he proudly stated:

> We no longer stand at the door of the House of Commons as supplicants; we no longer appear by proxy or by delegation; but as practical miners we march into the highest and greatest court of the realm by right; we take our stand on the floor of the House of Commons with power to discuss every line and clause of bills affecting the miners.[25]

All was not well in the Northumberland coalfields, however. The difficult economic problems facing the coal trade would culminate in a bitter strike in 1887, and Burt, who counselled against it, would endure another test of his leadership. While he surmounted this challenge, the strike would forever alter Burt's Northern world, which thereafter faced the presence of aggressive unionists and Socialists.

The North East experienced growing labour problems and worker militancy even before the Northumberland strike of 1887. An extremely divisive labour dispute racked the South Medomsley Colliery in County Durham during the winter of 1885-86. Boilermakers and shipwrights waged a strike on the Tyneside. A movement to elect independent labour candidates to Parliament emerged in 1885. Meetings in the Sandhill area of Newcastle, a popular congregating site for workers, were often critical of Burt's close ties to the Liberal Party.[26]

The Northumberland miners' strike was caused primarily by the coal trade's collapse, which exacerbated long-festering labour problems. Labourers and owners alike, as well as newspaper reporters, acknowledged that 1886 was one of the worst years for the coal industry in many decades. Large numbers of miners were laid off or put on short time, and some pits were closed.[27] The union provided relief for its members in distress. While membership of the NMA grew from 12,225 in early 1885 to 13,236 by December 1886, union funds dipped dangerously low because of payments to those out of work. A special levy for the unemployed was exacted from miners working at least eight days per fortnight, and in December 1886, the union borrowed £5,000 from its strike fund for relief measures. In October the NMA wrote off £5,752 deposited in the bankrupt Industrial Bank as unrecoverable.[28]

Both miners and owners complained about high royalty and wayleave payments. Royalty was paid to the holders of underground mineral rights, while wayleave rents were payments made for conveying coal from mine to market over privately held property. Miners were also frustrated that those receiving royalties, all too often absentee landowners, refused to contribute to miner distress funds. Burt addressed the royalty issue frequently in 1886, and on one occasion called for the state to lay claim to mineral rights 'for the advantage of the community'. Burt and the owners contended that royalty payments should be tied to the selling price of coal, much as wages were.[29]

In October 1886, owners announced that they would terminate the present sliding scale upon its expiration at the end of 1886 and wanted it replaced with one reflecting a lower base rate. In November, owners stated that they would no longer provide housing allowances to miners residing in non-company accommodation, and in December they demanded a 15 per cent reduction in wages.[30] Under pressure from the union, the owners dropped the reduction to 12.5 per cent and agreed not to cut off the housing allowance, but the union negotiating committee (which included Burt) was willing to go no further than a reduction of 10 per cent. As a result, negotiations broke off on 8 January 1887.[31] On 19 January union delegates approved a strike, and miners agreed with an overwhelming vote of 9,844 to 2,161.[32] The strike began on 27 January.

Miners were disaffected with union leadership over a variety of issues: some resented the handling of early mediation proposals[33] and reproached their negotiators for conceding *any* reduction in wages. Others, upset at the lack of funds available for the strike, contended that money had been poorly managed or wasted on parliamentary representatives. Certain miners believed that they would have been better off if they had never paid into the union at all.[34] Discontent peaked on 7 February, when more than 3,000 miners held an unauthorized protest meeting. On the same day, members of the executive committee and other NMA officials, including Burt, offered to resign from office, citing the extensive number of protests and votes of censure launched against them.[35] Burt did not favour the threat to resign, preferring instead to ride out the storm. He felt that the discontent arose from the unpopular advice he and others had offered, and to an incorrect belief that the officers did not resist the owners' demand for a wage reduction.[36] Many miners understood why the leaders threatened to resign, since the officials had consulted the miners, as required, yet were still subject to abuse and criticism.[37] As it was, the miners gave their leaders an overwhelming vote of confidence. The resignations never took place.[38]

The strike continued. Burt was politely received at various branch meetings, although he occasionally found himself on the defensive. At one gathering he revealed that he had refused an offer of a position at £900 per year because he intended to continue working on behalf of miners as long as they still wanted him.[39] (This position, which Burt did not explain to the group, was a general inspectorship at the Local Government Board.)[40] Under extraordinary pressure, the wages committee finally resigned in April, giving way to a new one.[41] In May, all officials, including Burt and Fenwick, agreed to receive only one-half their pay for the duration of the strike.[42] Finally, on 24 May after several votes and an authorization to the wages committee to gain the best terms available, the strike ended. The union accepted a reduction of 12.5 per cent with a promise by several owners to contribute payments for house rental.[43]

The strike failed for several reasons. The NMA had few financial resources, and an appeal by Burt to other unions and friends of labour had generated relatively little money.[44] Economic hardship among mining families was evident,[45] and officials obviously feared that if the strike was prolonged, miners would begin drifting back to work.[46] Because trade was depressed anyway, owners were not particularly harmed by the strike, since they had relatively few contracts to fill. They also knew that the union was financially strapped even before the strike began.[47]

Although he had advised against the strike, Burt dutifully carried out the functions of his office. When the strike was over, however, much of what he had laboured for so long lay in ruins. By May 1887, all the aid and strike funds were expended.[48] Officials testified that the union paid out £39,000 in benefits to the strikers, while the miners lost £180,000 in wages.[49] Disagreements between the miners and union officials over the leadership and direction of the NMA continued long after the strike. Several years of festering discontent would eventually lead some miners to advocate a move to the Miners' Federation of Great Britain. Moreover, outside political elements had entered the fray. Most immediately, however, Burt faced a major challenge just to continue as a spokesman for the miners in Parliament.

The end of the strike coincided with the union's annual meeting.

Angry, frustrated miners introduced resolutions either hostile to the leaders or to the direction of union affairs. The resolutions to abolish or reduce political salaries were ominous for Burt. A motion to reduce Burt's salary was defeated by a close delegate vote of 128 to 107.[50] The issue of financially supporting Burt's parliamentary efforts, or any of the union's political activities, was raised again in August 1887. Delegates approved a motion to hold a ballot of all members on the following resolution:

> Are you in favour of continuing to pay Mr. Burt his salary as Member of Parliament, and to guarantee to make up any deficiency due to Mr. Fenwick as agreed to previous to last election, and also for supporting other political matters in the past provided for in the objects of our association?

When the miners cast their ballots in September, 4,806 were opposed to continuing payments, and only 3,387 in favour.[51]

Why this refusal to continue paying Burt's parliamentary salary? Why this opposition to a man who had done so much to make the NMA one of the most secure, well-organized and respected unions in Britain? Burt's efforts first to avoid and finally to settle the strike, even at the cost of accepting a major wage reduction, had rankled many miners. Given the economic depression, the £850 needed to pay Burt and Fenwick was substantial.[52] Moreover, Burt's reluctance to use his political office to improve wages and gain economic benefits for miners led some to question the very concept of financial support. Socialist organizers, especially from London, encouraged the miners to switch their political allegiance to more forceful advocates of labour.

A significant number of Socialists appeared in the Northumberland area shortly after the strike began. J. L. Mahon and William Morris of the Socialist League were both present, as were John Williams, J. Hunter Watts, H. M. Hyndman and Tom Mann representing the Social Democratic Federation, and E. R. Pease, a Fabian Society leader. These organizers usually spoke before large and receptive audiences throughout the coalfields,[53] the most notable of which was a huge Socialist-organized gala at Horton on Easter Monday, 11 April.[54] Both Mann and Mahon remained in the North after the strike, setting up the short-lived North of England Socialist Federation.[55] Mahon, obviously directing his remarks at Burt, charged that labour MPs were ineffective representatives of the working class, a 'few limpid lisping weaklings, who always truckle to the party chiefs, who never yet distinguished themselves by standing out sturdily for the interests of labour – who indeed have either forgotten or never knew what the interests of labour mean'.[56] The Socialists were also present at a disorderly NMA picnic on 30 July 1887.[57]

Perhaps the main reason for the opposition of some miners to Burt stemmed from basic tension between miners and their union officials. In his study of the Durham miners, David Douglass argues convincingly that miners were independent simply by the nature of their work. Problems peculiar to each of the mines intensified this independence. Consequently, miners tended to distrust their union leaders, men who had been 'moderate, self-educated and temperate miners'. Miners often believed that union leaders, removed as they were from the everyday world of work, no longer appreciated the difficulties and conditions in individual mines. These leaders always seemed to counsel cooperation and conciliation.[58] Indeed, the role of union officer and negotiator was a difficult one. Each had to consider the democratic tendencies of miners in their lodges, while attempting to negotiate a county-wide contract with owners, a process which always required compromise. Natural suspicions were fuelled by the middle-class lifestyle that officers came to reflect. With his £500 annual income, his presence in London and his residence in Newcastle, Burt fit this middle-class image, no matter how much he claimed kinship with the hewers.

As it turned out, neither Burt nor Fenwick lost his parliamentary salary in 1887. In November of that year, another delegate meeting restored their pay by the slim vote of 125 to 100. At the request of several lodges,[59] a vote of all the miners was planned for March and April 1888. Before this decisive ballot, Burt wrote a lengthy circular to all miners.[60] This statement reflected his political and labour philosophy. He was opposed, he wrote, to a separate labour party, which he perceived as divisive, as well as restrictive of an MP's political judgement. His first loyalty was to the union, and he had therefore turned down offers of higher salaried positions. He took pride in his independence as an MP. Although loyal to union, constituents, and party, he would vote his own conscience. Burt enjoyed being an MP, but he was willing to give up his seat should the differences with his union or constituents become too great. Above all, the circular shows that Burt was a master at understanding and handling the miners. He detailed many of the services he had performed over the years and pointed out that the relationship between them was honourable and mutual. Differences should be openly discussed. He specifically stated that if miners were concerned over the amount of his pay, a special committee could examine the issue. Burt also played on the pride of the miners in their union. While miners' wages had suffered during the long depression, the union had remained special and unique: the NMA was the first union to elect and to pay one of its own as an MP; the miners were united, open and democratic.

During this entire dispute over their parliamentary salaries, Burt and Fenwick gained substantial support from both the local and national press. Most newspapers praised Burt as one who effectively represented his class and the miners in Parliament. Some feared that should the union fail to provide payment for MPs, the system, much used in Britain, could break down and hurt labour's representation.[61] There were exceptions to this support: the Socialist *Commonweal* sympathized with the miners' quest for a parliamentary voice not tied so closely to an established political party. *The Miner* reprimanded Burt and Fenwick for not voting in favour of the Eight-Hour Bill (this issue will be examined shortly).[62]

In early April 1888, the Northumberland miners, by a close vote of 4,572 to 4,278, agreed to continue paying Burt's and Fenwick's parliamentary salaries.[63] As Burt had recommended, the union created a special committee to examine the salaries of its agents and parliamentary representatives. Burt testified before the committee and voluntarily agreed to take a £100 reduction in pay, leaving him with a salary of £400. In November NMA delegates agreed to set Burt's salary at £400 and continue to pay Fenwick's salary for parliamentary duties.[64] This effectively ended the dispute, although unions throughout Britain remained divided over the funding of their parliamentary candidates. While the wealthy unions generally supported their own candidates – normally Lib-Labs like Burt – from their own union funds, the Socialists within the trade union ranks wanted a separate election fund set up on the national level, so that labour could support candidates not tied to the existing parties.[65]

The Socialists did not survive long in the North of England, and their hope in 1888 to mount a challenge to Burt and Fenwick at the next general election failed to materialize.[66] What proved a far greater challenge to Burt and his associates in the North was the Miners' Federation of Great Britain (MFGB), which attracted substantial support from the mining communities of Northumberland and Durham. We need to examine the emergence of the MFGB and Burt's attitude towards it, as well as the issue of the eight-hour day, which became the new organization's primary legislative goal.

At the NMA's annual meeting in May 1887, which came at the ending of the strike, delegates voted overwhelmingly to convene a 'conference of representatives from every mining district in the United Kingdom to consider the advisability of all miners' unions being amalgamated, and to adopt a uniform system of working not more then [sic] 7 hours a day and not more then [sic] 5 days per week'.[67] Presiding over this national meeting in October, Burt stated that he favoured a closer federation, believing that steps were needed to ensure that one area's output did not harm another's. But he was not enthusiastic about the possibility of a strong federation having the power to call strikes. To be effective, centralized organizations needed to wield power and control their funds, and district unions in the past had been reluctant at best to defer to a central authority. The miners, he warned, were 'simply deluding themselves if they were expected to be saved merely by federation'.[68] While there was considerable disagreement at the conference, representatives passed resolutions calling for a maximum eight-hour day and restrictions on production. Following the meeting at Edinburgh, delegates at an NMA meeting overwhelmingly approved these resolutions.[69]

After several more meetings, and with the stimulus of wage advances in many districts, the Miners' Federation was formed at Newport in November 1889. Burt usually represented the NMA at these meetings, although he did not preside. Ben Pickard of Yorkshire, the driving force behind the formation of the Federation, normally assumed that role.[70] Initially, the miners' leaders believed that the Federation and the Miners' National Union could peacefully co-exist, with the latter focusing on legislation and the Federation concentrating on the issues of the uniform national wage and the eight-hour day.[71] The differences between the two groups, however, were major. The miners' unions of the North East were powerful, well-established and, on the whole, able to command the loyalty, respect and obedience of their members. Miners in the North received adequate pay while working the shortest hours in the industry. Burt and other leaders had come to accept and defend wage fluctuations, as they believed that wages were closely tied to the selling price of coal. The price of north-eastern coal, because it was sold in the extremely competitive overseas market, varied considerably. Moreover, strikes were perceived as doing potentially permanent damage to that market. Burt was a confirmed free trader and frowned on the policy of driving up prices by restricting output. On the other hand, the Federation consisted of unions which, compared to those of the North East, were relatively new and lacking in individual strength and cohesiveness.[72] Morever, unlike the North East miners, the Federation unions' members produced primarily for the domestic market.

Leadership styles were noticeably different: Burt was quiet, gentle and polite, yet self-assured and firm. He was logical in his arguments, convincing in his carefully phrased speeches. He was an excellent if low-key negotiator. Many of the Federation leaders, however, viewed Burt as weak, too ready to yield to his opponents during hard bargaining sessions and too sympathetic with the economic views of mine owners. On the other hand, Burt viewed the Federation leaders as much too aggressive and abrasive. Pickard, who was particularly strong, single-minded, courageous and 'stubborn as a mule', possessed a leadership style which could offend miners.[73] Burt was above all a pragmatist: Why tamper with an organization which worked? Why endanger the NMA as well as the livelihood of miners by embarking on an untested venture? Why expect that a single union could gain national wage uniformity in an industry where local conditions such as coal type, seam size, market and season of the year were the primary determining trade factors?[74]

The differences between the two union groups proved too great to permit substantive cooperation. The gulf between them, which widened to a chasm when the North East stood apart from the Federation in the great lock-out of 1893, was already evident in the late 1880s over the eight-hour day movement, the issue that most divided the MNU and the Federation.[75] That movement emerged for all trades in the late 1880s, following the great London dock strike. Leaders within the labour movement were divided on the issue. Some advocated a universal eight-hour day law, others supported a law for specific industries, while some opposed legislation, advising instead that unions provide protection for their own workers.[76]

At the Edinburgh Conference in 1887 miners began their long, bitter and frustrating struggle for the eight-hour day, a goal that would not be reached until 1908. The phrase 'eight-hour day' for the mining industry normally meant from 'bank to bank', or from the moment the miners entered the shaft until they re-emerged. A shortened working day was needed, miners argued, to protect those working in conditions of exceptional danger, to prevent physical exhaustion of miners, to improve mining efficiency, and to provide workers with sufficient time for rest and recreation. A national eight-hour law would also benefit the entire industry by removing some instances of dangerous and unhealthy competition, and promoting industrial peace by eliminating differences in work hours. Federation leaders pushed their case for an eight-hour law at their own meetings, at the Trades Union Congress, before political leaders, and in Parliament.[77] The greatest opponent to their cause, they believed, was Thomas Burt.

Burt and the miners of the North East opposed the Eight-Hour Bill for many reasons. Burt was uncomfortable with State intervention in the economic life of the nation. Speaking before the Liberal Eighty Club in 1890, he concentrated on the very core of his political philosophy: the rights of the individual versus Socialism and State regulation. He stressed that certain restrictions – for example, the Factory Acts and the Mines Regulations Acts – were necessary and beneficial. 'My own bias, however, is very strongly towards self-help and mutual assistance. I trust for the future of the workmen mainly to their combinations, to education, to co-operation, and movements of that character.' Burt admitted that in some circumstances adult labour should be regulated, but these situations must be decided on their own merits. He also believed that an eight-hour act would not be effective or adequately enforced, since overtime would invariably continue and workers, often to their own detriment, would opt for longer hours and greater pay.[78] Burt often explained his views on the role of the State. In an 1889 article, he warned workers that when looking to the State for aid, they should 'bear in mind that State help always means management, control, and discipline by the State, and can be had only at the sacrifice of individual liberty'.[79]

Of greater concern to Burt than his theoretical dislike of State intervention, however, was the fact that hewers in the North East were already working a seven-hour day. This was made possible by a two-shift system, the shifts being from 4 a.m. to 11 a.m., and from 11 a.m. to 6 p.m. One ten-hour shift of putters and transit workers – most of whom were boys – provided the necessary support to both shifts of hewers. Miners in the North East could simply find no economic benefit in going to an eight-hour day. None of the possible options for administering the eight hours seemed satisfactory to the miners. A single eight-hour shift of both hewers and boys would increase the working day, lead to layoffs (since there would not be sufficient room in the pit for all of them), and force the pits to lie idle two-thirds of the time. A double eight-hour shift of men and boys would increase the men's hours, and miners feared that there would not be a sufficient number of boys for two shifts. Three eight-hour shifts of miners (this was done in some of the newer mines in the North East) and two eight-hour shifts of boys could result in overproduction. In addition, a third shift could disrupt home and social life, particularly for a female head of the family.[80] When Burt and Fenwick voted at a national miners' meeting in Birmingham in October 1889, in opposition to a resolution calling for Parliament to enact an eight-hour day law for all underground miners, they were following the instructions of the NMA miners.[81]

The most damaging charge against the NMA in this controversy was that adult miners who enjoyed a seven-hour day did so by exploiting boys who worked substantially longer hours. It was a charge that could not be denied. Burt and the miners were sensitive to this criticism and attempted to resolve the dilemma. A special NMA committee could not come up with a practical way to shorten the boys' hours while retaining the present benefits for the hewers. Delegates spent a day discussing the committee's report. They turned down various options providing an eight-hour day and voted simply to enforce an agreement that no boy work over ten hours a day.[82]

By 1891, Burt and the union had weathered the storm which began with the strike of 1887. Burt had overcome challenges to his leadership. The union leaders, with help from a moderate recovery in the coal trade, were able to retain their independence from the newly-formed Miners' Federation of Great Britain. Socialists, who had made so much noise during and shortly after the strike, were no longer a significant factor in the North. Burt enjoyed nationwide respect in political as well as labour circles. His prestige extended throughout much of Europe, where he was active in pioneering international labour organizations. Moreover, in 1891 he was selected to preside at the annual meeting of the Trades Union Congress at Newcastle.

Chapter 8

LABOUR LEADER AND ORGANIZATION MAN

Burt's prestige mounted in the early 1890s. He was widely respected for his efforts at conciliation and arbitration, within the British mining industry specifically and in the labour movement in general. He also took the lead in organizing conferences in Europe to strengthen unionization among the continent's coal miners and provide for peaceful resolution of international disputes. In addition, the British government appointed Burt representative to the International Labour Conference in Berlin in 1890, where delegates examined labour issues facing industrialized nations. As the leading labour union official in the North East, he presided at the annual meeting of the Trades Union Congress held in Newcastle in September 1891. Burt put an enormous physical effort into these activities, although he was not particularly well by this time. In these endeavours, Burt stressed to all participants a need for open discussion and reasonableness. Rational thought, oriented towards conciliation and arbitration, formed the core of his solutions for all problems.

Throughout his life Burt worked for international peace, especially by way of the International Arbitration League (originally the Workmen's Peace Association), a working-class society. As President of the IAL, he often chaired peace meetings. He also enjoyed a close relationship with the American steelmaker and philanthropist Andrew Carnegie, visiting him in Pittsburgh while touring the United States in 1883. Burt presided at a meeting in London in 1887, when Carnegie met with the IAL and several MPs, including Richard Haldane, the future Liberal Secretary of War, over arranging an arbitration treaty between the United States and Britain. Carnegie became a benefactor of the IAL.[1] Burt served many years as a vice-president of the International Arbitration and Peace Association and the Universal Peace Congress, a periodic gathering of peace society representatives from around the world.[2]

Through his close contact with IAL secretary W. R. Cremer, Burt became involved in the Inter-Parliamentary Union. In October 1888, thirty-four legislators from France and Britain, including Fenwick and Burt, met in Paris to discuss arbitration as an instrument of international peace. Burt was elected secretary of this conference. The following June a second meeting convened in Paris, out of which emerged the Inter-Parliamentary Union, an assembly of legislators devoted to the use of arbitration. Burt served as one of three secretaries in 1889. Permanently headquartered in Berne, the IPU became respectable in political circles. Leading politicians often attended its annual meetings, held in various major cities. At the 1906 meeting, British Prime Minister Henry Campbell-Bannerman uttered the famous words, 'The Duma is dead; long live the Duma', after the first Duma had been dismissed in Russia.[3] The IPU was the driving force behind the creation of a permanent international court of arbitration, set up by the Hague Conference of 1899.[4] Many of the large number of peace societies founded in the last quarter of the nineteenth century published an enormous amount of information emphasizing the importance of arbitration.

International cooperation took an unusual turn in 1889 when the young German Emperor, William II, called for a meeting in Berlin to deal with the problems of labour.[5] The Salisbury government appointed Burt to the British delegation attending this conference in March 1890, where he served on the committee on mining.[6] At a social gathering, William II remarked to Burt about the often violent and lawless nature of labour unions. Burt responded that 'all these disorders of which you speak are only the natural result of the policy of repression which has often been pursued by the authorities in dealing with working men's associations'. In England, he added, 'we have found no more sovereign remedy for these excesses than liberty'. By legalizing unions, Burt stressed, order had come to prevail in industry. When asked if he recommended that the Emperor ought to copy the English model, Burt said, 'Oh dear no. I left him to draw his own inferences, I thought I had put it quite plain enough.'[7] Burt was impressed with William's grasp of issues at the conference and offered this shrewd evaluation: 'He has certainly energy – perhaps too much – but the Hohenzollerns have always made reigning a business, and have conducted it with the same laboriousness, the same industry, and the same activity, as a man pursues a professional career.'[8]

The conferees met for two weeks, discussing extensively various aspects of labour, including mining, and women's and children's labour, and passing non-binding resolutions. While there were few meaningful results at the international level, the conference prodded Salisbury's government to raise the minimum age for children working in British factories and workshops from ten to eleven. Speaking in

Parliament, Burt pushed the government in that direction by pointing out that Britain permitted children to work in factories at a younger age than in most European nations.[9]

Shortly after the Berlin gathering Burt attended a miners' conference in Jolimont, a city in the heart of Belgium's coal mining region. Burt and Fenwick had taken the lead in setting up this conference, following two workers' meetings the previous year in Paris.[10] Burt presided at the opening session in Jolimont in May 1890. In his remarks, he urged the less-organized European miners to work hard at developing their unions, and to avoid harmful strikes by using arbitration and conciliation. Ironically, Burt and those representing the Miners' National Union were defeated by the Federation forces who, together with the continental miners, approved a motion calling for an eight-hour day through legislation. Burt was satisfied that the meeting had educated the Europeans to what he regarded as superior union organizations in Britain.[11] The Socialist press, however, referred to Burt as a 'fossil' of old unionism.[12]

The differences between the Federation and the MNU carried over to the next international miners' meeting. While the Northumberland miners voted not to send delegates to the 1891 meeting, Burt attended as a representative of the MNU, the president of the British section, the treasurer of the conference and a member of the International Committee. Differences at this meeting were substantial, particularly over the eight-hour day and a proposed international general strike.[13] In spite of all these problems, Burt continued his efforts and, in July 1891, presided at a meeting in Cologne that drew up a constitution for the International Miners' Federation.[14] Burt would long remain active in the International Federation, one of the first and largest of the international labour unions to emerge in the late nineteenth century.[15]

The miners' preoccupation with the eight-hour day, evident at the international meetings, also came to dominate the 1891 annual meeting of the Trades Union Congress in Newcastle. The TUC, a federation of British trade unions, had held its first annual meeting in 1868. Until the late 1880s, the organization consisted primarily of representatives of skilled trades, and worked for the right of unions to bargain for their own wages and working conditions. The labour scene in Britain began to change in the late 1880s as a wave of strikes among relatively unskilled labourers, such as dockers, gave rise to aggressive workers' organizations, the leaders of which were called New Unionists. Many New Unionists and Socialists demanded that the State provide protection for workers by enacting, among other · provisions, a maximum eight-hour day.

Burt attended the second TUC annual meeting in 1869. Forty-seven delegates gathered to hear papers on the value of arbitration and conciliation, emigration and working-class newspapers. Burt participated in a discussion on how to procure working-class representation in Parliament.[16] This conference must have appealed to Burt, who was at that time trying to shape the NMA into a union respected by coal owners. He did not speak highly of the TUC as it developed. By the early 1890s, he complained that its large annual meeting had become unwieldy and that the extensive agenda made it impossible to engage in meaningful debate.[17] Moreover, by the late 1880s TUC meetings had become ideological battlegrounds between old and new unionists.

If Burt represented the old unionists, Keir Hardie was the most visible of the new type of union leader who emerged in the late nineteenth century. Until the mid-1880s Hardie, the aggressive leader of the Scottish coal miners, was basically a Lib-Lab with some misgivings.[18] In 1887 he began publishing *The Miner*, a monthly journal. For the first issue Hardie requested that Burt contribute a piece on 'Self-Help'. In his article, Burt extolled the virtues of unionism, called on Scottish miners to be watchdogs over important legislation, and advised them not to expect immediate solutions to all their grievances. On the issue of reasonable work hours, the ever-cautious Burt encouraged the miners to depend on their own organization and not on Parliament, which was unlikely to set working hours for adult men.[19] In the following issue, *The Miner* contained an admiring article, probably by Cunninghame Graham, of Burt as a leader. Burt was described as a wise, cautious leader, who garnered the respect of politicians on working-class affairs, and of capitalists comfortable with his espousal of Political Economy. The writer mildly admonished Burt for refusing to support legislation to protect the adult working man, and stated that it was 'just possible that Mr. Burt has a little too much of the philosopher about him. A man may be "cautious overmuch"'.[20]

Hardie's grudging admiration of the Lib-Labs ended in 1887 with the growing industrial strife in the coalfields and the apparent unwillingness of the sitting labour MPs to deal with the issues. He and the Scottish miners desperately wanted an eight-hour day enacted, but the labour representatives, including Burt, were lukewarm in their support.[21] Hardie complained bitterly about the failure of the two political parties, including labour representatives in the Liberal Party, to be aggressive in the interests of the working class, and specifically charged that Burt wished to exclude most controversial issues from party consideration.[22] In 1888 Hardie formed the Scottish Labour Party and stood for Parliament at Mid-Lanark, his home district. He came in a distant third.[23] At an international labour conference in London in that same year, Hardie found British delegates 'dull' compared to the European Socialist representatives. According to Hardie, Burt appeared 'philosophic and gentle-looking as ever, taking no part in the proceedings, but, like the sailor's parrot, thinking a lot'.[24]

The central, often bitter, issue at the TUC conferences from 1887 into the 1890s was the eight-hour day.[25] The 1891 meeting began in Newcastle on Monday, 7 September. On the day before the conference opened, several meetings featured labour activists Keir Hardie, Cunninghame Graham and John Burns, calling for a state-mandated eight-hour day, higher wages, increased power for new unions, labour representation and a separate labour party. These open-air assemblies continued throughout the week,[26] while debate raged within the formal meeting itself.

As the leading union official from the Newcastle area, Burt served as presiding officer. Five hundred and fifty-two labour union representatives jammed into the Town Hall, a building ill-designed to house such a large gathering.[27] Burt gave his presidential address on Tuesday 8 September. As always, he praised the labour leaders for bringing respect to unions and for convincing political economists that workers were 'something more than machines', that they had a 'soul' and a 'will' and needed to be 'treated as men'. He called upon the Congress to increase the unionization of women and avoid 'barriers of race or colour'. Burt acknowledged the necessity of strikes but warned the new unions to be careful. The 'strike is an ugly weapon', much like a boomerang; 'if it is not skilfully thrown, it is apt to come back, and to hit and to wound the thrower'.[28] Burt earned exceptional praise for his address, even from the *Workman's Times*, a newspaper advocating an independent labour party.[29]

Burt's handling of the large rowdy gathering throughout the week was even more effective than his address. George Holyoake, a friend and admirer, found Burt's conduct of business a masterpiece:

> During the six days of discussion he stilled the wildest tempests, regulated the most confused debate, made every point of order lucid, arrested the impetuous, reconciled the offended, and decided points with promptness and fairness. Wit, humour, common-sense, and apt illustration delighted the delegates, won their confidence and admiration, maintained order and advanced business in a way no Speaker of the House of Commons could excel.[30]

The *Newcastle Daily Leader* praised Burt for dealing with 'this apparently untamable assembly'. He is 'thoroughly acquainted with the right methods of conducting business, understands how and when to interfere, and is not going to be bustled and humbugged out of his authority'.[31] Burt's sense of humour seems to have been central to maintaining some semblance of order. After one delegate complained about the weakness of the bell, a smiling Burt said: 'I quite agree with the speaker that we very well might have done with a better bell, but I must say that it is not with the bell that I have the most trouble at this meeting.'[32] Perhaps it was after this incident that he was given a larger bell, which he affectionately called 'Big Ben'.[33] The most celebrated confrontation at the 1891 meeting came when Keir Hardie and P. J. King distributed literature on the Eight-Hours Bill without the required approval of the standing order committee. Many unionists wanted the pair censured or even expelled, and there was great disorder in the hall. Burt finally interceded with a pointed admonition to all. The minutes include the interruptions from the audience:

> It would be very nice to expel Mr. King and Mr. Hardie – (laughter) – and in your present temper you would do it, but it would not bear the reflection of to-morrow morning. (Hear, hear.) Now the best thing you can do is to ignore it, and I hope that it will be a warning to Mr. Keir Hardie and Mr. King, and make them a little more careful in the future. (Hear, hear.) There may be other people who have not been found out who are quite as bad – (cheering) – they may be worse – (laughter and cheers) – and we will deal with them when we find them out, ... Now let us see if we can temper justice with mercy. Let the matter drop altogether – not another word about it. (Loud cheers).[34]

That ended the incident.

The most heated and tumultuous arguments occurred over several eight-hour day proposals. Sam Woods of the Miners' Federation specifically admonished Burt for using his 'great influence' to block the legislation. While gaining passage of the Eight-Hour Day resolution, the Federation lost the battle for representation on the all-important TUC Parliamentary Committee, which shaped the organization's legislative agenda.[35]

Following the meeting Burt, on behalf of himself and the Northumberland miners, replied to the critics of the eight-hour day. He emphasized that the miners had worked hard to reduce the boys' hours.[36] When Northumberland miners resoundingly rejected – by a vote of 8,720 to 2,689 – a resolution in late 1891 limiting boys' hours in the mines to eight per day, Burt expressed his belief that the vote did not mean that the miners opposed shorter hours or were satisfied with the present situation. Rather, the vote related the simple fact that, after careful consideration of all facets of the problem, they had not been able to find a solution. Moreover, the miners did not believe that Parliament should be asked to seek a solution.[37]

In 1892 the issue shifted to Parliament, where the Federation supported the Miners' Eight-Hour Bill introduced by Robert Leake, a Lancashire manufacturer. Burt led the opposition to the second reading of the Bill. His speech amending the Bill was probably the longest he had made in eighteen years in the Commons. His arguments were not new. While he very much favoured a shortened work day, the change should come through the effort of unions and not legislation. He explained that the Northumberland miners had considered the issue carefully over a period of several years and had recently voted decisively against an eight-hour day for boys.[38] Acting as a teller, Burt helped to scuttle the Bill by taking thirty-five Liberals with him into the opposition lobby.[39] Liberals and Radicals were characteristically divided over this issue which revolved around individualism versus State interference and much-needed child labour regulation.[40] The lack of unanimity among the miners, as well as the open opposition by the most respected mining political leader of the period, proved too much for eight-hour advocates to overcome.

While the eight-hour day was the most divisive issue between the Federation and the North East,[41] the parties also disagreed over the negotiation of wages on a national basis. The Federation, which did not include Scotland, South Wales or the North East, took advantage of economic recovery and a coal price increase to negotiate substantial wage advances from 1889 to 1891. When necessary, Federation areas had engaged in strikes to press for these advances.[42] Wages also improved in the North East, however. While the sliding scale was no longer formally used in Northumberland – it had been dropped in 1887 – wage negotiations there continued to reflect closely the selling price of coal.[43] Recovery of the Northumberland coal trade brought advances in late 1888 and early 1889, so that miners regained the 12.5 per cent they had lost at the settlement of the 1887 strike.[44]

Burt did not approve of the Federation's goal of a minimum wage, or its willingness to 'restrict' output to help control prices. In an attempt to use up surplus coal and stabilize prices and wages, the Federation closed the pits for one week in March 1892, and in the summer maintained a 'stop day', working five days per week instead of the normal six. Burt believed that each district had to make its own wage decision, reflecting local conditions.[45] Burt also could not accept Rule 20 of the Federation, which under certain circumstances called for all members to join a strike, even if action were taken only against one part.[46] What particularly bothered Burt was the Federation's claim of responsibility for wage advances, including those in the North East. Burt argued that the wage increases were made possible in all parts of England by the rise in coal prices. The unions had provided the means and pressure to make certain that miners benefited from improvement in trade. Burt contended that it had been the NMA, not the Federation, which had normally led in pay increases. Burt showed that by the end of 1890 Northumberland's advances had reached 43.75 per cent, the Federation's 40 per cent. The advances in Northumberland, he emphasized, were gained without stoppages, 'whereas in many other districts notices were served and the pits were stopped for a shorter or longer time before the wages were increased'.[47]

An economic downturn led the mine owners once again to demand wage reductions. In an attempt to resist reduction, the Durham miners refused arbitration and were locked-out in a bitter clash lasting three months in 1892.[48] Durham miners had become increasingly suspicious both of the sliding scale and of arbitration agreements between their leaders and the owners. Owners often favoured agreements that provided the flexibility to acquire a labour force whose wages reflected the prevailing state of the mining economy. On the other hand, union leaders found these agreements a means of controlling their often restless and demanding members. The Durham miners finally accepted a mediation effort by Bishop Westcott of Durham, agreeing to a 10 per cent reduction and the promise of a wage board to help settle future disputes. On 18 June 1892, shortly after the conclusion of the lock-out, the Durham miners agreed to join the Miners' Federation.[49]

Turmoil was once again descending on the coalfields throughout Britain. Under the leadership of Thomas Burt, by this time the miners' elder statesman, Northumberland had remained relatively peaceful. For the next two and one-half years, however, Burt devoted much of his time to London as a junior member of the Liberal government.

Chapter 9

AT THE BOARD OF TRADE

Respect for Thomas Burt's leadership reached its peak from 1892 to 1895. During this period he served the Liberal Government as Parliamentary Secretary of the Board of Trade and sat on several important royal commissions. Also, the splendid new offices of the Northumberland Miners' Association were named in his honour. At the same time, several critics questioned his leadership and the aggressive Miners' Federation attacked his conciliatory attitude towards labour–management relations.

Parliament was dissolved on 29 June 1892 and Burt once again ran unopposed. Elections were held in July and, by the time of the Northumberland miners' picnic on 9 July, Burt was welcoming the return of several miners' representatives to the House of Commons as well as the election of labour spokesmen Keir Hardie (South West Ham) and John Burns (Battersea). Burt deplored the defeat of colleague Henry Broadhurst because of his refusal to commit to the eight-hour day bill.[1] Salisbury, who had led the Conservative government since 1886, resigned in August 1892, after a vote of no confidence against his government. H. H. Asquith moved the amendment of no confidence; Burt seconded it.[2] Gladstone, with a majority made up of Liberal and Irish Home Rule MPs, formed a new government.

Gladstone asked Burt, a long-serving MP and a representative of labour, an important part of the Liberal constituency, to be Parliamentary Secretary of the Board of Trade, a position which did not carry cabinet rank. Burt was offered this office even though he had never been a member of the Liberal Party and did not accept the Party whip.[3] Although he was eager to accept this appointment, Burt stressed to Gladstone that while he would be relieved by the NMA of his secretarial duties, he hoped that he could 'still, in cases of emergency, be able to consult with and advise them'. Gladstone assured Burt that in those exceptional cases he would be free to give advice, although he should 'give such advice in a spirit of honourable and strict impartiality as between competing interests'.[4] Burt was determined to leave himself 'with a certain amount of freedom to still serve the Northumberland Miners', especially to confer with the wage and executive committees of the union.[5]

Burt's position at the Board of Trade carried a salary of £1,200 a year.[6] While employed by the government, he collected no salary from the NMA and did not write his monthly report, though he regularly attended NMA meetings. Although his name was not included on committee reports, a note such as the following, in reference to the wage committee reports on negotiations with the coal mine owners, was often added: 'Mr. Burt was present at the interview and at the meetings connected therewith, and concurred in what was done.'[7] The astute Burt made certain that he did not lose contact with the union and the miners.

In late December 1892, both the Northumberland miners and the local Liberal association held banquets to congratulate Burt on his appointment.[8] Not only was Burt honoured in Northumberland, but during his tenure at the Board of Trade, James Stevens (a timber merchant from Birmingham and a member of the Reform Club) bequeathed him £2,000 tax-free. According to Henry Lucy, Mr Stevens had never met Burt, but 'so much admired his public character and career that he desired to pay this mark of appreciation'.[9]

While many respected Burt as a political leader, some doubted his usefulness. In the late 1880s and early 1890s critics questioned the effectiveness of Lib-Labs operating within the scope of the Liberal Party. Hardie and others on the political left cited the Lib-Labs' lack of commitment to the interests of the working class, and Joseph Chamberlain attacked labour representatives as unproductive parliamentarians. Concern over labour came to the forefront in the 1880s in a variety of guises, including the visible problem of the unemployed, the emergence of the unskilled as a force through its use of strikes, and the expansion of the role of unions in the collective bargaining process. Labour had become a greater factor in national politics with the election of several working-class representatives to the House of Commons in 1885 and by Hardie's demand for a separate labour party.

Joseph Chamberlain was one of the most dynamic forces in British politics between 1870 and 1914.[10] An aggressive and enterprising politician, he served in Gladstone's cabinets in the early 1880s. He broke with Gladstone in 1886 over the issue of Home Rule for Ireland, although he had become increasingly frustrated with the Liberal leader's reluctance to actively support a programme of far-reaching social and political reform. Burt sponsored Chamberlain in the House of Commons in 1880 when the latter was sworn in after re-election (necessitated by having accepted a cabinet position). Burt and Chamberlain were kindred Radicals, holding many of the same political principles. Burt regarded Chamberlain as one of the great parliamentary debaters of the period.[11]

In 1891 and early 1892, as he edged ever nearer to an alliance with Salisbury's Conservative Party, Chamberlain renewed his call for reform. In November 1892, shortly after the Liberals formed a government, Chamberlain detailed the need for a variety of labour reforms in an article entitled 'The Labour Question'. He claimed, 'Almost all the legislation dealing with Labour questions has been initiated by Tory statesmen, and most of it has been passed by Tory Governments.'[12] Burt responded to Chamberlain in the next issue of the *Nineteenth Century*. To Chamberlain's assertion that the Tories had always provided impetus for social reform, Burt wrote: 'This is not a self-evident proposition; no proof is vouchsafed. It is enough, therefore, in the meantime to deny its correctness.' He reminded readers that a few years earlier Chamberlain had been extremely critical of the Tories. Burt contended that Chamberlain was simply wrong to claim that divisions between the Old and New Unionists were great, and that the New Unionists were the only vibrant element. Burt argued that Old Unionists had often supported the New. The New Unionists, Burt added, could be credited with relighting enthusiasm in the Old, 'while they in return have derived immense advantage from the knowledge and experience of the older societies. Both have benefited, and the Trade Union movement as a whole has been quickened, strengthened, solidified.'[13]

Later in the 1890s, Chamberlain continued his denunciation of labour leaders, calling into question the value of Lib-Labs as parliamentarians. In 1894 Chamberlain referred to trade unionists in Parliament as 'mere fetchers and carriers for the Gladstonian party', and, during the election campaign of September 1900, he contended that 'not one of those gentlemen had ever initiated or carried through legislation for the benefit of the working classes, though occasionally they had hindered such legislation'.[14] Chamberlain's criticisms were most effectively countered by George Howell in his book on labour legislation and leaders, published in 1902, wherein he compiled a detailed list of the legislative accomplishments of the Lib-Labs.[15] We have already seen that Burt contributed to bills associated with the interests of labour.

While Chamberlain criticized the Lib-Labs as ineffective MPs, Hardie formed a labour party independent of the two major political parties. Burt opposed a political party formed along class lines. Writing in 1889, he stressed that he had always believed that voters should elect an MP 'who is free from class bias, who looks at every question on broad grounds of justice and humanity, who will speak and vote for what is right'.[16] He contended that a labour party, committed solely to the concerns of the working man, would be too narrowly focused. No

MP could devote himself exclusively to the interests of his own class. Other great issues of state, including war and peace, had to be addressed by each MP. He also believed that a separate labour party would factionalize Parliament and impede the cooperation needed to pass legislation. In Burt's eyes, the Liberal Party was the one most willing to improve the lot of the working class. This Liberal Party contained a number of employers, including several mine owners, and Burt, as the great conciliator, regarded the interests of employers and labour as more alike than different. With his view of party and Parliament as one of reconciling the varied interests within the nation, Burt could accept the seeming limitations of the political system.[17] Hardie disagreed with this point of view. Cowen, Burt's old Radical friend, also considered Burt to be too closely tied to the Liberal Party.[18]

The Lib-Labs, primarily MPs supported by a specific union, were in a very difficult position, as they viewed themselves not only as independent and impartial MPs, but also as class representatives. As long as their numbers were small, they could be little more than a pressure group within Parliament. Cooperation with a major political party was necessary, even in drafting legislation.[19] The Lib-Labs were also a small but important Radical element within the Liberal Party. Burt and other Lib-Labs were strong proponents of Irish Home Rule, critics of privileged people and institutions, and advocates of change within framework of the law.

While maintaining a working relationship with the Liberal Party, the Lib-Labs also had to represent their unions. The Lib-Labs were spokesmen for their constituents, gaining, for example, appointment of working-class people as factory inspectors, and in Burt's case representing his union on the eight-hour day controversy.[20] Some present-day critics, such as Barker, see these union interests as narrowly defining the scope of the MPs, who thus found it difficult to speak for labour in general.[21] On the whole, Burt balanced this myriad of interests. He retained, partly because of his character, the respect and support of his union, his constituents, his political party, and, with some limitations, labour as a whole.

Burt was pleased to serve at the Board of Trade under A. J. Mundella, who had earned his fortune in the Nottingham hosiery industry. In the 1860s he had helped set up a conciliation board to settle disputes in that industry. A staunch Radical when he entered Parliament in 1868, Mundella aided the working class by expanding education and promoting laws to protect factory labourers and labour unions. He served Gladstone at the Board of Trade in the short-lived Liberal government of 1886, and returned to that office in 1892.[22]

Although Gladstone's government is best remembered for the House of Lords' veto of the Irish Home Rule bill in 1893, the Board of Trade was one of the most successful departments of the government, gaining parliamentary approval of several noteworthy laws benefiting the working class. Mundella was especially pleased with the creation of the Labour Department, which collected and disseminated labour statistics.[23] Some activists, though, wanted a much larger department, such as a Ministry of Labour. This was not to be, since the Treasury and the Home Office opposed such an expansion of responsibilities, and neither Mundella nor Burt advocated expanding the State's involvement in business or industry.[24]

Burt's services as Parliamentary Secretary of the Board of Trade did not put him before the public. Mundella conducted most of the Board's business in the House of Commons until he was forced to leave office in 1894 because of his connections with a bankrupt New Zealand company. While Burt seldom spoke for the Board during debates on major legislation, he was busy carrying out tasks behind the scenes. For example, he wrote to the Treasury in December 1892, justifying the proposal to expand the Labour Department. He saw the Department with a role in promoting industrial peace:

> The collection and circulation of useful information relating to Labour will be most serviceable in public and private discussions in directing the energies of those interested towards the right measures for improving the condition of the masses of the people, and in mitigating and diminishing those labour disputes between employer and employed which have so many baneful consequences both direct and indirect.[25]

The NMA had been pursuing and often gaining such statistical information in its negotiations with mine owners. Burt also advised Mundella on appointments to the Labour Department.[26] He sat on several committees and helped resolve issues between government departments, such as the Board of Trade and the Home Office.[27] From 1893 to 1895 he spent much of his time responding for the Board of Trade to a remarkable variety of questions in the House of Commons, including cattle-weighing machines, imported china and patents, as well as standard inquiries about railways and shipping.[28]

During this period, Burt served on two royal commissions. Following the Northumberland miners' strike of 1887, Burt had been instrumental in gaining the appointment of a commission to examine payment of royalties and wayleaves to property holders. Burt and other mining officials had complained that high payments to property owners, even when the price of coal was low, was an exceptional burden on the industry. The commission, which sat from 1889 to 1893, concluded that while royalties on the continent were often somewhat lower than in Britain, the charge there was also substantial. In some areas of Europe a portion of the royalty went to local government funds to benefit the community.[29] Burt also served on the Royal Commission on Labour which, like the royalty commission, was appointed by

Salisbury's government. The Labour Commission produced an enormous amount of material. Its final report of 1894 stressed the need for strong trade unions to help ensure industrial peace, as well as meaningful conciliation boards to settle differences between unions and management.[30] In the 1890s, Burt also served as a governor of the Imperial Institute, a body designed to foster public interest in and knowledge of Great Britain and its empire.[31]

Burt, the NMA and the Board of Trade were all affected by events in the coal industry in the 1890s. After the heady days of the late 1880s and very early 1890s, prices declined sharply. Northumberland miners suffered wage reductions in 1891, 1892 and early 1893.[32] Frustrated with reductions and rising unemployment, they turned their attention to the MFGB, whose leaders called for a basic minimum wage and the unity of all miners. Federation sympathizers criticized Burt for refusing to back the eight-hour day, particularly after he supported regulating the hours of railway workers.[33] In June of 1893 the Northumberland miners voted 6,730 to 5,807 to join the Miners' Federation.[34]

Northumberland's membership in the Federation proved to be stormy and short-lived. At the picnic on 24 June 1893, held just after the decision to join the Federation, Burt stressed that although he had no personal differences with Federation leaders, they did disagree over principles and policy. While Northumberland miners had to learn to cooperate with the Federation, Burt warned them not to get 'carried away into these difficulties and crises by mere sentiment without examining very carefully the road by which they were travelling'.[35] Burt's warning was prescient.

Northumberland and Durham's involvement with the MFGB coincided with the organization's preparation to wage a nationwide strike. The miners of the North East refused to participate in this venture.[36] When the Federation summoned an August meeting in London, the NMA did not attend. According to Welbourne, 'Burt would not go where his presence was unwelcome, and on his persuasion Northumberland failed to send a representative.'[37] Thus, the Federation lacked support of Northumberland and Durham miners' unions during the great coal lock-out of 1893, begun in July when miners refused to accept a wage reduction.[38]

The lock-out dragged on into the autumn of 1893, marred by occasional violence. The unprecedented scope of the lock-out affected coal availability, threatening supplies for industry and railroads, key to the nation's transportation. Because of the ramifications of the lock-out, the government finally took steps to end it.[39] While Lord Rosebery, the Foreign Secretary, is usually credited with playing a central role in mediating a settlement between Federation leaders and mineowners, Mundella and the Board of Trade actually laid the basis for the agreement.[40] The negotiated settlement allowed miners to return to work at their old wages. A conciliation board would be implemented the following February to determine subsequent wages.

Burt must have been delighted that the settlement of the 1893 lock-out provided for a conciliation board. He had continued to promote the use of conciliation and arbitration to settle labour disputes. In 1890, Burt had acted as an umpire in a dispute between shipwrights and joiners in the Tyneside shipyards.[41] In January 1894, he was the opening speaker at a conference on the development of conciliation boards. The meeting was sponsored by Bishop Westcott of Durham, whose arbitration had helped end the Durham miners' strike of 1892. In his speech, Burt, who was still at the Board of Trade, remarked that he looked to a time when there would be more 'harmonious relations between capital and labour', although he stressed that such a development would come by 'evolutionary rather than revolutionary methods'. Burt did not want arbitration to be compulsory, as one could not force a side to agree to terms of arbitration.[42] This meeting demonstrated that mine owners and union leaders in the North East were comfortable with conciliation and cooperation, believing that such an approach had brought stable relations to the coalfields. Industrial and union leaders formed what could be termed a mutual admiration society, as many of them held a common Liberal political ideology and opposed Socialism.[43]

In 1894, a wage conciliation board was instituted in the Northumberland coalfield.[44] Dissatisfaction with NMA leadership was still rife in some collieries, however. Miners at Burradon and elsewhere still zealously supported the Miners' Federation and its programme. Ashington miners had long been critical of Burt's leadership, contending that he cooperated with owners to the miners' detriment.[45] In the summer of 1894, Northumberland miners again voted to join the Miners' Federation, this time by a larger margin − 8,445 to 5,507.[46]

On 23 July 1894, the Federation's executive committee approved the NMA's application for membership, with the stipulation that Northumberland support the Federation on the eight-hour bill. In a proxy vote of the NMA lodges in the following month, a motion to withdraw opposition to the eight-hour bill was soundly defeated − 202 to 36.[47] NMA membership in the Federation was, in effect, stillborn. As a member of Gladstone's government, Burt actively opposed Federation-sponsored eight-hour bills in 1893 and 1894. In 1893 Sam Woods, a Lib-Lab MP and a leader of the Federation, gained substantial support in the House of Commons for the Miners' Eight-Hour Bill. As head of the Miners' National Union, Burt expressed his displeasure with Woods' bill, insisting on no parliamentary interference in the hours of the North East miners. Burt was one of only two members of Gladstone's government to oppose Woods' bill, which passed its second reading but died because the government could not afford it time for consideration.[48]

The split between North East and Federation miners over the eight-hour issue continued to manifest itself during several international miners' congresses in the 1890s. Burt attended most of these, often taking a turn as presiding officer. He continued to preach moderation, strongly counselling against an international strike over the issue in 1893. On that occasion he advised delegates not to utter threats they could not carry out. The motion for a general strike passed, and Burt's statement was greeted with marked coolness by continental miners; Federationists informed them that Burt preached a similar gospel in Britain.[49]

Labourers often expressed disdain for the policy of conciliation, which Burt so earnestly promoted. Conciliation boards usually did little more than reflect the price of coal when determining wages, and miners were frustrated when those deliberations led to decreases. By 1895, wages were again headed down because, according to Burt, production in both Britain and abroad was substantially up.[50] When miners expressed hostility towards the Conciliation Board, Burt explained that the board did not cause reductions; it was 'simply the system of registering facts, and they might as well blame the thermometer for the burning sun'.[51] Burt was the member of a conciliation group, the Industrial Union of Employers and Employed, which lasted from 1894 to 1896.[52]

On the whole, Burt was proud of the achievements of the Gladstone and Rosebery administrations on labour issues. Not only did he applaud the accomplishments of the Board of Trade, but he aggressively defended the entire government's labour record, citing as evidence the expansion of the mining and factory inspectorate and the extension of free education.[53] At the same time, he was very disappointed in the government's inability to carry other important legislative items, particularly an employers' liability bill in line with the TUC's recommendation for a ban on contracting out and an end to the doctrine of common employment. Burt submitted a memorandum from the Board of Trade in support of the bill, acted as a co-sponsor, and spoke briefly in its defence at the seconding reading.[54] Joseph Chamberlain led substantial Unionist opposition to the bill, which was finally killed in early 1894 after the House of Lords passed amendments permitting contracting out.[55]

The House of Lords defeated not only the Irish Home Rule Bill and the Employers' Liability Bill, but several other measures in 1894 and 1895. In an article in 1894, Burt referred to the House of Lords as a 'dangerous anachronism', an unrepresentative body in an age of representative government. The House of Lords was 'dangerous', not only because of the bills it killed, but because any Liberal government had to frame its legislation based on how the upper house would respond. Measures that Lords 'rejected, mutilated, or rendered futile' were not only constitutional issues, but those 'aiming to ameliorate the social and industrial condition of the people'. As the nation had become increasingly democratic, the House of Lords was 'year after year becoming more and more an unworkable and impossible part of the Constitution'. Burt warned that this body would eventually be stripped of its extraordinary power, the veto.[56]

In late 1894 and early 1895, Burt's family life underwent a troubling crisis. The very private Burt mentioned the development in a letter to W. T. Stead:

> P.S. *Private*. We have been passing through a terrible domestic trial. Our second son – a bright youth of 22 – went all wrong mentally and is now in the Asylum at Gosforth, where he has been for 4 months. It came with startling suddenness, and without a hint that anything was amiss. I cannot tell you but you can imagine – what a trial it has been. Happily he is much better, in fact, so far as I can judge, he is quite himself again, & we are hopeful that in a few weeks he will be with us again.[57]

No other evidence of this crisis exists, and this second son, Peter Burt, would later become an engineer.

While Burt was serving at the Board of Trade, a new office building for the NMA was being constructed in Newcastle. The offices on Picton Place had proved inadequate, and in late 1892 the NMA voted to build offices and a meeting hall on Northumberland Road. Called the 'Burt Memorial Hall',[58] the building was constructed of red Leicester-shire bricks and its front crowned by the figure of a miner. Still a familiar sight on the Newcastle skyline, the miner was based on Ralph Hedley's popular painting of 1888 entitled 'Going Home', which pictured two miners returning home after work in a colliery. The painting hangs today in the Laing Art Gallery in Newcastle.[59]

Opening ceremonies for the new hall, held on 14 September 1895, emphasized the congenial relationship between owners and miners in Northumberland. Newcastle newspapers waxed enthusiastic over the event, seeing the new hall as a symbol of union success and the prosperity of the coal trade. Burt was showered with praise. Deferential as ever, he stated that he had done nothing 'to merit such distinguished recognition', but that the ones truly deserving of credit were the thousands of miners who had remained united over the years, as well as the many union delegates who had served the Association.[60] The stone carving at the front of the building, still there today, reads 'In recognition of valuable services rendered by Thomas Burt, M.P., as their general secretary for 27 years; also to commemorate his appointment to the secretaryship of the Board of Trade in 1892'. The poem written by Matthew Tate for the occasion reflected the feelings of many. One of the stanzas reads:

This is the Burt Memorial Hall,
  What fitter name could we devise?
We should be proud, we miners all,
  To have in him so rare a prize.
Each man amongst us may lay claim
  To having done some little bit,
But his must be the crowning name,
And if this building honours him,
  I'm very sure he'll honour it.[61]

By the time of the opening of Burt Hall, Burt was no longer at the Board of Trade. The Rosebery government was defeated on a vote in July 1895, and resigned immediately. Salisbury formed a new government that included Joseph Chamberlain and four other former Liberals.

It is not easy to measure Burt's services at the Board of Trade. There are few contemporary evaluations of his effectiveness. Given his character and disposition, we know that he worked extremely hard and fulfilled all duties expected of him. As a result of preoccupation with his office, Burt had fewer opportunities to speak in the House of Commons and was less involved than usual with the mining industry and the NMA, which continued its struggle with the Federation.

Chapter 10

THE NORTHUMBERLAND MINERS' ASSOCIATION AND THE UNIONIST GOVERNMENT, 1895–1905

Burt's precarious health forced him to play a less active role in union and parliamentary affairs after 1895. Other agents and officers assisted with the expanding NMA, whose activities became increasingly complex. Burt's responsibilities decreased in 1898 when the Miners' National Union, which he had led for seventeen years, ceased to exist. Even though his public activities diminished, Burt remained a respected and powerful force in the community. At the turn of the century he focused his attention on the South African War and its aftermath. His opposition to the war brought about a strong challenge to his parliamentary seat in the election of 1900. Burt played a key role in the North East miners' protest against the government's levy on coal exports, and he became involved in the controversy surrounding the use of Chinese labour in the Transvaal.

After forming his Unionist government in June 1895, Salisbury called elections for the following month. For the first time since his election in 1874, Burt found his seat contested. His opponent was Maltman Barry, a most unusual man. Born in 1842, he had become a journalist 'of some talent', writing on parliamentary affairs for conservative London newspapers. He was a friend of Karl Marx, a member of the International Working Men's Association, and a supporter of the Independent Labour Party. Barry eventually became an adherent of the Tories' democratic wing, an avid imperialist, and a critic of Gladstone's Eastern policy.[1]

During the 1895 campaign, Barry charged that although Burt was originally elected to represent labour, he was no longer a champion of the workers but rather a main-line Liberal. Barry characterized himself as a defender of labour, calling for an old age pension for workers, a reduction of hours for boys in the mines, an employers' liability law without the option to contract out, and Home Rule for Ireland. In particular, he criticized the previous Liberal government, including Burt, for failing to aid the unemployed.[2]

There was no substantial difference between Burt and Barry on many issues. Burt usually defended the record of the Liberal government on workers' issues, claiming that it would have performed even better except for the interference of the undemocratic House of Lords.[3] He believed that his opponent stood little chance of winning the seat.[4] Barry often found himself baited by the miners, and he accepted this with generally good humour. He suffered 'no confidence' motions at the conclusion of each of four meetings held in mining communities.[5] Barry polled a respectable 1,235 votes, against 3,404 for Burt.[6] Among the casualties in the 1895 elections were Keir Hardie and John Morley, who lost the Newcastle seat he had occupied since 1883.[7]

Northumberland miners took actions not always approved by NMA officers. In late 1896 miners voted to abolish the Conciliation Board, much to Burt's displeasure. The Board, the victim of a marked downturn in wages, was not re-established until 1900.[8] In June 1897, Ashington colliery union leaders called a strike to force non-union miners to join the NMA.[9] Burt disliked using a strike for this purpose, regarding it as a form of tyranny akin to employers dismissing miners who were active in union affairs.[10] By the early 1900s, the Ashington miners were pressing the NMA to join the Miners' Federation. Established in 1849, the Ashington colliery was by the 1890s the largest colliery in Northumberland. Ashington miners often clashed with union leaders. Many of the Ashington miners were young or new to the area, and did not readily accept its religious, labour and political traditions.[11] The presence of a large labour force not steeped in the conciliatory tradition helps explain the willingness of these miners to accept new ideas and go their own way. An acrimonious three-month strike also flared up in Bedlington in 1897. Strikers were angry with Burt and the union, which forced them to return to work.[12] Yet, in spite of differences between owners, miners and union leaders during this period, most problems were amicably resolved through the Joint Committee, which Burt regarded as one of the NMA's great success stories.[13] Northumberland miners who pushed for membership in the MFGB gained relatively little support.

In 1898, the Miners' National Union – which Welbourne referred to as a 'relic of the past' – ceased to exist when the Durham miners withdrew their membership. Once encompassing several mining unions, by the 1890s the MNU included only those of Durham and Northumberland. In announcing its demise, Burt praised its long-time legislative efforts, especially in the areas of trade union rights and safety.[14] While Burt had always been comfortable in his association with the MNU, probably because of the limited scope of its activities, he remained sceptical of the value of the Trades Union Congress. He attended its annual meeting in 1899 and still found its membership too large for meaningful deliberation. Burt and Northumberland miners also had reservations about the attempt to create a Federation of Trade Unions in 1899.[15] In late 1897 and early 1898, the NMA generously supported the engineers' unsuccessful nationwide strike for an eight-hour day, after which Burt questioned the effectiveness of worker action on such a large scale.[16] As always, he looked to a strong local union as more valuable than any distant organization.

Burt remained interested in Britain's foreign and imperial policies, even though he seldom addressed these issues in Parliament. Speaking in Northumberland in 1896, he expressed his horror over the actions of the Turkish government, this time because of atrocities against the Armenians.[17] Speaking to his constituents in 1897, he charged that the British government in India had been far too aggressive. However, he stressed that he normally voted for a strong army and navy, as they were necessary for protection. He thought 'that England's rule was beneficent' and urged citizens to become more involved to ensure that it be a truly just empire.[18] He did not want military forces to be used aggressively and was appalled when the spectre of war between France and Britain raised its ugly head over Fashoda.[19] In 1898, Burt joined other union leaders to support W. T. Stead's 'Peace Crusade' for the Hague Peace Conference. Still the president of the International Arbitration League, Burt was pleased with that organization's promotion of the Tsar's peace effort.[20] Burt's optimistic view of a Britain promoting international peace and justice was rudely shaken in 1899 by the outbreak of war in South Africa.

South Africa's economic and political environment had been transformed following the discovery of gold in the South African Republic in the mid-1880s. The Boer republic not only became the centre of a huge gold-mining industry, but was also subjected to an influx of capitalists and miners, collectively called outlanders. Cultures clashed as the religiously and socially conservative Boers feared the overwhelming presence of the foreign mining community. Meanwhile, British elements within the Boer republic and in the neighbouring British-controlled Cape Colony resented the Boer government's attempts to tax the gold industry and restrict the political rights of the outlanders. The Jameson Raid of late 1895, an armed attempt by a small military force associated with Cecil Rhodes designed to overthrow the Boer government, not only failed miserably, but heightened tensions and led to war in October 1899.[21]

Burt's first known public statement on British conduct in South

Africa came in December 1897, when he spoke to his constituents about the Jameson Raid. Burt laid blame for the affair on Cecil Rhodes, a man who did not deserve to be called a hero. Burt believed that the House of Commons' committee investigating the Raid had made a big mistake in failing to examine all relevant telegrams. These might have clearly indicated British government complicity.[22] He also spoke about South Africa at the miners' picnic in July 1899, when war appeared a distinct possibility. By then Burt's son was working in the Boer republic. While Burt could 'sympathise' with outlanders, he thought problems could be 'solved by reasonable negotiation' and deemed it 'sheer criminality to plunge the country into war over the matter'.[23] Burt presided, albeit reluctantly, at a stormy anti-war meeting in Newcastle on 11 October, after Paul Kruger, president of the South African Republic, had issued his ultimatum to the British government. The hall was packed with supporters of the war, and none of the speakers could be heard over the extremely noisy and often orchestrated demonstrations of the crowd. While Burt had maintained order at the TUC annual meeting in 1891 in the very same hall, his gentle disposition counted for nothing in October 1899, and the meeting was abandoned before any substantial violence or injury occurred.[24]

In May 1901, Burt expressed disappointment with his own ineffective opposition to the war:

> I did indeed attempt to speak upon this question before the war was declared in favour of the dispute being referred to arbitration, but I was howled down. If I have any regret upon this question it is that I was perhaps too easily cowed, and that I should have protested more emphatically than I did against what I regarded as the most disgraceful war in our history.[25]

Burt was rather hard on himself, for he did actively oppose the war in several ways. Like most labour union leaders and working-class MPs, Burt mildly criticized the government's conduct leading up to the war and deplored the continuation of the conflict.[26] In June of 1899, the IAL, with Burt still president, called for both sides to exercise 'patience and forbearance' in attempting to resolve the grievances of the outlanders. The following year it published one pamphlet calling for arbitration to end the war and a second contending that the war was simply a disguised attempt to acquire cheap labour for the mines.[27] Burt attended an October 1899 meeting of the British section of the Inter-Parliamentary Union, which considered how to get as 'good a vote as possible' on the Stanhope amendment.[28] Burt, Fenwick and most other Lib-Labs voted in favour of Philip Stanhope's amendment protesting the government's conduct in negotiations with the Boer republic.[29] Burt was also active in the League of Liberals Against Aggression and

Militarism. At its formative meeting in February 1900, he made the seconding speech of David Lloyd George's resolution condemning the war.[30] Over the next three years, the League sponsored several meetings and publications critical of the conflict.[31]

By the spring of 1900, British forces were in the ascendancy in South Africa. The Unionist government, claiming that the war was virtually over and hoping to capitalize on the jingoism of the public, dissolved Parliament and held elections in October 1900. A few months earlier Burt had predicted that his position on the war would probably bring him an opponent in an election.[32] Not only did he face his old rival Maltman Barry, but Burt's margin of victory turned out to be the narrowest of his parliamentary career.

Barry campaigned ardently in support of the government's policy in South Africa and with enthusiastic promotion of the Empire. Tagging Burt as a member of the 'peace party', Barry charged that 'if they returned Mr. Burt to Parliament it was equivalent to returning a dozen ordinary pro-Boers in consequence of his great moral influence'. He urged voters to remove 'peace mongers' like Burt who failed to rally to the national defence. He insisted that Burt's promotion of arbitration was an unrealistic dream, as Britain could never gain a fair arbitrator amongst so many enemies.[33] Barry enjoyed greater backing from Conservative leaders and clubs, and a warmer response from the public, than in the previous election.[34] His greatest support came in Blyth, where posters proclaimed: 'Vote for Burt and down comes the Union Jack' and 'Every vote for Barry ensures the safety of the British Empire'.[35]

Shortly before the election, Burt's family suffered a personal tragedy. Burt's daughter Millie, who had shared his literary interests, died on 2 September, shortly after giving birth to a son. She had married Burt's friend, journalist James Annand, in September 1899. While her son Hamish (James) survived, the suddenness of her death was a shock to the family. At the beginning of the election campaign, Burt acknowledged the death but added that such an event was not unusual:

> That really belonged to the common lot of humanity – hearts were broken every day, tender friendships were severed, and they had to do the best they possibly could to brush aside their tears and to screw themselves up to face the troubles of life, remembering that their business was with the living, and not with those that are gone.[36]

Throughout the campaign, Burt criticized the government, in particular Alfred Milner, the British High Commissioner in South Africa, for breaking off negotiations in 1899 even though substantial progress had been made. Burt stressed the necessity of compromise in negotiation; otherwise, the whole process became simply a waste of time, and such had been the case with Milner. Burt believed that Britain should annex the Boer republics; since Britain had destroyed them, she was obligated to rebuild them.[37] Burt also charged the Unionist government with 'mismanagement and blundering' in running the war, accusing it of calling the election to take advantage of the country's 'emotions of patriotism and to exploit the bravery of the British soldiers in South Africa'.[38]

The Blyth Temperance Union backed Burt, and he received a strong endorsement from the United Irish League as one who had 'devoted a life's work to the working classes, and ... had been an earnest supporter of the cause of Ireland'.[39] Burt's greatest advantage in the election, according to the *Blyth News*, was his special relationship to the miners:

> There is a brotherhood which binds the hearts of Mr. Burt and the mining community in this district, which nature alone must sever. His career in the past lives in the memory of to-day, and though his physical abilities may not be as they were years ago, the faith and trust of the Morpeth Borough is still reposing in him, for his powerful mental capacity is still as active as ever it was.[40]

After the most heated campaign of his career, Burt won the election by a majority of 410, gaining 3,117 votes to 2,707 for Barry. Victory came from the solid support of loyal miners as well as Irish voters in Cowpen, Bebside and Bedlington.[41] The narrowness of the victory was explained particularly by Burt's opposition to the war,[42] and by the changing nature of his Morpeth constituency. Miners no longer dominated the voters' roll. The port of Blyth and its vicinity, where Barry garnered so many votes, had grown to constitute about one-half of the total electorate. Henry Pelling's contention that the North East's 'seafaring and shipbuilding combined with a military tradition to make for strong support for the war' may have translated into votes in the Blyth area for Burt's opponent.[43] Moreover, this region was under the influence of the Conservative landowner Sir Matthew White Ridley,[44] and the recently founded Blyth branch of the Primrose League – a grassroots Tory organization established in 1883 – was particularly active by the time of the South African War.[45]

Although Salisbury's government was returned to power with a large majority, the war dragged on until May 1902. At the miners' picnic in July 1901, Burt gave one of his most forceful speeches, accusing the government of waging a costly war in order to acquire gold mines. Franchise for outlanders was no longer an issue, but then, Burt added, why would one expect Salisbury, who had 'resisted the extension of the franchise at home', to support it elsewhere. Burt also wondered what the black South Africans must think seeing the two Christian peoples fighting with each other: 'If this was our Christianity ... we had better go back to our Paganism, ... we had better go back to the old gods – to Bacchus, to Mars, to Mammon, the gods we really worshipped.'[46] This speech, much applauded by the very large crowd of miners, was regarded by Ralph Young as 'the finest I fancy I ever heard him make ... It was straight[,]sound and delivered with so much earnestness and with so rare an eloquence that it made an enormous impression upon the audience [sic].'[47]

In late 1901 and early 1902, Burt often addressed the government's misconduct of the war. He criticized the government for demanding unconditional surrender of the Boers and attempting to 'destroy the spirit of nationality and subjugate if not exterminate a people'. A willingness to negotiate with the Boers would have avoided much suffering and death, including the terrible concentration camps, for which he blamed the government, not the soldiers, civilians or nurses. The government had to conciliate the Boers, he stressed, or face a constantly discontented people in South Africa, as in Ireland.[48]

A measure of prosperity had returned to the Northumberland coalfields by the beginning of the war. Much to Burt's delight, the Conciliation Board was reinstituted in 1900 and had the good fortune of being in place for a favourable year, with wage advances totalling 36.25 per cent over the four quarters.[49] By 1902 the NMA could proudly proclaim that it held £84,000 in property and investments, and had 23,880 members.[50] Not all miners were satisfied, however. At a well-attended gathering in January 1900, Ashington miners protested that the Conciliation Board restricted the ability of the union to make substantial gains.[51] Indeed, prosperity proved temporary. During the course of the year ending July 1902, Northumberland miners suffered a 12.5 per cent wage reduction.[52]

Burt was especially pleased with the establishment of the Northumberland Aged Miners' Homes Association (NAMHA) in 1900. When miners retired, they either had to leave company housing (unless they had at least two sons living at home who worked in the mine), or live with their offspring, which most independent-minded miners preferred not to do.[53] The NAMHA, while independent of the NMA, collected a significant initial contribution of £500 from the union, and received regular funding from a levy on miners' wages. Burt praised the efforts of miners in helping to provide housing for those who had contributed so much to the community by their labour. In his Monthly Circular, Burt cited John Ruskin's argument that a labourer working with his 'spade' deserved support from the community just as one of the 'middle ranks' earned it with his 'sword, pen, or lancet'. At a ceremonial laying of the first foundation stones, Burt spoke of the humaneness of the housing development and the importance of the miners' self-help movement.[54] The first cottages opened in East Chevington in 1902. Other cottages for aged miners, built usually in groups of ten and located in the various mining villages, were constructed over the years. By 1911 the number of cottages reached 148.[55]

The South African War was costly, and Sir Michael Hicks Beach, Chancellor of the Exchequer, helped finance it by raising income taxes, increasing duties on tea, tobacco and alcoholic drinks, and the issuing of several loans. In the 1901 budget he added a duty of 1s. per ton on exported coal. This tax was designed not only to raise revenue, but to reduce the flow of coal that was fuelling the industries and navies of Britain's European rivals.[56] There was widespread opposition to the coal tax throughout the North East, especially in 1901, although concern lasted until 1905. It was feared that the tax would restrict the sale of coal by those districts, such as Northumberland, which were heavily dependent on foreign markets.[57]

Throughout the North East, coal mine owners, miners, coal exporters and shipowners registered their concerns over the tax through a series of meetings. Burt played a leading role in marshalling these forces to denounce the tax. He helped to coordinate a national miners' conference in London, at which the normally moderate Northumberland miners were bellicose in advocating a strike. Speaking at this conference, even Burt was willing to support such a stoppage, although one was never called.[58] On the subject of the coal duty, Burt gave one of the longest parliamentary speeches of his career on 2 May 1901. He contended that the tax would affect one portion of the coal trade unfairly. Whenever possible, foreigners would purchase their coal from suppliers other than the British. As an exporter, Northumberland was particularly vulnerable, since 80 per cent of its coal was shipped to foreign markets. Burt stressed that a shilling tax per ton was a considerable amount in the competitive market, and that ultimately the miners would suffer through loss of trade and reduced wages.[59]

The Unionist government, with its large majority, easily defeated amendments to the budget. In his Monthly Circular, Burt claimed that pressure from coal-mining interests had forced Hicks Beach to agree to modifications to the tax, exempting existing coal contracts and excluding contracts below 6s. per ton.[60] The coal tax was collected even after the war ended. Burt and others regularly protested, to no avail, the detrimental impact of the tax on the export trade, as competitors invaded traditional British markets and as wages went down. The tax was finally dropped in 1906 after the Liberals came to power.[61]

By the 1900s Burt often curtailed his activities because of poor health, and William Straker increasingly relieved him of his union secretarial duties. Burt was severely ill with bronchial problems in early 1902. He was unable to write his Monthly Circular from February through April, and he reported to readers in June that he had not been able to keep up with all of the affairs. His comments at the July picnic were brief, since he was still recovering. In March 1904 he suffered a recurrence of his bronchial condition.[62]

Burt's illness in 1902 caused his absence from debates on the government's controversial Education Bill, which abolished local school boards and provided denominational schools with extensive government funding from local rates. In June Burt criticized the Education Bill as 'distinctly reactionary', and playing 'into the hands of the clerics and sectarians'. He believed that government funding of schools should include citizen control via 'popularly-elected representative bodies'.[63] On 8 October 1902, a banquet was given in Blyth to celebrate Burt's services to Liberalism and the restoration of his health. At that engagement, Burt criticized those who favoured the Education Bill as a means to save Christianity; he 'pitied Christianity if it depended on that'. He contended that religion should be taught in homes and churches, not in schools. Ultimately he held the citizens themselves responsible for neglecting the importance of education, as they were giving themselves to militarism while ignoring the loss of their liberties. Man was 'singing, till he was hoarse, "Rule Britannia", whilst his liberties were being filched away behind his back'.[64]

Burt retained his interest in temperance, which he saw as both a moral and a political issue. Before a rally of the United Kingdom Alliance at Newcastle in 1896, Burt reminded his listeners that England should be

> free and sober. A drunken people must be an enslaved people – a sober people only could be free. The vice that sapped the manhood of vast numbers of our population, that brutalised and degraded them, that made them the ready tools of greedy intriguers, struck a blow at the life and the soul of the nation.[65]

In 1904, the Unionist government introduced a new licensing bill. The bill shifted licensing authority from local magistrates to Justices of the Peace and provided monetary compensation for publicans who lost their licences. Temperance advocates were furious over the bill, which they saw as supporting the brewing industry. In a major speech on 9 May, Burt moved the rejection of the government's Licensing Bill. While Meech regarded it as one of Burt's better parliamentary addresses, a correspondent for the *Newcastle Daily Chronicle* said that Burt was so tentative at the beginning that he 'gave one the impression of being somewhat overweighted with responsibility. For a time, indeed, he seemed quite nervous and ill at ease.' He eventually gained his composure and delivered a 'harangue' which was 'loudly cheered by Liberals'.[66] Burt feared that the bill would neither reduce drunkenness nor encourage temperance. He was especially concerned about the removal of licensing authority from local magistrates. Perhaps because they were more directly responsible to the citizens than were the Justices of the Peace, magistrates had recently responded to the wishes of the people and closed some public houses. He also accused the government of inordinately enhancing the value of a licence by compensating its removal. Some of Burt's remarks were clever. For instance, he insisted on not criticizing publicans, whom he found to be good people: 'Many of them are my friends, and some of them have even voted for me. And considering that I am not one of their best customers, I think it was very disinterested of them to treat me so kindly.' He expressed the moral dimension of the issue when referring to John Bull's 'very big and heterogeneous family. Many of his children are in rags, living on the verge of starvation, and their poverty, their misery, and their crime is largely caused by the traffic in intoxicating liquor.'[67] In spite of substantial opposition, the Licensing Bill passed.

The issue of Chinese coolie labour in the Transvaal generated even more dramatic public controversy than the disputes surrounding the Education and Licensing Acts. Alfred Milner, British High Commissioner in South Africa, was convinced that stability in the former Boer republic was dependent on a return of prosperity to their mines. Productive mines would ensure jobs for British workers, whose influx would bring British population and culture to South Africa. The mines, however, needed a large amount of unskilled labour to become productive once again. Unskilled British labour was deemed too expensive, and native labour was not available in sufficient numbers, so owners sought Chinese labour under restricted contract. Alfred Lyttelton, who had replaced Joseph Chamberlain as Colonial Secretary, approved a hiring scheme, and in February 1904 the Transvaal Council approved the Chinese Labour Ordinance to procure the labourers, tens of thousands of whom would arrive over the next few months. By February and March 1904, British humanitarian and economic interests reacted angrily to the use of Chinese 'slaves' to aid mining magnates in the Transvaal.[68]

Burt began to criticize the use of Chinese labour earlier than most public figures. In August 1903, Burt objected to employing imported labour in the South African mines. He understood why native labourers were reluctant to toil in the mines, as their already low wages of 2s. or 2s. 6d. per day had been reduced to a mere 1s. after the war. Moreover, mortality and illness rates were extremely high. To get labour, Burt stressed, 'good pay, fair treatment, safe and healthy conditions, are necessary'.[69] In January 1904, drawing primarily on South African sources for information, Burt devoted over three pages of his Monthly Circular to this issue. The affair, Burt said, was economically important to the people of Northumberland since they had many companions working there, and prosperity 'will afford profitable employment for thousands of white men'. Instead, owners seeking Chinese workers 'want not only cheap labour, but still more docile, submissive, uncomplaining labour – serfs and chattels, not free, independent workers'. Burt stressed that his concern had 'nothing to do with racial or colour prejudices or antagonisms', but with the fact that conditions under which the Chinese would serve, confined within compounds and with restricted rights, was 'in its essence slavery'. Burt also charged that the people in the Transvaal were not able to express their own views as the issue was being manipulated by mine owners and the mine-controlled Transvaal press.[70] Burt continued his attack in March and April 1904. He was particularly upset that certain types of labour were being presented as degrading and therefore beneath the dignity of whites to perform. There should be nothing wrong, he stressed, with honest labour.[71] In May the NMA delegate council passed a resolution reflecting Burt's viewpoint:

> That this Council condemns the action of the Government in introducing Chinese and servile labour into the Transvaal as being a direct attack on the freedom and dignity of labour. One of the objects of the South African War was declared in the high authority to be to obtain equal rights for all men and for all races, and now we see the Government violating that principle by seeking to secure cheap and servile labour for the benefit of the mining magnates, who were the chief instigators and promoters of the war.[72]

In late 1904 and early 1905 Burt and his wife visited South Africa for about three months. They wished to see their two sons there (one son, Robert, died in South Africa in 1906 at the age of twenty-three), and hoped that the trip would improve the elder Burt's health. He intended to learn for himself the conditions of labourers in the country.[73] Following his return, Burt published a short account of the trip entitled *A Visit to the Transvaal*. He certainly held some stereotypical racist views of the period. He admired the muscular strength of the Zulus, who did 'their heavy work in the broiling sun with apparent ease and playfulness. Never had I seen workers play with hard work and enjoy it as did these Zulus.' Whites, he said, did not have the strength to do hard manual labour like the 'coloured', but it was only 'when intellect, skill, special training are required that the white man's superiority makes itself manifest'. On the whole, white men did not flourish in the environment: 'Not that the individual withers and degenerates, but the race – the superior race – does not multiply and flourish. Here one may travel, as I have done, day after day for miles over hills and veldt ... without seeing the face of a white man.' At the same time, he emphasized that the common criticism of black Africans as being lazy and no good was simply incorrect. He rather admired, but also feared, the Chinese: 'this mental alertness of the Chinaman; his readiness to learn new things and to adapt himself to altered conditions will make him, directly and indirectly, a formidable competitor to the white man'. Burt contended that there seemed to have been sufficient native labour available, but mine owners had not made use of it, determined instead to gain ever more inexpensive labour. After the war, employers decreased the pay of black Africans while extracting more labour from them. 'To me,' Burt added, 'it is amazing that shrewd employers, short of labour, should have been able to devise no better method of attracting it than by reducing wages to nearly half of what they had been before the war.' On the whole, Burt found the Chinese looking healthy, living in clean facilities, and eating good food. The illness and death rates, however, were much too high. Moreover, the Chinese had been recruited under false pretences, as they had not expected to work underground and were paid much less than anticipated. Burt returned from South Africa convinced that the use of the Chinese labour was unacceptable, equating it to convict labour: 'I have a profound, an ineradicable objection to the importation and deportation of human beings in droves, and of shackling them by all sorts of galling restrictions and disabilities.'[74]

Conservative opponents seized upon Burt's description of the acceptable conditions in which the Chinese lived as evidence that he endorsed the use of Chinese labour. In fact, he returned from the trip even more opposed to the system than before. In his Monthly Circular of June 1905, he listed evidence that the Chinese were being flogged for even the 'most trivial offences'. The following month, Burt reported to miners that the press had picked up his comments on flogging. On several occasions in Parliament during July, Burt forcefully charged that various sources indicated that illegal flogging and imprisonment (often without interpreters present) was rather common.[75] Only in late 1905 did the British government finally recognize that even Milner had permitted corporal punishment without due process. In December 1905, Burt reported to the miners that support for coolie labour, even among mine owners, had sharply diminished, and that he looked forward to the new Liberal government, which had just taken office, bringing the practice to an end.[76]

The Unionist government, under the leadership of Arthur Balfour since the retirement of his uncle Lord Salisbury in 1902, resigned in December 1905. The South African War, once so popular, had dragged on until 1902 and raised serious questions about the government's handling of the conflict. In addition, the Unionist Party split in 1903 when Joseph Chamberlain resigned as Colonial Secretary to pursue his dream of establishing a tariff on goods that would help rejuvenate the British economy. Liberals rallied, not only in defence of free trade, but over the controversies surrounding the Licensing and Education Acts, and the issue of Chinese labour. Throughout the period, Burt played a quiet role, criticizing the government for pursuing a militaristic goal while ignoring what he believed to be pressing social needs at home.

Chapter 11

BURT AND THE LABOUR MOVEMENT UNDER THE LIBERAL GOVERNMENT, 1905–14

The period from 1905 to 1914 brought political, economic and social change on both the national and local levels. After ten years in the political wilderness, the Liberal Party used its huge majority from the 1906 election as a mandate to pass a series of reform bills, including measures addressing the economic and social problems of the working class. The House of Lords was shorn of its veto power following a protracted showdown over the 1909 budget. The Liberals confronted the issue of women's suffrage, addressed a wave of labour unrest which swept the nation after 1910, and worked to solve the extraordinary dilemma of Irish Home Rule. During this period the Liberal Party was challenged not only by its traditional opponent, the Conservative Party, but also by the recently formed Labour Party, which gained political credibility by electing a substantial number of MPs in 1906.

Thomas Burt and the people of Northumberland were very much a part of these changes. The Northumberland miners, ending their county independence, finally agreed to support the eight-hour day and join the Miners' Federation. Strikes racked the Northumberland coal fields as miners adjusted uneasily to their new work schedules while collaborating their activities with the national union. Burt overcame a major challenge from the Labour Party between 1906 and 1909, when it questioned his effectiveness as an MP. Often in weak health, Burt seldom spoke in Parliament, although he readily defended the Liberal Party to his constituency and wrote an article in support of old age pensions. By now, most of his long-time political and union allies from Northumberland had died. Throughout the period, however, Burt retained his unique respect and popularity throughout the North East.

While Burt's union and parliamentary salary was paid entirely by the

NMA, his and Fenwick's election expenses were borne by the Liberal Association.[1] These contributions helped to cover the cost of an election agent shared by the Wansbeck and Morpeth divisions. Money for the election fund came primarily from wealthy Liberal industrialists and landowners. Walter Runciman, son of a wealthy Newcastle shipowner and later a member of H. H. Asquith's Liberal government, solicited these financial contributions.[2] Coal mine owners Lord Durham and Sir James Joicey contributed 'substantial assistance towards Burt's election expenses' in 1906, and G. O. Trevelyan, historian, politician and owner of the country estate of Wallington in Northumberland, sent £25 in 1905 to Runciman, who was soliciting support for Burt, with the note: 'It is fortunate that you have taken the matter in hand. People sometimes, when on the aggressive, omit to secure their strongholds, with disastrous results. I would not have anything happen to Burt for a king's ransom.'[3] Burt was comfortable accepting contributions from wealthy industrialists because he viewed the production of goods as a cooperative venture between owner and labourer. As A. W. Purdue emphasizes, the Lib-Labs also shared with the Liberal industrialists a common concern over 'great moral issues such as arose from religion, Ireland, or foreign policy'.[4]

Burt's opponent in the January 1906, election was thirty-seven-year-old businessman Stuart A. Coats, a resident of Mayfair, London, and heir to the head of the family thread-making firm of J. & P. Coats.[5] His chance of winning the Morpeth seat became virtually impossible when, in late December 1905, the government announced that Burt was named Privy Councillor. Burt was flooded with congratulatory messages from throughout the nation. Newcastle-area newspapers applauded the honour and, before the commencement of many campaign rallies, notice was given of the well-deserved tribute. Few candidates for Parliament ever enjoyed such positive publicity on the eve of an election. Burt's friend Aaron Watson later contended that Burt should have been awarded a cabinet position, although he admitted that Prime Minister Campbell-Bannerman had a large number of ambitious candidates from which to choose.[6] In fact, Burt was beyond his prime in political influence as well as in health. In early 1904 sickness forced Burt to recruit others to speak at his constituency meetings.[7] He was also extremely worried about his daughter, Stella, who had nearly died in 1902. In order to avoid the northern cold she spent the entire winter of 1906 in Bournemouth.[8] Stella died in 1908 at the age of thirty-three.

Coats, a Unionist, had the unenviable task of defending the past government's positions on licensing, education and coolie labour, all very unpopular in Northumberland. However, the central issue in the local campaign, as Burt stressed, was free trade versus protection. Coats avidly defended the tariff on goods to protect and promote

British manufacturing, while Burt continued to advocate free trade for a British economy heavily oriented towards exporting its manufactured articles.[9] Although the campaign was spirited, the outcome was never in doubt, and Burt won by 5,518 to 1,919.[10] The election proved bitter-sweet, however, as his son-in-law and friend James Annand, elected to Parliament for the first time, died before he was seated.[11]

In 1906 the NMA narrowly approved the Eight-Hour Bill by a vote of 9,251 to 8,786, ending the divisiveness which had long separated the union from the MFGB. The following year, NMA miners voted to join the MFGB, 16,108 to 3,613.[12] Durham followed shortly thereafter. Thus ended the independent county unions of Northumberland and Durham, which Burt had helped to develop and which he had nurtured for so long. The change from conciliatory county unions to a more combative national organization was not sudden. Critics of the conciliatory approach had become more numerous and vocal since the 1880s. Moreover, by the early 1900s, coal mining in the North East had changed, as the number of hewers – long the most powerful within the workforce – decreased in proportion to other labourers. Also, as the mining industry expanded and the workforce increased, a wave of new immigrants poured into the villages of the North East. Many of these new miners did not share the traditions of Nonconformity, cooperation and Radicalism, which had for so long shaped the NMA.[13] Moreover, the Independent Labour Party, under the leadership of Keir Hardie, became very active in the northern coalfields starting in 1905. The number of local branches of the ILP in the North East increased dramatically, and the party pushed especially hard for approval of the miners' Eight-Hour Bill.[14] Hardie dominated the 1906 picnic with his dynamic and energetic style. Compared to Hardie, Burt's 'figure was most pathetic. The never-robust voice was most quavery and at times it appeared as if he would break down altogether.'[15]

These momentous changes for the NMA were accompanied by changes in union leadership. Ralph Young, who had long assisted Burt in his secretarial duties, died suddenly on 4 December 1904. Young had been an outspoken opponent of the eight-hour day and an avid champion of conciliation. Hugh Boyle, elected president of the NMA in 1896, died in 1907. Both Young and Boyle had served on elected local government boards, and both were strong Radicals. Young was particularly opposed to Socialism.[16] Those who replaced Young and Boyle, particularly William Straker (corresponding secretary after 1905 and in reality the one who carried out most of Burt's secretarial duties), John Cairns (elected agent in 1906), and Joseph English (Boyle's replacement as president in 1907) had religious and political back-grounds similar to the older leaders. However, they were of the next generation and more open to the new political and economic ideas in vogue in the twentieth century.[17] Burt was the last surviving officer of his generation. Other friends and colleagues from the North East had also recently died, including James Trotter in 1899, Joseph Cowen in 1900, and W. E. Adams in 1906.[18]

The greatest personal test facing Burt after 1906 centred on the close affiliation between the NMA and the Liberal Party, and the challenge posed to that relationship by the Labour Party. While Hardie and the ILP waxed enthusiastic and optimistic over the future of the Labour Party in Northumberland, Burt and many miners would remain faithful Liberals. The public argument over Burt's and Fenwick's political futures dominated Northumberland politics from 1906 to 1910. The national press closely followed the course of this controversy.

The connection between the rise of the Labour Party and the demise of the Liberal Party constitutes an important historical debate. It is not intended here to examine this debate in any detail.[19] There is no doubt that the Labour Party made considerable inroads into the traditional Liberal stronghold of Northumberland mining communities before the Great War. Nevertheless, the Liberal Party remained powerful in these districts, where loyalty to Burt and Fenwick continued to be strong. But the Liberal Party was more than Burt, Fenwick and the miners. It was well organized locally, whereas the Labour Party, for all the enthusiasm of its backers, was new and lacked the resources, especially financial, of the older party. Moreover, many miners who had long been active in the leadership of the local Liberal Party were not about to abandon their positions, believing, as did Burt and Fenwick, in the Liberal political philosophy which had served them so well.

The ILP, formed by Keir Hardie in 1893, was one of several Socialist organizations that, along with the labour unions, combined to form the Labour Party in 1900. The ILP formed its first Northumberland branch in Ashington in 1905, and others quickly followed.[20] During the summer of 1906 several ILP rallies were held in Bedlington at the Cross. One of the meetings became rather lively after Burt and Fenwick were referred to as dogs who were 'simply carrying the lamp for the Liberal Party, members of which exploited the working classes of this country'. The Liberal Party countered with its own rallies.[21] ILP organizer M. T. Simm wrote of the formidable obstacle to his work:

When I undertook propaganda work in Northumberland twelve months ago, the preliminary warning everywhere was – 'Ye monna say nowt agyen Burt and Fenwick.' Among the older school, to agree with Messrs. Burt and Fenwick was apparently a religious duty accepted by the old and imposed upon the young.[22]

In September 1906, Socialists roundly criticized Burt for having charged that ILP supporters encouraged workers to desert their unions; Burt contended that he was misquoted by the press.[23] About the same time, the ILP censured the Lib-Labs, including Burt and Fenwick, for preaching class cooperation, for failing to address the issue of poverty, and for collaborating with industrialists.[24]

Burt had often been critical of Socialists. Although he admitted in 1898 that they were good at drawing attention to major social issues, and he agreed that the industrial system often did not equitably distribute wealth, Burt sought change by evolution, not revolution, and he did not consider nationalization a practical solution.[25] In 1903–04, Burt served as president of the Northern Liberal Federation which, according to Bealey and Pelling, 'launched a deliberate campaign against independent Labour men'.[26] While Burt found that, following the 1906 parliamentary session, Labour Party MPs almost always voted with the Liberals and Radicals, he feared that the emergence of voting blocks would factionalize the body politic, as had happened recently in Europe, and make it difficult to maintain a 'strong, powerful, and coherent Government'.[27] Burt also observed that all too often Socialists voiced opinions on social issues without carefully studying the problems. He called upon the Socialists 'to now and again say something about duty as well as about rights ... and do not let us imagine that it is only the rich and well-to-do who have duties'.[28] Burt defended the new Liberal government against Socialist criticism by contending that its bills, such as the Merchant Shipping Act and the Trades Disputes Act, directly benefited labourers.[29]

One matter particularly dear to Burt's heart, a state-sponsored old age pension programme, finally reached fruition in 1908. The proportion of the elderly dependent on Poor Law relief – 30 per cent of those aged 65 and over – became evident for the first time in 1890. This information, which emphasized the need for old age pensions, was presented to Parliament in response to a question by Burt.[30] The issue of aid to the elderly gained increasing attention in the 1880s and 1890s, especially after Charles Booth, who had studied the needs of the poor and elderly, proposed a non-contributory pension plan (paid for by the state with no contributions by employers or workers). New Zealand's adoption of a non-contributory pension plan spurred renewed interest in Britain in 1898 and 1899. Francis Herbert Stead, W. T. Stead's brother, was instrumental in developing support for Booth's plan.[31]

Henry Pelling contends that neither the working class nor the Lib-Labs supported non-contributory old age pensions before 1906.[32] Burt was an exception. While often praising the Northumberland and Durham Miners' Permanent Relief Fund for helping to care for the elderly, he also stressed the need for a system to aid everyone.[33] Although initially concerned about the cost of such a scheme, Burt eventually strongly supported a universal pension paid out of the government's general tax fund, along the lines of the plan promoted by Booth.[34] In January 1899, Burt hosted a private meeting in Burt Hall, during which Booth presented his proposal to one hundred delegates from trade unions, cooperative societies and friendly societies. Booth gained unanimous support for his scheme from these labour representatives. Burt also served on the executive committee of the National Committee of Organized Labour on Old Age Pensions, which was set up in 1899.[35] However, the old age pensions plan languished after 1899 because of its cost, as well as the government's preoccupation with the South African War.[36]

On 4 April 1906, three months after the election, Burt chaired a meeting of old and new Labour MPs who, as a group, decided to push for old age pensions. Shortly thereafter he led committees to meet with the Chancellor of the Exchequer Henry Asquith, and with Campbell-Bannerman. Burt found the new Liberal government disposed towards a non-contributory universal program.[37] In September 1906, Burt wrote an article promoting old age pensions for workers. Many labourers, he said, had struggled to raise their families on meagre wages and could not be expected to contribute monetarily to the plan. He eloquently explained that workers produced enormous wealth for the nation and thus deserved a modest pension from the State. They warranted the support of the nation, he insisted, as much as a government official or a member of the military.[38] Burt also presided over a large demonstration in favour of old age pensions at Newcastle in December 1907.[39] While judging certain provisions in the final bill of 1908 as too restrictive (5s. pension a week to those over 70 years old earning not more than 10s.), Burt still praised the government for laying a good 'foundation-stone'.[40] Stead later wrote that of all the Lib-Labs, Burt had been especially helpful in advancing the pension plan in Parliament.[41]

For labour unions, the most important measure passed by the Liberal government was the Trades Disputes Act. It stemmed from a 1901 judicial decision on the Taff Vale case, which determined that a union could be held liable, and fined, for actions of its members. The decision also threatened a union's use of a strike. While some union leaders saw this as an opportunity to gain a more clearly defined legal status for unions and give leaders more authority in dealing with dissident or irresponsible union members, labour unions came to demand immunity from such liability.[42]

Burt followed the Taff Vale dispute before it entered the courts. In August 1900, he criticized the Taff Vale railway workers for waging a strike without union approval. The union also erred, Burt added, by condemning the strike while supporting it financially. Following the decision rendered by the House of Lords, Burt contended that the judgment did not endanger the survival of unions, which were strong and would 'not collapse because they can be sued at law'. The decision might, he thought, actually strengthen unions when employers refused to negotiate or recognize the associations. As he had contended for years, Burt believed that unions had to wield their power with responsibility, although 'whatever responsibilities and duties may properly be thrown upon Trades Unions should and must apply equally to combinations of employers'.[43] In 1902, Burt commented on the implications of Taff Vale: 'Trade unionists, who have always rightly contended for civil equality for themselves, cannot logically and justly demand special exemption and privileges for their organisations.'[44] Burt, however, became concerned about the costs of litigation and fines, as well as restrictions on picketing and the practice of judge-made laws. By late 1902 he called for legislation to straighten out the complicated issues.[45]

The ineffectiveness of the Parliamentary Committee of the TUC, coupled with the threat to the unions posed by new and powerful employer organizations as well as the adverse court decisions of the 1890s, led to the formation of the Labour Representation Committee in 1900 (known after 1906 as the Labour Party). The Taff Vale judgment of 1901 brought to the new Labour Party substantial support from union members and contributed to the separation of Labour from the Liberals.[46] The Liberal government's legislative proposal tried to place unions within the law and deny them complete immunity from liability. The Labour Party, on the other hand, wanted a total reversal of the Taff Vale decision, and offered its own bill. Prime Minister Campbell-Bannerman, recognizing the importance of the labour vote, accepted the Labour Party bill, which was eventually enacted as the Trades Disputes Act of 1906. The Act, which provided full immunity to the unions,[47] was not what Burt thought to be appropriate. His comments on the Taff Vale dispute did not endear him to the Labour Party.

Burt's parliamentary career had always been closely tied to his position in the NMA, which had paid his legislative salary. By early 1908, Burt's parliamentary salary of £350 per annum was met by the MFGB, while the NMA paid his union salary of £100.[48] In 1908, the MFGB voted to join the Labour Party,[49] enormously complicating Burt's dual roles as MP and labour union leader.

Early on, Burt carefully spelled out his problems should the MFGB join the Labour Party. He would have to abide by the constitution of the Labour Party, which required that an endorsed candidate could not support any other party's candidate in any constituency under any circumstances. Also, the candidate had to accept the decisions of the Party. 'In other words,' Burt wrote, 'the member is asked to pledge himself in advance to act and vote with a certain party, irrespective of his own opinions and convictions, and without regard to the views of his constituents.'[50] If one totally agreed with the Labour Party, then these requirements, Burt said, would pose no problem. On the other hand, an MP who took pride in his 'independent judgement' and 'convictions' would find this conformism intolerable.[51]

In late 1908 the NMA delegate assembly voted to set up a nine-member parliamentary election committee which would, in conformity with the Labour Party constitution, prepare for a general election or possible by-election.[52] On 15 September 1909, the election committee announced that both Burt and Fenwick had refused to pledge agreement to the Labour Party's constitution.[53] Following a series of meetings involving NMA representatives and local Labour and Liberal parties, the NMA announced that it was severing its long-standing ties with the Liberal associations. T. C. Heatley, chairman of the Morpeth Liberal Council, indicated that local Liberal associations had every intention of offering Burt and Fenwick as their candidates, even without the formal support of the NMA.[54]

The NMA's election committee found itself in a difficult position. Supporters of Burt and Fenwick charged that the miners, when voting in 1908 to recommend that the MFGB join the Labour Party, had not recognized the implications this would have on the relationship of these two MPs to the Liberal Party. Clearly this charge was incorrect, as the implications of that vote had been carefully spelled out.[55] At a meeting of the NMA and Labour Party representatives, William Straker, corresponding secretary of the NMA and member of the election committee, emphasized that although miners still wanted Burt and Fenwick to represent them, that had become impossible. He stressed that the NMA, now under the rules of the Labour Party, could not both support Burt and Fenwick and remain members of the MFGB and the Labour Party. Another problem became evident at this meeting: representatives of other local Labour Party-affiliated organizations (such as trades councils, cooperative societies, Mechanics' Institutes, and Socialist societies) felt snubbed by the NMA's election committee, which had apparently not joined with other local Labour Party committees and appeared determined to impose its own candidates on the two districts. This meeting became very passionate, which must have amused Burt.[56] Two weeks later the NMA Council held a three-day, closed-door session to discuss this divisive political situation. According to the *Morpeth Herald*, Burt made a 'fighting speech', vowing to defend his parliamentary seat.[57]

Newspapers throughout England followed the story unfolding in the northern coalfields. While Socialist and Labour papers defended the actions of the NMA and the Labour Party, virtually all others were extremely critical of any attempt to end the political careers of Burt and Fenwick. Not only did these newspapers admire the two MPs, whom they respected as hard-working and dignified spokesmen for their class and for all people, but some newspapers were outspokenly opposed to the Socialist element which permeated the coalfields.[58]

Political interest was at its height in late 1909, not only concerning the fate of the local MPs, but also because of the national debate over David Lloyd George's proposed budget. Burt gave annual reports to large and wildly enthusiastic audiences of his constituents at Morpeth and Blyth on 29 and 30 October. While he discussed the budget, both speeches centred on the controversy surrounding his seat in Parliament. He was determined to defend it, even if he did not gain the approval of the NMA, which was after all his paymaster. He reiterated why he opposed signing the constitution of the Labour Party: it restricted his freedom to support candidates from other parties and, by requiring that he agree to party direction on issues, effectively disregarded the wishes of his constituents. Burt stressed that under no circumstances did he want the NMA to break from the MFGB in order to resolve the issue. As an alternative, he thought that the NMA should simply run no candidate for the seat. T. C. Heatley, the presiding Liberal official at these meetings, argued that while there were 4,000 miners in the constituency, the 6,000 others also had an interest in the seat.[59] The Liberal Party, he said, 'would stand by Mr. Burt and fight all comers'. Appealing to the sentimental feelings of the audience, he also added that should Burt be returned at the next election, he would be the Father of the House of Commons, that is, the longest serving member in the present body.[60]

The Labour Party was deeply split over the events in Northumberland. Most leaders of the Northumberland ILP branches wanted desperately to run candidates against the sitting MPs. Other Labour leaders, local and national, feared that opposing Burt was not only futile but might endanger the NMA's ties to the Labour Party.[61] In late 1909, the national executive of the Labour Party decided not to approve a candidate for Morpeth, arguing 'that the Party could not encourage such selection so long as the seat was held by a nominee of the Miners' Federation'. As Gregory pointed out, this was a 'curious' justification, as the Labour Party well knew that Burt was 'no longer a nominee of the M.F.G.B.'.[62]

Meanwhile, NMA officials continued to struggle with the issue of Burt's and Fenwick's candidacy. The Association wanted miners to occupy the two seats, but running other mining candidates against the two long-time respected and dearly loved MPs could well split the union. On the other hand, the union could not back Burt and Fenwick, for the MFGB prohibited endorsing candidates who were not approved by the Labour Party.[63] Moreover, the NMA, by late 1909, very much needed the support of the national MFGB, as the Northumberland union was preparing for a struggle with mine owners over the application of the Eight-Hour Act, due to begin in the North East in January 1910.[64] At a special delegate assembly on 14 December, Burt argued that there was insufficient time for the union to field additional candidates, and therefore he should be permitted to run again to make certain that a Tory did not slip in. Burt thought that he should be able to retain his position of union general secretary while serving in Parliament. Should this prove a conflict with the MFGB, however, 'he was prepared to give up his secretarial connection rather than allow Northumberland to be severed from the Federation'.[65] Finally, in December 1909, in a complex series of ballots, the NMA voted not to run candidates in the election, a suggestion made much earlier by Burt himself.[66]

The Liberal government responded to the House of Lords' veto of Lloyd George's 1909 budget by calling an election for early 1910. Burt's opponent was Jasper Ridley, a young man in his thirties, member of a local land-owning family. Ridley was an exceptionally strong proponent of a tariff to protect Britain and the Empire. He charged the Liberal government with mismanaging the financial resources of the country and failing to maintain a powerful navy and a united empire.[67] Like Coats in 1906, Ridley faced an uphill battle in contesting Burt's seat. In January 1910, the *Morpeth Herald* carried serialized installments of Aaron Watson's *A Great Labour Leader*, a biography of Burt. Ridley also discovered that miners were exceptionally loyal to Burt.[68]

Burt was quite ill in late 1909 and did not begin campaigning until 30 December. As usual, he defended the government's legislation, including the measures setting up labour exchanges and providing for old age pensions, and attacked the House of Lords for obstructing the will of the people.[69] The spirited campaign generated a turnout of about 88 per cent of the registered voters. Burt easily won, gaining 5,874 votes to Ridley's 3,009. In Wansbeck, Fenwick overwhelmed Charles Percy, 10,872 to 4,650.[70]

The election of early 1910 brought substantial changes to the political scene. While Burt and Fenwick felt vindicated for their refusal to join the ranks of the Labour Party and for their defence of the Liberal-Radical tradition, Lib-Lab was all but dead. Only seven Lib-Labs, including Burt, Fenwick and Wilson, were returned to Westminster. Most Lib-Labs had joined the Labour Party. At the same time, the Labour Party had absorbed MPs who were more Liberal than Labour in their political orientation. Also, the Liberal Party's huge majority had disappeared, and Asquith's government was thereafter dependent on the votes of the Irish Home Rulers and Labour to remain in power.[71]

Burt and Fenwick lost their parliamentary salaries provided by the MFGB. Subsequently, Burt received some private funding from supporters; for example, he received a cheque for £260 from the Liberal coal mine owner Lord Joicey, much to the dismay of the Socialists.[72] The state paid all MPs annual salaries of £400 beginning in 1911. Throughout this period Burt continued to receive his salary as secretary of the NMA.

After the January 1910 election, the NMA took no meaningful steps to sponsor a candidate in opposition to Burt or Fenwick. In the spring of 1910, the union voted not to run a Labour candidate in an upcoming election.[73] Thus, Burt and Fenwick faced no opposition in the December 1910 election, as Conservatives deemed those seats unassailable.[74] In 1911 the NMA agreed to set up an election committee for the Morpeth and Wansbeck divisions and select candidates in the event of a vacancy. It was made clear, however, that Burt and Fenwick could retain their seats as long as they wished.[75] The Labour Party languished in the mining communities of Northumberland before the Great War because the industrial working class remained loyal to the Liberal Party and the Labour Party lacked strong local associations. The NMA, for example, did not help set up local Labour Party organizations until 1912 and 1913.[76]

In addition to political issues, Northumberland miners were heavily immersed in a series of labour disputes from 1909 to 1913. The application of the Eight-Hour Act in January 1910 brought on the costliest strike in the history of the NMA.[77] In 1912 the NMA participated in the nation-wide strike that led to the passage of a minimum wage for miners.[78] There is little evidence that Burt was involved in many of these county or national negotiations from 1910 to 1913, as poor health restricted his activities. William Straker was generally the main spokesman for the NMA. Even Burt, however, found the owners inflexible and reluctantly agreed in 1911 that occasionally strikes were a necessary weapon.[79] While he supported the Labour Party's proposal for a 5s. per day minimum wage for miners and 2s. for boys,[80] he preferred that the issue be settled through negotiation rather than legislation.[81] In late 1911, just before the national strike, Burt complained that the Federation not only attempted to do too much but that some of its actions were too hasty.[82] Certainly Burt's model of industrial negotiations, in which wages reflected the selling price of coal and disputes were settled by strong local unions operating on the premise of conciliation, free of government interference, was no longer the accepted norm in Northumberland.

Burt seldom spoke in Parliament after 1910. His public remarks on current issues came primarily through local speeches or in his Monthly Circular. Not even the actions of extreme suffragettes altered his support for women's suffrage.[83] He viewed the passage of the National Insurance Bill of 1911 – which provided for health service and unemployment benefits for the workers – as timely,[84] and he remained committed to Home Rule as the solution to Ireland's problems.[85]

Burt's health, long a concern, markedly deteriorated by 1913. Bronchial problems, identified by Watson as asthma, so weakened him in 1912 that he had to forego many functions, including the miners' picnic, the first he had ever missed for health reasons.[86] On 10 February 1913, Burt informed William Straker that, as a result of poor health, he would resign as general secretary of the NMA effective with the upcoming annual meeting. He thanked Straker and others for having relieved him for quite some time of many of the burdensome duties of the office. He then concluded:

> But there is a certain responsibility attaching to office, and no one can take away, or diminish that responsibility.
>
> I need not say that, after nearly fifty years of service, the wrench is a severe and painful one; but I feel that it is better both for me and for the Association, that the official connection should now cease.
>
> It occurred to me that the Annual Meeting is the fitting time to convey this intimation.
>
> With kindest regards,
> I am truly yours
> Thos. Burt[87]

At the annual meeting on 17 May, Burt declined to reconsider his resignation but accepted the appointment of adviser to the union for life. He told union officials: 'I might be asked for advice, but I am perfectly sure it will never be taken.'[88] Thus ended his nearly forty-eight years of service as general secretary of the NMA. He was succeeded by William Straker.

Burt wrote his last Monthly Circular in June 1913. Ever gracious, he thanked the miners for allowing him the opportunity to serve them. He closed by offering the miners the same advice he had tendered in the 1860s:

> I trust and believe that you will continue to stand closely and resolutely together, and I hope, too, that you will ever make your appeal to reason, rather than to passion, in the settlement of all disputes. Never forget, as there seems at times a tendency to forget, that in the armies of industry, as in those that fight on the battle-field, order, discipline, and strict adherence to rule are absolutely necessary to permanency and success.[89]

Chapter 12

HONOURS AND THE LAST YEARS

Every aspect of Burt's life was intimately tied to the coal industry. When he retired in 1913, Britain's coal production was still a major factor in the national economy and throughout the world. Coal production in the North East was at a peak, as was the number of miners, estimated at 224,500.[1] While accidental deaths in mining continued to decrease throughout Burt's long term as secretary, the industry remained a dangerous one.[2] The repetitive descriptions by agent Joseph English of the causes of death in 1907 and 1908 graphically attest to the perils of coal mining.[3] From 1854 to 1908, sixty-seven miners were killed at Dudley Colliery,[4] and in 1912 there were 10,000 accidents in Northumberland, involving two out of every nine labourers at the mines.[5] Socialists often castigated Burt and other Lib-Lab miners' MPs for being too closely allied to the owners to promote essential safety measures.[6] This was an unfair criticism of Burt, who always worked with the union and in Parliament to implement stronger safety measures. After a notable pit accident or disaster, he invariably expressed his sympathy for the victims and usually called for an investigation into its cause. Burt was fortunate that during his years as secretary from 1865 to 1913 Northumberland suffered no great pit disasters.[7]

During his last decade of public service, Burt was publicly honoured on many occasions for his contributions to society. The first, as noted earlier, was his appointment to the Privy Council in 1906. In 1907, George Spencer Watson's large portrait of Burt was unveiled at the Newcastle Liberal Club, which Burt had served as president. The portrait was reproduced as the frontispiece in Aaron Watson's 1908 biography of Burt.[8] In June 1911, Durham University honoured him with the degree of Doctor of Civil Law,[9] and in December the borough of Morpeth made Burt its first honourary freeman.[10] One month later the city of Newcastle added Burt to its list of distinguished freemen for his services towards the peaceful settlement of industrial disputes, for work towards international peace, and for efforts to improve conditions in mining communities.[11] On 5 May 1913, the Labour Party hosted a dinner for Burt at the House of Commons that was attended by the majority of Labour MPs as well as trade union representatives. While both the Labour Party and Burt readily acknowledged their differences, they also recognized their common interest in the service of labour.[12] Not all labour organizations were pleased with the dinner, however. The Ashington ILP, which had waged a frustrating battle against Burt and Fenwick since 1906, protested the affair, 'believing that the recipient not only does not represent the aspirations of the workers, but has been against many forward movements in the Labour world, viz., the Northumberland miners joining the Miners' Federation, the Federation joining the Labour Party, etc.'[13]

In January 1914, Burt became very ill after attending a union meeting. In the NMA newsletter, Straker wrote: 'Probably the illness of no other man in the north would give rise to so many anxious enquiries.' Whether in Parliament or in union affairs, Straker stressed, Burt attracted the 'affection' of others, including those who disagreed with him. Why this attraction?

> The secret lies in his marvellous personality; in his purity of soul; in his unselfishness of character; and in his integrity of conduct. He compels the respect and love of others by first respecting and loving them.[14]

No greater show of affection was showered on Burt than on 17 June 1914, when over 300 people gathered in London to pay tribute to his efforts to maintain international peace. The banquet was sponsored by the International Arbitration League (which Burt still served as president),[15] and was chaired by his friend Andrew Carnegie. Among the large number of politicians and public figures in attendance were Israel Zangwill, Jewish playwright and Zionist; Sir John Brunner and Sir Alfred Mond, MP, industrialists; G. P. Gooch, historian; Charles Booth, businessman turned sociologist; Harold Begbie, writer and journalist; and Thomas Fisher Unwin, publisher.[16] Burt, ever the optimist, refused to accept the inevitability of war. At the banquet he commented on the serious situation in the Balkans:

> I think I see signs of improvement in many directions. If we look even at the Balkan wars, with their heroisms and their horrors, with their self-sacrifices and their sordidness, we yet see that at any rate the area of conflict was narrowed, and I venture to say that probably in no previous period of our history, with such racial hatred, with such conflicting interests, should we have avoided a conflict among the Great Powers of Europe.[17]

Less than two weeks after the banquet, Crown Prince Francis Ferdinand was assassinated in Sarajevo. By 4 August, Great Britain was at war with Germany and the Great War began. On 5 August, the *Newcastle Daily Chronicle* quoted Burt's opposition to Britain's participation: 'The Government has striven to the utmost to prevent war, and in my opinion nothing has yet occurred to justify our active intervention in the strife.'[18] He eventually came to support the war, believing that a small nation like Belgium had to be defended against an aggressor like Germany.[19] At his eightieth birthday celebration in 1917 he expressed the hope that the conflict would finally lead to the 'doing away with militarism, and setting up some kind of international method of settling the international disputes, which must inevitably arise, by an appeal to reason'.[20] While a critic of war, Burt had never claimed to be a pacifist. He recognized that Britain had been partly responsible for the arms race in the decade before the Great War. He believed, as did many of his labour associates, that certain wars were justified.[21] It was the duty of a nation like Britain to defend the weak against the wanton and irresponsible behaviour of the powerful. War should be an absolute last resort; every opportunity should be given for sanity and reason to triumph.

A few honours were bestowed on Burt during the war. On 21 September 1915, Charles Fenwick unveiled a bust of Burt, paid for by public subscription and placed in the Newcastle Public Library.[22] In the 1980s, Burt's grandson, Peter Burt Jr, traced the bust to the cellar of the Scotswood Library. It was brought out for a Burt exhibition in 1987 and is now on display in the old Town Hall in the centre of Morpeth.[23] In 1917, the NMA gave Burt a small party on the occasion of his eightieth birthday.[24]

Burt apparently had no personal financial concerns following his retirement as a union official in 1913. Two years earlier, the Liberal Council of Morpeth presented him with a silver plate valued at £30 and a cheque for £803, plus a gold bracelet for his wife.[25] In 1919 Andrew Carnegie bequeathed him a £1,000 annuity.[26] Burt continued to draw his parliamentary stipend until 1918. At the time of his death in 1922, his estate was valued at £5,017.[27]

Burt announced in 1915 that he would not seek re-election to Parliament. He was by that time no longer active in politics. When elections were held in December 1918, Labour candidate John Cairns, who had served as a union officer with Burt and had been a Liberal until shortly before the war, was elected MP for the Morpeth constituency in a five-person contest. F. C. Thornborough, a Liberal, came in a close second.[28]

For the last three years of his life, Burt was confined to bed with a respiratory condition.[29] He died at his home in Burdon Terrace on 13 April 1922, aged eighty-four and mentally alert to the end. His funeral was 'one of the largest [gatherings] ever seen in Newcastle'. People lined the streets while the procession made its way from Burdon

Terrace, down Osborne Road and along Jesmond Road, to the Old Jesmond Cemetery (now Newcastle General Cemetery).[30]

Burt's death brought forth an exceptional outpouring of local and national adulation for his distinguished career.[31] Many obituaries gave detailed accounts of his public life, including the opposition he faced within labour circles. The *Manchester Guardian* stressed that Burt was regarded by many parliamentarians as 'one of the best public men of their times'.[32] His honesty, openness, courage of convictions, and optimism were seen as vital aspects of his 'character'. The *Newcastle Daily Chronicle* emphasized that Burt, who believed deeply in democracy, warned that the duties of citizenship were as important as its rights:

> The lessons that he was sent to teach are that there is no royal road to social wellbeing and individual happiness; that while each man has inherent rights he has ... duties which if left unperformed will destroy his own soul and the soul of the nation as well; that good laws may make it easier for the citizen to walk uprightly, but that to build up a great and noble State we must make of ourselves noble citizens.[33]

The London *Daily News*, which had followed the course of his life from an early period, underscored how closely the people of the North – particularly the miners – had identified with him, making him 'beloved and revered almost beyond any man of his time. And the humblest loved him the most. The Northumbrian miner felt himself a nobleman by his kinship to "Tommy Bort". He was his own, flesh of his flesh and bone of his bone.'[34] The *Durham Chronicle*, concentrating its remarks on the conciliatory nature of Burt's leadership, reminded readers that Burt had grown up with trade unionism, that he had 'helped to nurse it, to rear it, to tend it, and to bring it to an honourable manhood'.[35]

From the 1930s to the 1980s, people in the North East appear not to have been aware of the important role Burt had played in the life of their region. By 1987, however, interest heightened as preparations were made to celebrate the 150th anniversary of his birth. Several individuals and institutions played an important role in preserving and extending appreciation of Burt's career. On 12 November 1987, the 150th anniversary of Burt's birth, Dr Eric Wade of the Open University gave the memorial address, 'Thomas Burt: His Life and Ideas'. A Burt exhibition was on display at the Northumberland County Hall in Morpeth and was subsequently shown elsewhere. A likeness of Burt is now included among the engravings on display in the County Hall. A short, interesting illustrated account of Burt's life, *A Howky Gan te Parliement*, first written in the 1970s, was revised and republished for the 150th anniversary. Burt's grandson, Peter Burt Jr, and great-granddaughter, Rosemary Halsey, have made family material available to the public. Some of the memorabilia from the 1987 exhibition is now part of the Burt display at the Woodhorn Colliery Museum. The Stephenson Railway Museum, located near Murton Row, where Burt was born, has a steam engine named the 'Thomas Burt'. Built in 1950, the engine was renamed the 'Thomas Burt' in 1991, to provide an identity for the museum and for the area.[36]

A visit to the North East today offers other physical evidence of the public role Thomas Burt played in the region. The aged miners' homes at Choppington, under construction at the time of Burt's death, were named the Burt Memorial Homes.[37] They still stand, occupied by retired miners. Several streets in the North East are named in his honour.[38] The greatest living memorial to Burt and to the North-umberland Miners' Association is Burt Hall, located on Northumberland Road in downtown Newcastle. It is owned by the University of Northumbria and is used for its Arts and Design programme. The plaque dedicating the hall to Burt is on the side of the building facing Northumberland Road. At the Newcastle General Cemetery one can see the gravemarker for Thomas Burt and many of his family members.

Chapter 13

CONCLUSION

Thomas Burt was arguably the most beloved and respected labour leader in late nineteenth-century Britain. He helped make 'labour' and trade unionism acceptable to the public and to the working class itself. The respect he gained came primarily from his relationship with the Northumberland miners and their union.

When Burt died, the entire issue of the Monthly Circular of the NMA was devoted to a review of his public life. The review's author, William Straker, an occasional critic of Burt, spelled out why Burt had been such a remarkable and successful leader of the Northumberland miners: (1) Burt had made it possible for the fledgling union to survive its infancy. Taking over in the midst of the notorious Cramlington strike, he had used 'the cruelty inflicted on the men, women, and children, as an object lesson' for the need of a strong union. He had brought a union but recently born to a walking stage during the Cramlington affair. (2) In spite of what contemporary critics said, Burt was a man of great courage and 'fight'. While he was reluctant to use the strike as a weapon (for he regarded the miners as the 'greatest sufferers by stoppages'), he accepted its use when 'right and reason failed to move the other side'. (3) Advocacy of 'conciliation' early in his career had fit the period and had protected the union: 'With employers, Press and public against trades unionism, and the men themselves only half-convinced of its utility, any other sort of leader would have smashed the young Association to pieces in a few months. He saw his objective, and was wise enough to take the road that led nearest to it. To regard this as weakness is but to misunderstand good generalship.' (4) Early on, especially in the 1870s, Burt had indicated that he would be forthright with the miners when they were wrong, and would accept no irrational criticism from them. On the whole, Straker stressed, miners of Northumberland, even during periods of distress, supported their leaders. 'I once heard Mr. Burt declare,' he added, 'that often the members of his Association had kicked him; but they would never allow anybody else to do so.'[1] Straker saw Burt's effective guidance of the NMA in its formative stage as the key to his long-term success as a leader.

Critics, during Burt's lifetime and today, often see him as wedded to the market system and being little more than an accomplice of the industrialists. This, however, misses an important point. Burt gained the cooperation of the mine owners only because he had already earned the respect of the miners, both as a leader and as a member of the mining community. Burt regarded himself a miner throughout his life, and miners themselves viewed him as one of their own. He embodied many of the principal movements defining his community. He had close connections with Primitive Methodism while at the same time embracing the secularism of the period. He was an enthusiastic proponent of the cooperative movement and the Mechanics' Institutes. In addition, he was very bright and, although self-educated, the intellectual equal of anyone.

Socialists opened their attack on Burt and the Lib-Labs in the 1880s and continued their criticism throughout the rest of his career. Except in the latter stages of his career, these criticisms gained little hearing among the miners, because they had done quite well with Liberalism. Key Liberal principles, including individualism and self-help, fit their labour in the mines. Moreover, the Liberal Party cooperated closely with miners, supporting their parliamentary candidates in both Morpeth and Wansbeck, and incorporating them as officials within the party.

Had Burt retired from politics or joined the Labour Party in 1909–10, he would be highly regarded today in Labour Party circles. He apparently never considered enlisting in the Labour Party because of his fundamental differences with it. His lifelong commitment to conciliation, in industrial bargaining and in politics, required coopera-tion – not the confrontation which he found in the new party. Moreover, he believed that signing the Labour Party constitution would obligate him to support issues and candidates before careful examination. He refused to accept blindly the dictates of any party or organization. While the Independent Labour Party, for example, stressed the independence of the 'party', Burt viewed the independence of the 'self' as more important. A person's judgement of an issue should not be restricted by any organization. The Labour Party also would not permit its members to endorse a parliamentary candidate from another party or lend support by appearing on the same platform. Burt had always argued that the individual was more important than party, class or occupation. When defending himself against union critics in 1872, Burt declared: 'I came to you as a free man, and I only can continue with you as such.'[2]

One might charge that Burt subordinated himself to the dictates of his own union. Burt believed otherwise. The union was a direct expression of the miner's interest and world. In that union, Burt and all others were free to argue. Individual lodges were constantly bringing forth matters for argument and vote at delegate meetings. The eight-hour day issue was a primary example of open, vigorous debate within the union. Critics charged Burt with leading the opposition to the eight-hour day, but in fact he was effectively expressing the wishes of the majority of his miners. Ultimately, decisions were made, and Burt was occasionally required to implement policy which he judged wrong. He had no trouble with that, as long as decisions had come after due deliberation. Burt could possibly have accepted a Labour Party which arrived at commitments only after free and open discussion. He was not unalterably opposed to certain Labour Party proposals, such as the nationalization of the railroads. He was sceptical, however, that government could run such a business, because the government was not always efficient.

Burt would have been uncomfortable with the increasingly class-oriented nature of politics and labour–management relations of the post-World War I era. His great hope had not been a classless society, but one wherein classes would respect each other and work for the common good. To him, political parties were secondary to the importance of the individual and the advancement of his or her rights and dignity. Burt the Radical constantly advocated the development of the individual through his support of educational facilities, Irish Home Rule, universal suffrage, religious equality and the peaceful solution of international disputes. Burt's devotion to his union was directed towards similar goals. Satisfactory working conditions and a decent standard of living were for Burt not ends in themselves, but rather the means for the individual miner and his family to develop intellectually and morally. Indeed, Thomas Burt's life embodied the goals he sought for others.

At the core of Burt's philosophy was 'conciliation'. His relations with workers and management centred on peaceful resolution of disputes. Parliament operated on the basis of vigorous debate tempered with compromise. Governments, spurred on by the democratic and peace-loving orientation of the working class, resolved international disputes through diplomacy and arbitration. Conciliation did not always work. Nations waged war, bitter strikes divided owners and labourers, and Parliament raged against its own members. None of this surprised Burt, but it never deterred him from striving for his ideal.

NOTES

Chapter 1

1. *Shields Evening News*, 18 January 1939, p. 4f.
2. Much of the material on Burt's family and childhood comes from Thomas Burt, *An Autobiography*, supplementary chapters by Aaron Watson (London, 1924).
3. List in exhibit at Woodhorn Colliery Museum.
4. Burt, *Autobiography*, p. 25.
5. *Biograph and Review*, May 1881, p. 443.
6. Roy Church, *The History of the British Coal Industry. Vol. 3. 1830–1913: Victorian Pre-eminence* (Oxford, 1986), pp. 10, 18, 35.
7. J. A. Jaffe, 'Competition and the Size of Firms in the North-East Coal Trade, 1800–1850', *Northern History*, 25 (1989), 235–55.
8. Carol Jones, 'Experiences of a Strike: The North East Coalowners and the Pitmen, 1831–1832', in R. W. Sturgess (ed.), *Pitmen, Viewers, and Coalmasters: Essays in North East Coal Mining in the Nineteenth Century* (1986), pp. 27–54; James Jaffe, *The Struggle for Market Power: Industrial Relations in the British Coal Industry, 1800–1840* (Cambridge, 1991), pp. 150–89; Robert Colls, *The Pitmen of the Northern Coalfield: Work, Culture and Protest, 1790–1850* (Manchester, 1987), pp. 44–51, 64–73, 88–99.
9. Burt, *Autobiography*, pp. 24–5.
10. Richard Fynes, *The Miners of Northumberland and Durham* (Newcastle, 1986; first published 1873), pp. 37–112; Raymond Challinor and Brian Ripley, *The Miners' Association: A Trade Union in the Age of the Chartists* (London, 1968).
11. Burt, *Autobiography*, pp. 33–42.
12. Challinor and Ripley, *Miners' Association*, p. 245.
13. *Newcastle Weekly Chronicle*, 13 November 1875, p. 5g.
14. Burt, *Autobiography*, pp. 31–2, 43–9; J. R. Leifchild, *Our Coal and Our Coal-Pits* (London, 1968; reprint, first pub., 1856), pp. 208–15; Jules Ginswick (ed.), *Labour and the Poor in England and Wales, 1849–1851* (London, 1983), vol. II, p. 58.
15. Children's Employment Commission, Appendix to First Report, Part I,

1842 (381), XVI, 533, 715, 716; Report from the Commissioner ... Mining Districts, 1846 (737), XXIV, p. 47.

16. Colls, *Pitmen*, pp. 146–61; P. Stigant, 'Wesleyan Methodism and Working-Class Radicalism in the North, 1792–1821', *Northern History*, 6 (1971), 98–116; Julia Stewart Werner, *The Primitive Methodist Connexion* (Madison, 1984).

17. Thomas Burt, 'Methodism and the Northern Miners', *Primitive Methodist Quarterly Review*, July 1882, 387, 390–1; Burt, *Autobiography*, pp. 84–8.

18. Burt, 'Methodism', pp. 393–4.

19. Report ... Mining Districts, 1846 (737), XXIV, 8, 25.

20. R. F. Wearmouth, *Methodism and the Working-Class Movements of England, 1800–1850* (Clifton, NJ, 1972; reprint, first pub. 1937), pp. 227–9.

21. Burt, 'Methodism', p. 394.

22. J. A. Jaffe, 'The "Chiliasm of Despair" Reconsidered: Revivalism and Working-Class Agitation in County Durham', *Journal of British Studies*, 28 (January 1989), 41.

23. Francis Hearn, *Domination, Legislation, and Resistance: The Incorporation of the Nineteenth-Century English Working Class* (Westport, CT, 1978), p. 199.

24. John Benson, *British Coalminers in the Nineteenth Century: A Social History* (Dublin, 1980), pp. 28–63; Church, *British Coal Industry*, pp. 321–5.

25. Fynes, *Miners*, pp. 164–7; George Clemerson Greenwell, *A Glossary of Terms Used in the Coal Trade of Northumberland and Durham*, (London, 1888; 3rd edn), p. 19.

26. Burt, *Autobiography*, pp. 50, 55–62, 73, 80, 84. For a description of a young person working in the mines thirty-five years later, see Bill Williamson, *Class, Culture and Community: A Biographical Study of Social Change in Mining* (London, 1982), pp. 17–54.

27. Burt, *Autobiography*, pp. 89–112; David Douglass, 'The Durham Pitman', in Raphael Samuel (ed.), *Miners, Quarreymen and Saltworkers* (London, 1977), pp. 229–33; M. J. Daunton, 'The Export Coalfields: South Wales and North East England, 1870–1914', in Sturgess, *Pitmen*, pp. 143–5.

28. Burt, *Autobiography*, pp. 113–27.

29. Ibid., pp. 128–36; Burt, 'Methodism', pp. 394–5; Aaron Watson, *A Great Labour Leader* (London, 1908), pp. 68–70; Fynes, *Miners*, pp. 181–3.

30. Northumberland Record Office [NRO], Marriage Records, Bedlington, 1860, p. 136; Burt, *Autobiography*, pp. 138–9.

31. NRO, Parish Records, Bedlington, 1861/22, RG9/3873 (69).

32. *Newcastle Weekly Chronicle*, 12 April 1873, p. 2e-f.

33. Burt, *Autobiography*, pp. 139–40; NRO, Bedlington-area coal mines: Choppington.

34. R. W. Martin (collector), *An Interesting Collection Commencing in 1645 of the Freemen of Newcastle-upon-Tyne, down to 1928*. Bound volume of letters located in Local History, Newcastle Public Library. There is no indication to whom the letter was directed, and it was probably not

published, as Burt stated that his first published letter came in 1862; Burt, *Autobiography*, pp. 154–5.

35. Ibid., pp. 137–8.
36. NRO, Bedlington-area coal mines: Choppington; *Newcastle Weekly Chronicle*, 12 April 1873, p. 2e-f.
37. Alan Lee, 'Ruskin and Political Economy: *Unto This Last*', in Robert Hewison (ed.), *New Approaches to Ruskin* (London, 1981), pp. 83–5; John Ruskin, '*Unto This Last*' (London, 1934), pp. 29–33, 66–73.
38. Burt, *Autobiography*, pp. 144–6.

Chapter 2

1. Fynes, *Miners*, pp. 171–9; Helen and Baron Duckham, *Great Pit Disasters* (Newton Abbot, 1973), pp. 95–114.
2. Fynes, *Miners*, pp. 196–206; *Newcastle Weekly Chronicle*, 1 February 1862, pp. 2e-3a, 4c-d; Home Office Papers, HO 45/3 & 45/7349; John Elliott McCutcheon, *The Hartley Colliery Disaster, 1862* (Seaham County Durham, 1963), pp. 136–43.
3. *Newcastle Weekly Chronicle*, 14 June 1862, p. 3a, 28 June 1862, p. 2a; Northumberland and Durham Permanent Relief Fund Records, Tyne and Wear 919/38, Report for 1912, pp. 29–31.
4. The Steam Colliery Association, founded in 1852, handled prices and wages until 1871, when the Steam Collieries Defence Association was established. This Association, renamed the Northumberland Coal Owners Association in 1889, 'represented employers' interests up until Nationalisation in 1947'. Robin Gard, 'The Northumberland Pitman', *Bulletin of the North East Group for the Study of Labour History*, 6 (1972), 19–20.
5. Northumberland and Durham Coal Owners Association Records [NDCOA Records], NRO 238, minutes, Steam Collieries' Association, 11 November and 13 December 1862.
6. Daunton, 'Export Coalfield', in Sturgess, *Pitmen*, pp. 134–5.
7. NDCOA Records, NRO 263, minutes, Steam Collieries' Association, 23 December 1862.
8. *Newcastle Weekly Chronicle*, 27 December 1862, p. 7b-c. According to David Neville, the term Folly 'derives from its nickname of "Polly's Folly"', a corruption of "Paully's Folly". The man who built the Inn was Paul Jameison. People thought he was making a big mistake but "Paully" got to know that a colliery village (Shankhouse) was to be built. A successful Folly!' NRO, Cramlington Colliery-Klondike. Northumberland Miners' Mutual Confidence Association, *Northumberland Miners' Union Centenary Brochure, 1863–1963* (1963), p. 11, located in Ashington Mineworkers' Federation Minutes, NRO 1286/5.
9. Burt, *Autobiography*, pp. 156–7.
10. NDCOA Records, NRO 263, minutes, Steam Collieries' Association, 27 December 1862, 13 January 1863.
11. *British Miner and General Newsman*, 17 January 1863, pp. 8c-9a; Benson Papers, NRO 768/F/20, Rules of the Northumberland & Durham Miners Mutual Confidence Association, 1863, p. 2; Fynes, *Miners' Unions*,

pp. 208–9; *Newcastle Weekly Chronicle*, 3 January 1863, p. 2d-e, 14 February p. 6b, 4 April, p. 8b-c, 13 June, p. 5a.

12. Ibid., 4 July 1863, p. 5b, 12 March 1864, p. 5c, 6 August 1864, p. 5a.
13. For detailed coverage, see the *Durham Chronicle, Newcastle Weekly Chronicle*, and *Miner and Workman's Advocate*, for 1863 and 1864.
14. Burt, *Autobiography*, pp. 157–62.
15. *Morpeth Herald*, 11 June 1864, p. 5a-b; *Miner and Workman's Advocate*, 11 June 1864, p. 5a; Burt, *Autobiography*, pp. 162–3; Fynes, *Miners*, pp. 247–8.
16. E. Allen, *The Durham Miners' Association* (Durham, 1969), pp. 8–10.
17. Burt, *Autobiography*, pp. 163–5; Report from the Select Committee on Mines, 1866 (431), XIV, pp. 1–13.
18. E. Welbourne, *The Miners' Unions of Northumberland and Durham* (Cambridge, 1923), p. 127; Burt, *Autobiography*, pp. 166–8; Fynes, *Miners*, p. 248; Northumberland Branch of the National Union of Miners Records [hereafter NB–NUM Records], NRO 3793/301, NMA expense book.
19. The first picnic was held in 1864 at Polly's Folly. I have not been able to determine the precise date. The second was held on 11 June 1865, in a field at Blyth Link House (*Morpeth Herald*, 17 June 1865, p. 5a). The third was on 11 June 1866, at Blyth. Brochures for the annual picnic of the Northumberland miners have incorrect dates for the first few picnics.
20. E. J. Hobsbawm, *Worlds of Labour: Further Studies in the History of Labour* (London, 1984), pp. 76–7.
21. Burt, *Autobiography*, pp. 171–3.
22. Welbourne, *Miners' Unions*, p. 127; *Newcastle Daily Chronicle*, 24 June 1865, p. 3b.
23. Ibid., 1 August 1865, p. 3d.
24. Ibid., 10 August 1865, p. 4b.
25. *Morpeth Herald*, 2 September 1865, p. 4e; 16 September, p. 6d-e.
26. NDCOA Records, NRO 263, minutes, Steam Collieries' Association, 30 September 1865.
27. Home Office Papers, HO 45/7692, Cramlington colliery evictions, various letters; *Newcastle Daily Chronicle*, 12 October 1865, p. 2e-f; *Newcastle Daily Journal*, 13 October 1865, p. 3a.
28. *Newcastle Daily Chronicle*, 14 October 1865, p. 3d-e; *Morpeth Herald*, 28 October 1865, p. 4b-c.
29. NDCOA Records, NRO 263, minutes, Steam Collieries' Association, 28 October and 11 November 1865; Home Office Papers, HO 45/7692, Cramlington evictions, A. Brown to George Grey, 29 November 1865; *Workmen's Advocate*, 25 November 1865, p. 1c; Burt, *Autobiography*, p. 181.
30. *Newcastle Daily Chronicle*, 22 November 1865, p. 3c-f, 24 November p. 3f.
31. *Morpeth Herald*, 11 November 1865, p. 4b-c.
32. *Newcastle Daily Chronicle*, 24 November 1865, pp. 3f, 4a. This letter also appeared in the *Newcastle Daily Journal*, 24 November 1865, p. 2e-f; Burt's response did not.
33. *Newcastle Daily Chronicle*, 25 November 1865, p. 3e; Burt, *Autobiography*, p. 184.

34. *Newcastle Daily Chronicle*, 28 November 1865, p. 4a-b; Watson, *Leader*, pp. 91–5, reproduces most of this long letter.
35. *Newcastle Daily Chronicle*, 29 November 1865, p. 2d-e.
36. Nigel Todd, *The Militant Democracy: Joseph Cowen and Victorian Radicalism* (Tyne and Wear, 1991), pp. 53, 59–60.
37. Burt, *Autobiography*, p. 185.
38. Owen R. Ashton, *W. E. Adams: Chartist, Radical and Journalist 1832–1906* (Tyne and Wear, 1991).
39. *Newcastle Daily Chronicle*, 7 December 1865, p. 3a-b; *Newcastle Guardian*, 8 December 1865, pp. 8a, 5b; Welbourne, pp. 129–31. See *Dusty Diamonds*, an interesting novel that details the Cramlington strike and the resentment towards the Cornishmen. Welbourne lists the author as David Addy, publication date 1900, while the Newcastle Central Library's copy gives it as [1910].
40. *Newcastle Weekly Chronicle*, 6 January 1866, p. 8b; *Newcastle Daily Chronicle*, 6 January 1866, p. 3c-f; NB–NUM Records, NRO 3793/301, NMA expense record, October to December 1865; Burt, *Autobiography*, p. 179.
41. Welbourne, *Miners' Unions*, p. 129; Burt, *Autobiography*, pp. 182–3. His chapter title on the Cramlington strike bears this phrase.
42. Webb Trade Union Collection, Sect. A, Vol. XXVIII, ff. 218-26, Memorandum on NMA rules from Ralph Young, a long-time NMA official, to the Webbs, date not given but some time in the 1890s; Northumberland Miners' Mutual Confidence Association Records [Hereafter NMMCA Records], NRO 759/1, minutes, delegate meeting, 30 September 1873, pp. 220–2.
43. *Newcastle Weekly Chronicle*, 10 October 1868, p. 8d-e.
44. Ibid., 23 January 1869, p. 4c.
45. NMMCA Records, NRO 759/68, report on the picnic, 11 July 1908, p. 23.
46. Arthur J. McIvor, 'Employers' Organisation and Strikebreaking in Britain, 1880–1914', *International Review of Social History*, 29 (1984), 5; E. Allen *et al.*, *The North-East Engineers' Strikes of 1871: The Nine Hours League* (Newcastle-upon-Tyne, 1971), pp. 106–7, 126; Richard Price, *Labour in British Society: An Interpretative History* (London, 1986), p. 135, mentions that collective bargaining began in several sectors in the North East shortly after the Reform Act of 1867 and the Ballot Act of 1871.
47. Fynes, *Miners*, p. 253.
48. *Newcastle Weekly Chronicle*, 22 July 1871, p. 7c-e.
49. Fynes, *Miners*, p. 253; *Newcastle Weekly Chronicle*, 9 December 1871, p. 5b-c.
50. NB–NUM Records, NRO 3793/350, circular from Burt, 4 December 1871.
51. Ibid., NRO 3793/59, Young's diary, 23 December 1871, 1 January 1872.
52. *Newcastle Weekly Chronicle*, 9 December 1871, p. 4b, e.
53. NB–NUM Records, NRO 3793/59, Young's diary, 27, 30 January and 3, 8, February 1872; *Newcastle Weekly Chronicle*, 10 February 1872, p. 5b-c.
54. Church, *British Coal Industry*, p. 658, quoting the minutes, Steam Collieries' Association.

55. Fynes, *Miners*, pp. 254–5; *Newcastle Daily Chronicle*, 10 April 1872, p. 3a.
56. *Newcastle Daily Chronicle*, 10 April 1872, p. 3e; *Newcastle Weekly Chronicle*, 13 April 1872, p. 5c; and in large part in Fynes, *Miners*, pp. 255–7.
57. NB–NUM Records, NRO 3793/350, minutes, delegate meeting, 13 May 1872.
58. Fynes, *Miners*, p. 257.
59. NB–NUM Records, NRO 3793/59, Young's diary, 13 July, 3 August 1872, 22, 27 February 1873.
60. *Daily News*, 27 September 1872, p. 2b; *Newcastle Weekly Chronicle*, 3 August 1872, p. 8f, 10 August, p. 4f-g.
61. Burt, *Autobiography*, pp. 190–5.
62. *Dictionary of National Biography* (Oxford University Press), entry on Thornton.
63. Adam Smith, *An Inquiry into the Nature and Causes of the Wealth of Nations* (New York, 1937), pp. 66–7; John Stuart Mill, *Principles of Political Economy* (New York, 1901), vol. 2, p. 553; William Thornton, *On Labour* (Shannon, Ireland, 1971; reprint of 2nd edn, 1870), pp. 251–8, 322.
64. Mill, *Political Economy*, vol. 1, pp. 420–4, vol. 2, pp. 549–51.
65. Burt, *Autobiography*, pp. 193–4; Thornton, *On Labour*, pp. 82–91.
66. Eugenio F. Biagini, 'British Trade Unions and Popular Political Economy', *Historical Journal*, 30 (December 1987), 822–8.
67. Thornton, *On Labour*, p. 232.
68. Burt, *Autobiography*, p. 200.
69. NB–NUM Records, NRO 3793/59, Young's diary, 25 June 1872. Young's diaries show a variety of intellectual interests.
70. Burt, *Autobiography*, pp. 199–200; Fynes, *Miners*, p. 254; Watson, *Leader*, p. 117.
71. On his off nights, he addressed groups on such topics as temperance, education and politics; Burt, *Autobiography*, p. 198.
72. NMMCA Records, NRO 759/1, minutes, executive committee meeting, 18 February 1873, pp. 29–30, and delegate meeting, 1 March 1873, p. 33.
73. Church, *British Coal Industry*, p. 658.
74. NMMCA Records, NRO 759/1, Report from the Coal Trade, which was adopted by the Steam Collieries' Association on 1 February 1873 (a cutting included in the bound handwritten minutes of the NMA), and minutes, executive committee meeting, 12 February 1873, pp. 13–15, and delegate meeting, 27 February 1873, p. 32.
75. 'Industrial Harmony: How Attained', *Shipping World*, 15 April 1908, pp. 434–6, also reproduced with slight omissions in Burt's *Autobiography*, pp. 201–6.
76. Raymond Challinor, *The Lancashire and Cheshire Miners* (Newcastle upon Tyne, 1972), pp. 91–6.
77. See K. Burgess, *The Origins of British Industrial Relations: The Nineteenth Century Experience* (London, 1975); Challinor, *Miners*; Royden Harrison (ed.), *Independent Collier: The Coal Miner as Archtypal Proletarian Reconsidered* (New York, 1978); Gordon M. Wilson, *Alexander McDonald, Leader of the Miners* (Aberdeen, 1982);

B. R. Mitchell, *Economic Development of the British Coal Industry 1880–1914* (New York, 1984); Church, *British Coal Industry*, pp. 680–7, provides a brief review of unionizing activity from the 1850s to the 1880s, and G. D. H. Cole, *A Short History of the British Working Class Movement 1789–1937* (London, 1937), vol. 2, pp. 70–3, summarizes the interests of the two associations.

78. See Burt's letters to the editor, *Newcastle Weekly Chronicle*, 5 March 1870, pp. 4g-5a, and 12 March, p. 5a-b, his attendance and testimony at public meetings, 19 March, p. 5d-e, his remarks at annual picnic, 18 June, p. 5g, his speech at MNA meeting, 14 January 1871, p. 7e.
79. Fynes, *Miners*, pp. 264–9.
80. *Newcastle Weekly Chronicle*, 15 June 1872, p. 7d.
81. *Daily News*, 3 October 1872, p. 5e-f; *Miners' National Gazette*, 21 April 1883, p. 14.

Chapter 3

1. W. Hamish Fraser, *Trade Unions and Society: The Struggle for Acceptance, 1850-1880* (Totowa, NJ, 1974), ch. 5; T. J. Nossiter, *Influence, Opinion and Political Idioms in England: Case Studies from the North East 1832–1874* (Hassocks, 1974).
2. Ashton, *Adams*, pp. 109–11.
3. *Newcastle Daily Chronicle*, 13 December 1866, p. 3a-f.
4. Ibid., 29 January 1867, pp. 4–6.
5. Norman Gash, *Politics in the Age of Peel* (London, 1953), pp. 215, 432.
6. Basic information is from William H. Maehl, Jr 'The Northeastern Miners' Struggle for the Franchise, 1872–74', *International Review of Social History*, 20 (1975), 198–219; Eugenio Biagini, *Liberty, Retrenchment and Reform: Popular Liberalism in the Age of Gladstone, 1860–1880* (Cambridge, 1992), pp. 278–88; and an article written by a participant in *Newcastle Weekly Chronicle*, 21 February 1874, p. 3f-g.
7. *Morpeth Herald*, 13 October 1900, p. 2d.
8. Burt, *Autobiography*, pp. 210–12; W. E. Adams, *Memoirs of a Social Atom* (New York, 1968; reprint of first edn of 1903), vol. 2, pp. 538–9; Maehl, 'Franchise', pp. 201–2.
9. Ashton, *Adams*, p. 112.
10. *Newcastle Weekly Chronicle*, 13 July 1872, p. 4h, 20 July, p. 5f, and subsequent issues.
11. Burt, *Autobiography*, pp. 209–10.
12. *Newcastle Weekly Chronicle*, 28 September 1872, p. 4a.
13. *Morpeth Herald*, 10 August 1872, pp. 3c-e, 4a.
14. Adams, *Memoirs*, vol. 2, pp. 541–4; Burt, *Autobiography*, p. 211–12.
15. *Daily News*, 30 September 1872, p. 2a-b.
16. Maehl, 'Franchise', pp. 206–7; *Newcastle Weekly Chronicle*, 4 January 1873, p. 8g; Biagini, *Liberty*, pp. 282, 287.
17. Cowen Papers; *Newcastle Weekly Chronicle*, Supplement, 19 April 1873.
18. Maehl, pp. 209–10.

19. Todd, *Cowen*, p. 113; *Newcastle Daily Chronicle*, 12 November 1873, p. 3f-h.
20. *Newcastle Weekly Chronicle*, 4 October 1873, p. 4c-d; Adams, *Memoirs*, vol. 2, p. 545.
21. NMMCA Records, NRO 759/1, minutes, delegate meeting, 30 September 1873, pp. 218–19.
22. *Newcastle Weekly Chronicle*, 25 October 1873, supplement; *Biograph and Review*, May 1881, V, 447; NB–NUM Records, NRO 3793/59, Young's diary, 18 October 1873.
23. *Biograph and Review*, May 1881, V, 446; John Shepherd, 'Labour and Parliament: The Lib.-Labs. as the First Working-class MPs, 1885–1906', in Eugenio Biagini and Alastair J. Reid (eds), *Currents of Radicalism* (Cambridge, 1991), p. 191.
24. Cowen Papers, B 154, typescript copy of speech.
25. *Biograph and Review*, May 1881, V, 446–7; *Newcastle Weekly Chronicle*, 25 October 1873, supplement, p. 2b.
26. Adams, *Memoirs*, vol. 2, pp. 545–6; NMMCA Records, NRO 759/1, minutes, executive committee meeting, 26 January 1874, p. 289; *Biograph and Review*, May 1881, V, 447; *Morpeth Herald*, 31 January 1874, p. 4c, 7 February, p. 2e. William Gwyn, *Democracy and the Cost of Politics* (London, 1962), pp. 147–53, writes about the cost of elections.
27. Burt, *Autobiography*, pp. 214–15.
28. *Morpeth Herald*, 31 January 1874, p. 4b-c, 7 February, p. 4e.
29. *Newcastle Weekly Chronicle*, 15 November 1873, p. 8f.
30. *Morpeth Herald*, 31 January 1874, p. 3e.
31. *Newcastle Weekly Chronicle*, 10 January 1874, p. 8b-c.
32. Watson, *Leader*, p. 166.
33. Burt, 'Methodism', p. 387.
34. Watson, *Leader*, p. 165. Street moved to Belfast in 1870; Church of Divine Unity Papers, Tyne and Wear Archives, 1787/161/2.
35. Ibid., cuttings book, 1867.
36. *Newcastle Weekly Chronicle*, 12 April 1873, p. 2f.
37. *Morpeth Herald*, 31 January 1874, pp. 3e-4a; *Biograph and Review*, May 1881, V, 448.
38. *Morpeth Herald*, 31 January 1874, p. 4a-c, 7 February, p. 3a-d.
39. Biagini, *Liberty*, pp. 347–50; *Morpeth Herald*, 7 February 1874, p. 4a-b; Burt, *Autobiography*, pp. 218–19, 221–2.
40. *Morpeth Herald*, 7 February 1874, p. 4b.
41. *A Howky Gan Te Parliement* (Northumberland County Council, [1987]), pages not numbered.
42. *Morpeth Herald*, 7 March 1874, pp. 2e, 3a-c; Watson, *Leader*, pp. 145–52; Burt, *Autobiography*, pp. 224–8.
43. *Newcastle Weekly Chronicle*, 17 November 1888, p. 8b.
44. *Newcastle Critic*, 14 February 1874, pp. 108–9, at Durham County Record Office, NCB I/RS/408.
45. *Miners' Advocate and Record*, 17 January 1874, p. 5b, 14 February, p. 4b.
46. Todd, *Cowen*, pp. 115–19.
47. *Newcastle Weekly Chronicle*, 21 March 1874, p. 3e; *Bee-Hive*, 21 March 1874, p. 10.

48. 3 *Hansard*, CCXIX, 222–3; the bill was defeated.
49. *Newcastle Daily Chronicle*, 15 May 1874, p. 2h.
50. Quoted in *Newcastle Weekly Chronicle*, 23 May 1874, p. 8f.

Chapter Four

1. Church, *British Coal Industry*, pp. 559, 561–3.
2. *Newcastle Daily Chronicle*, 26 October 1874, p. 3c.
3. NB–NUM Records, NRO 3793/59, Young's diary, 30 January, 3 February 1875; Roger Cawley, *British Coal Owners, 1881–1893: The Search for Structure* (SUNY, Binghamton, 1984), pp. 86–8.
4. NB–NUM Records, NRO 3793/215, minutes of the arbitration hearing and decision.
5. Ibid., NRO 3793/350, p. 7, cuttings on award, dated 1 February 1876.
6. NMMCA Records, NRO 759/2 & 3, minutes, committee meetings, 1874–77, reflect these stoppages; *Newcastle Weekly Chronicle*, 25 March 1876, p. 8f, 2 December, p. 8b.
7. NMMCA Records, NRO 759/2, minutes, delegate meeting, 4 September 1874.
8. NB–NUM Records, NRO 3793/59, Young's diary, 27 April 1875; *Newcastle Weekly Chronicle*, 1 May 1875, p. 4g.
9. Ibid., 6 February 1875, p. 8d, 20 March, p. 4b-d; Challinor, *Miners*, pp. 151–2.
10. Webb Collection, Sect. A, Vol. XXVIII, ff. 230–4, a list of NMA strikes, their causes, duration, cost, from beginning of union to 1880, provided by Ralph Young.
11. *Newcastle Weekly Chronicle*, 31 October 1874, p. 5c, 9 January 1875, p. 5b; *Newcastle Daily Chronicle*, 28 October 1874, p. 3e; NMMCA Records, NRO 759/2, minutes, executive committee meetings, 28 October, 6 November 1874; ibid., NRO 759/68, minutes, executive committee meeting, 5 November 1875; NB–NUM Records, NRO 3793/58, Young's diary, 20, 21, 22 January 1875, 19 January 1876.
12. NB–NUM Records, NRO 3793/59, Young's diary, 1 May, 7 August 1875; NMMCA Records, NRO 759/2, minutes, delegate meeting, 5 February 1876, and executive committee meeting, 22 February 1876.
13. *Newcastle Weekly Chronicle*, 12 August 1876, p. 8e, 19 August, p. 8b; *Newcastle Daily Chronicle*, 28 November 1876, p. 3h, 26 December, 3f-g; *Bee-Hive*, 28 April 1877, p. 7; NB–NUM Records, NRO 3793/59, Young's diary, 13, 14, 26 August 1876; NMMCA Records, NRO 759/3, minutes, executive committee meeting, 15 December 1876.
14. *Newcastle Weekly Chronicle*, 19 June 1875, p. 5d, 17 April 1876, p. 5g; A. Potts and E. Wade, *Stand True* (Blyth, 1975), pp. 4–8.
15. *Morpeth Herald*, 21 November 1874, pp. 2e-3a; Benson, *British Coalminers*, p. 92.
16. NB–NUM Records, NRO 3793/59, prospectus included loose-leaf in Young's diary for 1872; *Newcastle Weekly Chronicle*, 28 December 1872, p. 5g.
17. NB–NUM Records, NRO 3793/350, cuttings file, report of delegate meeting, 24 March 1873, and minutes, delegate meeting, June 20–23,

1873; John Wilson, *A History of the Durham Miners' Association, 1870–1904* (Durham, 1907), pp. 110–11; *Newcastle Daily Chronicle*, 23 December 1874, p. 3a-b; *Newcastle Weekly Chronicle*, 2 October 1875, p. 5f-h.

18. *Co-operative News*, 25 September 1875, p. 503, 14 October 1876, pp. 540–2, 28 October, pp. 568–9; *Newcastle Weekly Chronicle*, 14 December 1872, p. 8d; *Newcastle Daily Chronicle*, 27 November 1876, p. 3d; NMMCA Records, NRO 759/3, minutes, executive committee meeting, 20 June 1877.

19. *Durham Chronicle*, 9 July 1875, p. 6c-d; *Bee-Hive*, 26 February 1876, p. 6; *Newcastle Weekly Chronicle*, 10 June 1876, p. 8c-d, 8 July, p. 8e-f.

20. NDCOA Records, NRO 263, minutes, Steam Collieries Association, 7 April 1877; NMMCA Records, NRO 759/3, minutes, delegate meeting, 18 April 1877; *Newcastle Daily Chronicle*, 1 May 1877, p. 4; NB–NUB Records, NRO 3793/350, cuttings, Burt letter undated.

21. NMMCA Records, NRO 759/3, minutes, delegate meeting, 25 May 1877; *Newcastle Daily Chronicle*, 26 May 1877, p. 3g.

22. *Capital and Labour*, 30 May 1877, p. 302; *Newcastle Daily Journal*, 28 May 1877, p. 2h; *Colliery Guardian*, 1 June 1877, pp. 847a, 850b-c; *Northern Echo*, 30 May 1877, pp. 3f-4; *Durham Chronicle*, 1 June 1877, p. 6a-e.

23. *Newcastle Daily Chronicle*, 2 June 1877, p. 4c.

24. *Newcastle Weekly Chronicle*, 16 June 1877, p. 8d; *Newcastle Daily Chronicle*, 5 June 1877, p. 8d, 6 June, p. 4a-c; *Capital and Labour*, 13 June 1877, pp. 319–20.

25. Letter from José Maria d'Eça de Queiróz to Portuguese Foreign Minister, 10 July 1877, Alan Freeland, trans. and ed., 'Letters of a Portuguese Consul, 1877–79', *Bulletin of the North East Labour History Society*, (1984), 33.

26. *Newcastle Daily Chronicle*, 8 June 1877, p. 4b.

27. NB–NUM Records, NRO, 3793/350, undated circular, but clearly mid-June 1877, by NMA deputation reporting on meeting with owners.

28. Ibid., minutes, delegate meeting, 23 June 1877.

29. *Newcastle Weekly Chronicle*, 29 September 1877, p. 3e-h.

30. NB–NUM Records, NRO 3793/350, circular dated 4 September 1877, and two undated documents in reference to Herschell's award; NDCOA Records, NRO 263, minutes, Steam Collieries' Association meeting, 20 October 1877.

31. *Newcastle Weekly Chronicle*, 27 October 1877, p. 8f.

32. Ibid., 8 December 1877, p. 8c-d, 15 December, p. 5h; NDCOA Records, NRO 263, minutes, Steam Collieries' Association meeting, 12 December 1877; *Newcastle Daily Chronicle*, 26 December 1877, p. 3f; NMMCA Records, NRO 759/3, minutes, delegate meeting, 15 December 1877.

33. *Newcastle Daily Chronicle*, 24 December 1877, p. 3e-f.

34. Ibid., 28 December 1877, p. 4a-b, 31 December, pp. 2–3; *Miners' Watchman and Labour Sentinel*, 5 January 1878, pp. 2, 9; *Newcastle Courant*, 28 December 1877, p. 4e-f.

35. *Capital and Labour*, 2 January 1878, pp. 5–6.

36. *Newcastle Daily Chronicle*, 1 January 1878, p. 3f.

37. NMMCA Records, NRO 759/3, minutes, delegate meeting, 15 November 1877, and executive committee meeting, 11 December 1878; *Newcastle Weekly Chronicle*, 17 November 1877, p. 8d, 12 January 1878, p. 8f.

38. *Newcastle Daily Chronicle*, 26 December 1877, p. 3f, 14 January 1878, p. 3f-g; NMMCA Records, NRO 759/3, minutes, executive committee meeting, 26 December 1877.

39. Welbourne, *Miners' Unions*, p. 184; José Maria d'Eça de Queiróz to Portuguese Foreign Minister, 18 January 1878, Freeland, 'Letters', p. 36; *Morpeth Herald*, 12 January 1878, p. 4a, 2 February, p. 3f; *Blyth Weekly News*, 12 January 1878, p. 3e.

40. *Bee-Hive*, 22 December 1877, pp. 6–7.

41. *Newcastle Daily Chronicle*, 5 February 1878, p. 4c, 9 February, p. 4d; *Newcastle Daily Journal*, 6 December 1877, p. 4b, 19 December, p. 3c.

42. *Capital and Labour*, 13 February 1878, p. 109.

43. NB–NUM Records, NRO 3793/350, minutes, executive committee meeting, 9 February 1878; *Newcastle Daily Chronicle*, 13 February 1878, p. 3g.

44. *Blyth Weekly News*, 16 February 1878, p. 3f-g; *Newcastle Daily Journal*, 14 February 1878, p. 3e; *Newcastle Daily Chronicle*, 13 February 1878, p. 3g, 14 February 1878, p. 3g; NMMCA Records, NRO 759/3, minutes, executive committee meetings of February and March 1878.

45. *Miners' Watchman*, 2 March 1878, pp. 4–5.

46. NB–NUM Records, NRO 3793/350, minutes, delegate meeting, 22, 24 June 1878.

47. Ibid., Burt circular to miners, 4 November 1878; *Newcastle Daily Chronicle*, 12 November 1878, p. 3f, 14 November, p. 3c, and 18 November, p. 3e.

48. Webb Collection, Sect. A, Vol. XXVIII, ff. 230–4, Young's list of NMA strikes; NMMCA Records, NRO 759/4, minutes, executive committee meetings, 14 August, 13 October 1879; *Newcastle Daily Chronicle*, 10 May 1879, p. 3f.

49. National Coal Board Records, NRO 538/259, addresses, pp. 1–18 in minutes for NMMCA for 1879.

50. Burt to Stead, 29 September 1879, Stead Papers, STED 1/2.

51. Welbourne, *Miners' Unions*, pp. 177–81, 185–95.

52. Mitchell, *Economic Development*, pp. 4–9.

53. NMMCA Records, NRO 759/3, minutes, executive committee meeting, 28 April 1879; *Newcastle Daily Chronicle*, 14 May 1879, p. 3g, 20 June, p. 3d.

Chapter 5

1. Thomas Burt, 'Forty Years in the House', *Strand Magazine*, 50 (1915), 493.

2. Todd, *Cowen*, pp. 126–7; *Newcastle Weekly Chronicle*, 5 August 1876, p. 4h; Roy Jenkins, *Sir Charles Dilke: A Victorian Tragedy* (London, 1958), p. 100.

3. Todd, *Cowen*, p. 128.

4. Thomas Burt, 'Labour in Parliament', *Contemporary Review*, 55 (May 1889), 679.

5. Shepherd, 'Labour', pp. 190–1.
6. Gwyn, *Democracy*, pp. 151–2.
7. *Newcastle Daily Chronicle*, 18 December 1879, p. 4d.
8. *Newcastle Weekly Chronicle*, 24 January 1880, p. 3g.
9. These three principles were also a basic part of Victorian Liberalism: Shepherd, 'Labour', p. 199.
10. Kenneth Brown, 'Trade Unions and the Law', in Chris Wrigley (ed.), *A History of British Industrial Relations 1875–1914*, (Amherst, 1982), pp. 117–19; Royden Harrison, *Before the Socialists* (London, 1965), pp. 284–302.
11. W. H. G. Armytage, *A. J. Mundella, 1825–1897: The Liberal Background to the Labour Movement* (London, 1951), pp. 164–7; Wilson, *McDonald*, pp. 164–7; B. C. Roberts, *The Trades Union Congress, 1868–1921* (Cambridge, 1958), pp. 87–8; Harrison, *Socialists*, pp. 302–5.
12. 3 *Hansard*, CCXXV (28 June 1875), 681, and (16 July 1875), 1587–8; Watson, *Leader*, p. 177.
13. P. W. J. Bartrip and S. B. Burman, *The Wounded Soldiers of Industry: Industrial Compensation Policy, 1883–1897* (Oxford, 1983), pp. 103–16, 124–7.
14. 3 *Hansard*, CCXXIX (24 May 1876), 1160–1, 1179–81.
15. Ibid., CCXXXIX (10 April 1878), 1061–2.
16. Home Office Papers, HO 45/9458/727 31A, documents on bills introduced on employers' liability, 1871–79; Cawley, 'Coal Owners', pp. 126–53.
17. Bartrip and Burman, *Wounded Soldiers*, pp. 149–57.
18. 3 *Hansard*, CCLII (3 June 1880), 1135–6; CCLV (4 August 1880), 246–7, (6 August 1880), 585–6.
19. *Newcastle Daily Chronicle*, 19 July 1880, p. 4a; Welbourne, *Miners' Unions*, pp. 200–1.
20. *Newcastle Daily Chronicle*, 19 July 1880, p. 4c.
21. *Newcastle Weekly Chronicle*, 28 August 1880, p. 4b-d.
22. Bartrip and Burman, *Wounded Soldiers*, p. 163; *Newcastle Daily Chronicle*, 12 January 1881, p. 3g.
23. Ibid., 31 January 1881, p. 4a.
24. Bartrip and Burman, *Wounded Soldiers*, pp. 158–73; Geoffrey Alderman, *The Railway Interest* (Leicester, 1973), pp. 74, 78.
25. Home Office Papers, HO 45/9786/B3028C, abstract of inspectors' reports, dated 20 August 1889, of the mining districts that had contracted out of the Employers' Liability Act, 1880.
26. Norbert Soldon, 'Laissez-Faire as Dogma: The Liberty and Property Defence League, 1882–1914', in Kenneth D. Brown (ed.), *Essays in Anti-Labour History* (Hamden, CT., 1974), pp. 211–14.
27. NMMCA Records, NRO 759/68, Burt's address to delegate meeting, 21 May 1883; *Miners' National Gazette*, 26 May 1883, pp. 49, 56; Webb Collection, Sec. B, Vol. LXIV, no. 13, circular by Burt, as President of the MNU, and William Crawford, May 1883; *Newcastle Daily Chronicle*, 23 July 1883, p. 4b; Edward Bristow, *Individualism Versus Socialism in Britain, 1880–1914* (New York, 1987), pp. 129–30.
28. Trades Union Congress [TUC], minutes, annual meeting, 4 September 1884, pp. 22–3.

29. Bartrip and Burman, *Wounded Soldiers*, pp. 174–82; D. G. Hanes, *The First British Workman's Compensation Act, 1897* (New Haven, 1968).

30. Paul Smith, *Disraelian Conservatism and Social Reform* (London, 1967).

31. *Bee-Hive*, 22 April 1876, p. 13; 3 *Hansard*, CCXXVIII (23 March 1876), 531–2, CCXXXIV (9 May 1877), 585; *Morpeth Herald*, 27 January 1877, p. 4a-c. Burt served on a Parliamentary committee in 1878 to examine seamen; Report from the Select Committee on Merchant Seamen Bill, 1878, (205), XVI.

32. 3 *Hansard*, CCLIII (16 June 1880), 157–9.

33. *Newcastle Weekly Chronicle*, 21 August 1880, p. 4a-b.

34. 3 *Hansard*, CCXLII (8 August 1878), 1553.

35. *Durham Chronicle*, 12 July 1878, p. 6c-d, 31 July 1885, p. 6e.

36. Burt to Harcourt, 20 January 1899, William Harcourt Papers, MS 240/fols. 151–2; Burt to Harcourt, 3 March 1904, MS 245/fols. 70–1; Burt, *Autobiography*, pp. 259–60.

37. Webb Collection, Sect. B, Vol. XXIV, No. 11, report on trade union deputation to William Harcourt, 2 July 1884.

38. 3 *Hansard*, CCXC (4 July 1884), 76–81.

39. Ibid., 84–8.

40. *Newcastle Weekly Chronicle*, 12 September 1885, p. 8c.

41. Preliminary Report of Her Majesty's Commissioners Appointed to Inquire into Accidents in Mines, 1881 (C. 3036), XXVI; Final Report, 1886 (C. 4699), XVI.

42. Burt presided at a national meeting of miners in 20–22 April 1887 to examine and discuss the provisions of the bill; Webb Collection, Sect. B, Vol. LXIV, No. 15, minutes, Miners' National Conference, and *Newcastle Daily Leader*, 21 April 1887, p. 5d-e.

43. 3 *Hansard*, CCCXVI (20 June 1887), 636.

44. Ibid., CCCXIX (15 August 1887), 501, 511, 520–1, 529, (16 August), 714–16.

45. Ibid., CCCXVI (22 June 1887), 706, 724.

46. In *Liberty*, Biagini stresses that Liberalism was generally not laissez-faire, but included the right of government to aid and protect people.

47. *Newcastle Weekly Chronicle*, 23 October 1875, p. 8d.

48. Ibid., 3 May 1884, p. 8g, July 5, p. 3a.

49. TUC, minutes, annual meeting, 1891, p. 32.

50. Angela John, *By the Sweat of Their Brow* (London, 1980), pp. 11, 144–5; Wilson, *McDonald*, pp. 98, 106.

51. *Birmingham Daily Post*, 23 January 1886, p. 6f. John, *Sweat of Brow*, p. 145, indicates that the resolution was Burt's, but provides no reference to confirm it. Neither the *Birmingham Daily Post* just cited nor the account in the *The Times*, 25 January 1886, p. 7b, refers to the resolution as Burt's.

52. *Birmingham Daily Post*, 19 March 1886, p. 3e-f.

53. *Labour Tribune*, 19 February 1887, p. 4d.

54. 3 *Hansard*, CCCXVI (20 June 1887), 635, 646, 659.

55. Ibid., 636, 648–9, (23 June 1887), 792.

56. Ibid., 822–4.

57. *Englishwoman's Review*, N.S. CLIV, February 1886, 49–58.

58. Ibid., N.S. CLVII, May 1886, 225–7; *St. Helens Newspaper & Advertiser*, 27 April 1886, p. 4e.
59. Bristow, *Individualism*, pp. 102–4; Soldon, 'Laissez-Faire', pp. 215–16; John, *Sweat of Brow*, pp. 148, 155–8, 203–5.
60. *Morpeth Herald*, 26 December 1874, p. 4c.
61. 3 *Hansard*, CCXXIX (30 May 1876), 1466.
62. *Morpeth Herald*, 11 December 1875, p. 4b-c, 3 February 1877, p. 4a-b; *Newcastle Weekly Chronicle*, 28 April 1877, p. 4b-c.
63. *Newcastle Daily Chronicle*, 24 September 1883, pp. 5–6, 27 October 1884, p. 4a-f.
64. Ibid., 30 June 1884, p. 4b.
65. *Morpeth Herald*, 7 February 1885, p. 3c.
66. Walter Arnstein, *The Bradlaugh Case; A Study in Late Victorian Opinion and Politics* (Oxford, 1965), pp. 5–6.
67. Edward Royle, *Radicals, Secularists and Republicans: Popular Free Thought in Britain, 1866–1915* (Manchester, 1980), pp. 64–5; Watson, *Leader*, pp. 165–71.
68. NMMCA Records, NRO 759/68, Monthly Report, February 1891, pp. 7–8.
69. Burt to Stead, 27 May 1880, Stead Papers, STED 1/12.
70. *Newcastle Daily Chronicle*, 16 December 1880, p. 3e.
71. Ibid., 25 July 1881, p. 4b-c.
72. 3 *Hansard*, CCLXIV (3 August 1881), 715–16.
73. *Newcastle Weekly Chronicle*, 6 August 1881, p. 5f.
74. 3 *Hansard*, CCLXXXIV (11 February 1884), 485.
75. Burt to Trotter, 12 February 1884, Trotter Papers, NRO 1980/34.
76. Arnstein, *Bradlaugh*, pp. 313–19.
77. *Newcastle Daily Leader*, 21 December 1901, p. 8c.
78. Watson, *Leader*, p. 104.
79. For developments in education during this period, see J. S. Hurt, *Elementary Schooling and the Working Class 1860–1918* (London, 1979), and John Lawson and Harold Silver, *A Social History of Education in England* (London, 1973).
80. *Morpeth Herald*, 6 February 1875, p. 2b.
81. *Newcastle Weekly Chronicle*, 2 December 1876, p. 5f.
82. Ibid., 16 December 1876, p. 5c-d.
83. Ibid., p. 4d.
84. Alon Kadish, 'University Extension and the Working Classes: The Case of the Northumberland Miners', *Historical Research*, LX (June 1987), 188–207.
85. John Wigley, *The Rise and Fall of the Victorian Sunday* (Manchester, 1980), p. 132.
86. *Morpeth Herald*, 13 November 1875, p. 4c-d.
87. 3 *Hansard*, CCLXIX (19 May 1882), 1152–4.
88. Wigley, *Victorian Sunday*, pp. 147–8.
89. *Morpeth Herald*, 6 February 1875, p. 2b.
90. 3 *Hansard*, CCXLV (2 April 1879), 232–3; *Newcastle Weekly Chronicle*, 10 March 1877, p. 4a-b.
91. 3 *Hansard*, CCCXXVII (14 June 1888), 163–5.

92. Watson, *Leader*, p. 253.
93. *Newcastle Daily Chronicle*, 15 April 1922, p. 2d; Burt, *Autobiography*, p. 138; Lilian Lewis Shiman, *Crusade against Drink in Victorian England* (New York, 1988).
94. *Newcastle Weekly Chronicle*, 12 September 1874, p. 5d, 10 June 1876, p. 7b.
95. Shiman, *Crusade*, pp. 82–4; A. E. Dingle, *The Campaign for Prohibition in Victorian England* (New Brunswick, NJ, 1980), pp. 16–30.
96. 3 *Hansard*, CCXXV (16 June 1875), 71–4, (14 June 1881); CCLXII, 538–40; Biagini, *Liberty*, pp. 175–9.
97. 3 *Hansard*, CCLI (5 March 1880), 464.
98. *Newcastle Daily Leader*, 8 November 1886, p. 8b, 9 November, p. 8b-c, 3 January 1888, p. 6a.

Chapter 6

1. In 1880, for example, the MNU contributed toward his expenses; letter, Burt to James Trotter, 13 May 1880, printed in *Morpeth Herald*, 29 May 1880, p. 2f.
2. Burt to Trotter, 22 November 1878, Trotter Papers, NRO 1980/12, 16 March 1880, NRO 1980/15, 4 December 1880, NRO 1980/23, 30 October 1881, NRO 1980/28.
3. Burt to Trotter, 1 April 1880, ibid., NRO 1980/16, and 3 July 1880, NRO 1980/20.
4. Burt to Trotter, 16 March 1880, ibid., NRO 1980/15, and 30 June 1880, NRO 1980/19.
5. Burt to Trotter, 8 June 1882, ibid., NRO 1980/30, and 28 June 1882, NRO 1980/32.
6. Burt to Trotter, 12 February 1884, ibid., NRO 1980/34, 4 September 1884, NRO 1980/36; Burt, *Autobiography*, p. 212.
7. *Newcastle Weekly Chronicle*, series began on 17 February 1877.
8. Burt to Stead, 16 January 1878, Stead Papers, STED 1/12.
9. Information from a photograph owned by Rosemary Halsey, Burt's great-granddaughter.
10. *Newcastle Weekly Chronicle*, 30 April 1881, p. 8b, and 18 June 1881.
11. 3 *Hansard*, CCLXXVII (6 April 1883), 1632.
12. Martin Pugh, *The Making of Modern British Politics* (New York, 1982), p. 74.
13. 3 *Hansard*, CCXLIV (12 March 1879), 762.
14. *Newcastle Weekly Chronicle*, 17 August 1878, p. 7g.
15. Burt to Stead, 14 January 1879, Stead Papers, STED 1/2; Burt to R. S. Watson, 15 January 1880, Weiss Papers.
16. Burt to Stead, 29 October 1879, and 15 November 1881, Stead Papers, STED 1/12.
17. *Pall Mall Gazette*, 7 December 1883, p. 1b, and 10 December 1883, p. 1b; thanks to Owen Ashton for the reference. Aaron Watson, *A Newspaper Man's Memoirs* (London, [1925]), pp. 27, 59–69.
18. Geo. B. Hodgson, *From Smithy to Senate: The Life Story of James Annand* (London, 1908), pp. 53–120; E. I. Waitt, 'John Morley, Joseph Cowen and

Robert Spence Watson: Liberal Divisions in Newcastle Politics, 1873–1895'
(PhD dissertation, University of Manchester, 1972), p. 460, biographical
sketch, and *passim* for disputes between Cowen and Liberal leaders; Maurice
Milne, *The Newspapers of Northumberland and Durham* (Newcastle upon
Tyne, [1971]), pp. 128–30; Todd, *Cowen*, pp. 120–1, 130–59.

19. Philip Magnus, *Gladstone* (New York, 1964), pp. 207–11; Elizabeth
Longford, *Victoria R. I.* (London, 1964), pp. 376–96.

20. 3 *Hansard*, CCXXI (30 July 1874), 978–9.

21. Ibid., CCXXV (8 July 1875), 1157, (15 July 1875), 1525.

22. Many MPs were opposed to India being expected to contribute to this
visit. As it was, the government of India eventually contributed about
£100,000 to help cover the expenses of the visit. Philip Magnus, *King
Edward the Seventh* (New York, 1964), p. 133.

23. *Morpeth Herald*, 3 February 1877, p. 4a-b.

24. 3 *Hansard*, CCXLII (31 July 1878), 780–4.

25. Ibid., CCCXXXVIII (29 July 1889), 1613–14.

26. George Earle Buckle, *The Life of Benjamin Disraeli* (London, 1920),
vol. 6, pp. 436–9; Theo Aronson, *Queen Victoria and the Bonapartes*
(Indianapolis, 1972), pp. 160–95.

27. 3 *Hansard*, CCXLIX (8 August 1879), 544–5.

28. *Newcastle Daily Chronicle*, 19 July 1880, p. 4c.

29. 3 *Hansard*, CCLIV (16 July 1880), 698–730.

30. Owen Ashton, 'W. E. Adams and Working Class Opposition to Empire
1878–80: Cyprus and Afghanistan', *North East Labour History Bulletin*,
No. 27 (1993), 60–7; Walter Wirthwein, *Britain and the Balkan Crisis,
1875–1878* (New York, 1966; first pubished 1935), pp. 367–9.

31. *Newcastle Weekly Chronicle*, 16 September 1876, p. 8b.

32. *Morpeth Herald*, 27 January 1877, p. 4a-c.

33. E. P. Thompson, *William Morris, Romantic to Revolutionary* (New
York, 1977; rev. edn), p. 214; Labour Representation League Minutes,
minutes, 11 May 1877; Ann Pottinger Saab, *Reluctant Icon: Gladstone,
Bulgaria, and the Working Classes, 1856–1878* (Cambridge, MA: Harvard
University Press, 1991), pp. 136–7.

34. *Reynolds's Newspaper*, 14 April 1878, p. 6e; *The Times*, 11 April 1878,
p. 10d-e.

35. *World Encyclopedia of Peace* (Oxford, 1986), vol. 3, pp. 197–9; pamphlet
on the International Arbitration League, bound with other IAL
pamphlets, at the British Library; Howard Evans, *Sir Randal Cremer*
(Boston, 1910).

36. Roger Chickering, *Imperial Germany and a World Without War: The
Peace Movement and German Society, 1892–1914* (Princeton, 1975),
pp. 6–8.

37. *Newcastle Weekly Chronicle*, 10 August 1872, p. 2b.

38. NMMCA Records, NRO 759/1, minutes, delegate meeting, 29 March
1873, p. 73, minutes, executive committee meeting, 4 April 1873, pp. 83–4.

39. *Newcastle Weekly Chronicle*, 6 February 1875, p. 3e-f.

40. The precise date when Burt became the president is not known. Watson
wrote that when he was honoured in June 1914, for his long-time service
to the League, he had served for thirty-two years as the president; in his

speech at that meeting, Burt referred to his thirty-five years of presidency; Burt, *Autobiography*, pp. 308, 312.

41. Burt to Stead, 19 December 1877, Stead Papers, STED 1/12.
42. NMMCA Records, NRO 759/3, minutes, executive committee meeting, 7 January 1878.
43. *Newcastle Daily Chronicle*, 20 May 1878, p. 4a-c.
44. Ibid., pp. 2h-3a; Todd, *Cowen*, pp. 131–4.
45. *Newcastle Weekly Chronicle*, 1 February 1879, p. 8d.
46. *Newcastle Daily Chronicle*, 4 December 1878, p. 3f.
47. 3 *Hansard*, CCXLIII (13 December 1878), 787–90.
48. Robert Blake, *Disraeli* (New York, 1967), p. 663.
49. *Newcastle Weekly Chronicle*, 24 January 1880, p. 3f-g.
50. Tingfu Tsiang, *Labor and Empire: A Study of the Reaction of British Labor, Mainly as Represented in Parliament, to British Imperialism Since 1880* (New York, 1923), pp. 215–17.
51. 3 *Hansard*, CCLXXXVI (20 March 1884), 275; CCLXXXVIII (15 May 1884), 426–7; CCCL (17 February 1891), 835–6, (19 February 1891), 1058–9.
52. Ibid., CCCVIII (30 August 1886), 839–41; Tsiang, *Labor and Empire*, pp. 33–4.
53. Muriel Chamberlain, *'Pax Britannica'? British Foreign Policy, 1789–1914* (New York, 1988), pp. 144–5.
54. *Newcastle Daily Chronicle*, 22 June 1882, p. 3e; *The Times*, 21 June 1882, p. 13f.
55. Thomas Burt, 'Working Men and War', *Fortnightly Review*, 32 (December 1882), 718–27.
56. *Newcastle Daily Chronicle*, 3 February 1883, p. 3e, 30 January 1884, p. 4c.
57. 3 *Hansard*, CCLXXVIII (19 April 1883), 695.
58. *Newcastle Daily Chronicle*, 7 February 1885, p. 3f; Tsiang, *Labor and Empire*, pp. 63–4.
59. *Arbitrator*, February 1885, p. 14.
60. Ibid., pp. 8–13, and April 1885, pp. 5–7; Evans, *Cremer*, pp. 111, 113.
61. *Newcastle Daily Chronicle*, 1 August 1874, p. 3a; T. M. Healy, *Letters and Leaders of My Day* (New York, 1929), vol. 1, pp. 34–5.
62. F. S. L. Lyons, *Charles Stuart Parnell* (New York, 1977), pp. 57–64.
63. Alan O'Day, *The English Face of Irish Nationalism* (Toronto, 1977), p. 54.
64. *Newcastle Daily Chronicle*, 16 December 1880, p. 3f, 8 January 1881, p. 5e; *Newcastle Weekly Chronicle*, 1 January 1881, p. 5d-f.
65. Thomas Heyck, *The Dimensions of British Radicalism: The Case of Ireland 1874–1895* (Urbana, 1974), pp. 54–6, 61–7; see also T. A. Jenkins, *The Liberal Ascendancy, 1830–86* (New York, 1994), pp. 172–7.
66. Conor Cruise O'Brien, *Parnell and His Party, 1880–90* (Oxford, 1957), p. 57; *Newcastle Daily Chronicle*, 17 January 1881, p. 3f.
67. *Newcastle Weekly Chronicle*, 29 January 1881, p. 5c-e.
68. *Newcastle Daily Chronicle*, 31 January 1881, p. 3d.
69. Burt to Trotter, 27 January 1881, Trotter Papers, NRO 1980/24.
70. O'Brien, *Parnell*, pp. 58–9.
71. Burt, 'Forty Years', p. 499.

72. *Newcastle Daily Chronicle*, 22 April 1881, p. 3e-f.

73. Todd, *Cowen*, pp. 138–9.

74. Burt to Trotter, 19 February 1881, Trotter Papers, NRO 1980/25.

75. Thomas Burt, 'Working Men and the Political Situation', *Nineteenth Century*, 9 (April 1881), 611–22.

76. L. P. Curtis, Jr, *Coercion and Conciliation in Ireland, 1880–1892: A Study in Conservative Unionism* (Princeton, 1963), pp. 9–10.

77. Heyck, *Dimensions*, pp. 67–71; O'Brien, *Parnell*, pp. 69–74.

78. *Newcastle Daily Chronicle*, 15 October 1881, p. 3g.

79. Todd, *Cowen*, pp. 140–3, 149–50.

80. *Newcastle Daily Chronicle*, 24 October 1881, p. 2g-3d, 27 October, p. 3d, 28 October, p. 3e-f.

81. It would be distributed nation-wide in pamphlet form by the National Liberal Federation; Watson, *Leader*, p. 265.

82. The printed account, 'Address by Mr. T. Burt, M.P., at Bedlington', is available in Local Tracts, 1881, Newcastle Public Library.

83. *Newcastle Daily Chronicle*, 10 November 1881, p. 3g-h.

84. *Tyneside Daily Echo*, 10 November 1881, p. 3c-d.

85. *Newcastle Daily Chronicle*, 11 November 1881, p. 4d-e.

86. Burt to Howell, 12 November 1881, George Howell Papers, Correspondence.

87. *Newcastle Daily Chronicle*, 14 November 1881, p. 3c, and 15 November 1881.

88. Ibid., 18 November 1881, p. 3f-g.

89. Ibid., 1 December 1881, p. 3c-e.

90. Heyck, *Dimensions*, pp. 71–81.

91. Burt to Trotter, 21 May 1882, Trotter Papers, NRO 1980/29. In his letter, Burt is apparently referring to the vote on the second reading, held 19 May 1882, as Burt is not listed as voting; 3 *Hansard*, CCLXIX (19 May 1882), 1145–8. Burt voted more often against than in favour of the amendments, which were designed to weaken the coercion bill of 1882; *Newcastle Weekly Chronicle*, 24 June 1882, p. 8g. According to Todd, *Cowen*, p. 143, Burt generally supported the bill.

92. *Newcastle Daily Chronicle*, 3 February 1883, p. 3e-f.

93. Ibid., 30 January 1884, p. 4c.

94. *Newcastle Daily Leader*, 26 April 1886, p. 8a-b.

95. Burt to Stead, 20 December 1886, Stead Papers, STED 1/12.

96. Hodgson, *Annand*, p. 100.

97. *Newcastle Daily Chronicle*, 25 July 1887, p. 5e; *Newcastle Daily Leader*, 4 February 1888, p. 5c-d.

98. 3 *Hansard*, CCCXXII (17 February 1888), 787–8.

Chapter 7

1. South Wales was not a part of the MFGB in the early 1890s.

2. NMMCA Records, NRO 759/68, emigration circular dated 18 July 1881, quarterly financial statements, 1881–83.

3. Notices of payments to 'sacrificed' members are scattered throughout NMA minutes during the 1880s; one example is to a Mr Cox, ibid.,

minutes, executive committee meeting, 5 February 1885, p. 7.

4. Ibid., agenda and minutes, delegate meeting, 20 and 22 May 1882, pp. 17–18, 23–4; minutes and letter, house-rent committee, 10, 26 July, 22 August 1882, pp. 9–15.

5. L. L. F. R. Price, *Industrial Peace* (London, 1887), p. 38; NMMCA Records, NRO 759/68, minutes, joint committee meetings.

6. Ibid., circular on federation talks, 26 January 1882; minutes, executive committee meeting, 27 February 1882, p. 12; agenda, delegate meeting, 20 May 1882, pp. 6–7; federation board minutes, 8 August, 4 October 1882, 20 November 1883. H. A. Clegg, Alan Fox, and A. F. Thompson, *A History of the British Trade Unions Since 1889. Vol. 1, 1889–1910* (Oxford, 1964), p. 103.

7. NMMCA Records, NRO 759/68, agenda and minutes, delegate meeting, 18, 20 November 1882, p. 25; agenda, delegate meeting, 17 May 1884, p. 6.

8. Welbourne, *Miners' Unions*, pp. 206, 212–23.

9. NMMCA Records, NRO 759/68, minutes, delegate meeting, 2, 4 April 1881, pp. 4–5; agenda and minutes, delegate meeting, 19 November 1881, p. 31.

10. Ibid., accountant's report, 31 March 1881, p. 16.

11. John G. Treble, 'Sliding Scales and Conciliation Boards: Risk-Sharing in the Late 19th Century British Coal Industry', *Oxford Economic Papers*, 39 (December 1987), 679–98.

12. *Newcastle Weekly Chronicle*, 8 May 1880, p. 8c.

13. Price, *Industrial Peace*, pp. xxvii, 75–9.

14. *Newcastle Weekly Chronicle*, 31 July 1880, p. 4a-d, 29 July 1882, pp. 4h-5a, 5 August 1882, pp. 4h-5a.

15. Ibid., 17 December 1881, p. 8e, 2 September 1882, p. 5g.

16. Ibid., 16 September 1882, p. 8e; NMMCA Records, NRO 759/68, minutes, executive committee meeting, 20 January 1883, p. 10, 2 June 1885, p. 30.

17. *Newcastle Daily Chronicle*, 7 July 1884, p. 4c; *Labour Tribune*, 27 November 1886, p. 2b.

18. NMMCA Records, NRO 759/68, minutes, delegate meeting, 18, 20 November 1882, pp. 16, 23.

19. Ibid., report, sliding-scale committee, 17 November 1882, pp. 18–27; minutes, executive committee, 27 December 1882, p. 47.

20. Ibid., minutes, executive committee meeting, 1 February 1883, p. 13.

21. Ibid., sliding-scale agreement, 9 March 1883, and sliding-scale committee's report, 10 March 1883, pp. 8–10.

22. Clegg, *Unions*, p. 19; J. H. Porter, 'Wage Bargaining under Conciliation Agreements, 1860–1914', *Economic History Review*, 2nd ser., 23 (1970), 474–5; V. L. Allen, *The Sociology of Industrial Relations* (London, 1971), p. 82; R. Page Arnot, *The Miners: A History of the Miners' Federation of Great Britain, 1889–1910* (London, 1949), p. 60, quoting Webb, *History of Trade Unionism*, p. 340.

23. Burt, 'Industrial Harmony', pp. 434–6, largely reproduced in Burt, *Autobiography*, pp. 201–6.

24. *Newcastle Weekly Chronicle*, 18 July 1885, p. 8e; NMMCA Records,

NRO 759/68, minutes, executive committee meetings, 18, 27 June, 20 July 1885, pp. 34–44; minutes, delegate meeting, 21 November 1885, pp. 27–8; voting results on Fenwick's salary, 4 December 1885, pp. 4–5; *Manchester Guardian*, 28 February 1888, p. 5h.

25. *Newcastle Daily Leader*, 21 January 1886, p. 8a.
26. Ashton, *Adams*, pp. 162–4.
27. NMMCA Records, NRO 759/68, address on short time and relief, February 1886, p. 3; *Newcastle Daily Chronicle*, 12 April 1886, p. 5d, 4 October p. 5e-f; *Newcastle Daily Leader*, 28 December 1886, p. 5a-b.
28. NMMCA Records, NRO 759/68, quarterly balance sheets for years 1885 and 1886; minutes, rent committee meeting, 8 August 1886, p. 8; minutes, delegate meeting, 18 September 1886, pp. 31–4, 18 December, pp. 48–9; minutes, executive committee meeting, 21 October 1886, p. 56.
29. *Newcastle Daily Leader*, 29 April 1886, p. 8a-b, 1 November, p. 8b, 23 December, p. 5a-b.
30. NMMCA Records, NRO 759/68, minutes, executive committee meeting, 6 October 1886, p. 52; addresses on house rent, 8, 18 November 1886, pp. 5–8; report, miners committee, 10 December 1886, pp. 11–14.
31. NDCOA Records, NRO 263, minutes, Steam Collieries' Defence Association, for various committees and meetings from October 1886, to April 1887; NMMCA Records, NRO 759/68, address by union negotiators, 8 January 1887, pp. 3–6; *Newcastle Daily Leader*, 10 January 1887, p. 4c-e.
32. NMMCA Records, NRO 759/68, minutes, delegate meeting, 19 January 1887, pp. 6–7; results of voting, 1887 strike, pp. 3–4.
33. NDCOA Records, NRO 263, minutes, Steam Collieries Defence Association meeting, 28 May 1887; NMMCA Records, NRO 759/68, addresses, dated 1, 2 February 1887, pp. 8–9; results of voting, 1887 strike, pp. 3–4; *Tyneside Echo*, 27 January 1887, p. 3c; Bill Williamson, 'The 1887 Lock-out and Strike in the Northumberland Coalfield', in Sturgess, *Pitmen*, pp. 111–12.
34. *Newcastle Daily Chronicle*, 17 December 1886, p. 5b, 31 January 1887, p. 5c-d, 11 February, p. 5e-f; *Newcastle Daily Leader*, 31 January 1887, p. 8a.
35. *Newcastle Daily Chronicle*, 8 February 1887, p. 5e-f; NMMCA Records, NRO 759/68, letters, dated 7, 8 February 1887, pp. 12–13.
36. *Labour Tribune*, 19 February 1887, p. 5a-b; *Newcastle Daily Chronicle*, 18 February 1887, p. 8b.
37. Ibid., 11 February 1887, p. 5e-f.
38. *Newcastle Daily Leader*, 14 February 1887, p. 5d, 15 February, p. 4g.
39. *Newcastle Daily Leader*, 18 April 1887, p. 5d, 23 April, p. 8d, 25 April, p. 5f.
40. Burt, *Autobiography*, pp. 236–7; Burt to Dilke, 25 April 1888, Dilke Papers, Add. MS 43914, fols. 63–4.
41. *Newcastle Daily Leader*, 19 April 1887, p. 5d; *Newcastle Daily Chronicle*, 29 April 1887, p. 8d; NMMCA Records, NRO 759/68, results of voting on 1887 strike, p. 7.
42. *Miner*, May 1887, p. 79.
43. *Newcastle Daily Chronicle*, 23 May 1887, p. 4f; NMMCA Records, NRO 759/68, wage committee report, 25 May 1887, pp. 23–7; NDCOA Records, NRO 263, minutes, Steam Collieries' Defence Association meetings, 7, 23, 24, 28 May 1887.

44. Welbourne, *Miners' Unions*, pp. 238–9; NMMCA Records, NRO 759/68, financial statement for 1887 indicated that £10,888 had been received during the strike.
45. *Newcastle Weekly Chronicle*, 16 April 1887, p. 5a; *Labour Tribune*, 28 May 1887, p. 4c. Williamson, '1887 Lock-out', pp. 114–16, describes life in pit villages during the strike.
46. *Newcastle Daily Chronicle*, 19 April 1887, p. 8d-e.
47. *Colliery Guardian*, 4 February 1887, p. 167a.
48. NMMCA Records, NRO 759/68, see quarterly statements, especially for 1886 and 1887.
49. First Report of the Royal Commission on Labour, 1892 (C. 6708), XXXIV, 122.
50. NMMCA Records, NRO 759/68, agenda and minutes, delegate meeting, 21, 24 May 1887, pp. 29–46.
51. Ibid., voting results of the August meeting resolution, p. 14.
52. *Manchester Guardian*, 28 February 1888, p. 5h.
53. David Howell, *British Workers and the Independent Labour Party, 1888–1906* (New York, 1983), pp. 42–51; Thompson, *Morris*, pp. 439–45, 464–6; Tom Mann, *Memoirs* (London, 1923), pp. 65–6; Dona Torr, *Tom Mann and His Times* (London, 1956), vol. 1, pp. 236–51; Chushichi Tsuzuki, *Tom Mann, 1856–1941* (Oxford, 1991), pp. 26–9; Williamson, '1887 Lock-out', pp. 116–20.
54. *Newcastle Daily Leader*, 12 April 1887, p. 3e-f; *Newcastle Daily Chronicle*, 12 April 1887, pp. 4d-f, 5a.
55. Ian Hunter, 'Labour in Local Government on Tyneside, 1883–1921', in M. Callcott and R. Challinor (eds), *Working Class Politics in North East England* (Newcastle upon Tyne, 1983), p. 25.
56. J. L. Mahon, *A Plea for Socialism. Delivered in the Course of a Socialist Campaign Amongst the Miners on Strike in Northumberland* (London, 1887), pp. 5–6.
57. *Newcastle Weekly Chronicle*, 6 August 1887, pp. 5a, 6b-d.
58. Douglass, 'Pitman', pp. 255, 281–2.
59. NMMCA Records, NRO 759/68, minutes, delegate meeting, 19 November 1887, p. 61; agenda and minutes, delegate meeting, 18 February 1888, pp. 3–4, 8; *Newcastle Weekly Chronicle*, 26 November 1887, p. 4e; *Miner*, March 1888, p. 33c.
60. NMMCA Records, NRO 759/68, address by Burt on pay issue, 3 March 1888, pp. 1–7.
61. *Daily News*, 22 September 1887, p. 4f-g; *Labour Tribune*, 18 February 1888, p. 4c-d; *Newcastle Daily Leader*, 12 March 1888, p. 4b-d; *Newcastle Daily Journal*, 21 September 1887, p. 4d-e; *Northern Echo*, 13 March 1888, p. 3a-b. *Newcastle Daily Leader*, 21 September 1887, p. 8a, *Newcastle Weekly Chronicle*, 24 September 1887, p. 5e, and *Labour Tribune*, 24 March 1888, p. 6b-c, ran excerpts from various newspapers.
62. *Commonweal*, 25 February 1888, p. 62; *Miner*, March 1888, p. 33c.
63. NMMCA Records, NRO 759/68, minutes, executive committee meeting, 7 April 1888, pp. 25–6.
64. Ibid., report, Committee on Wages and Salaries, 30 July 1888, pp. 20–7;

agenda and minutes, delegate meeting, 15 November 1888, pp. 27–9, 35–6.

65. Gwyn, *Democracy*, pp. 152–3.
66. *Newcastle Daily Leader*, 20 February 1888, p. 5f.
67. NMMCA Records, NRO 759/68, minutes, delegate meeting, 21, 24 May 1887, p. 42.
68. Arnot, *Miners, 1889–1910*, p. 84; Webb Collection, Sect. B., vol. LXIV, no. 16, minutes, national miners' conference, 11–14 October 1887.
69. NMMCA Records, NRO 759/68, voting of delegates, 18 November 1887, p. 19.
70. Ibid., minutes, executive committee meeting, 27 March 1889, p. 21; Arnot, *Miners, 1889–1910*, pp. 91–109.
71. Ibid., pp. 94–5.
72. *Newcastle Weekly Chronicle*, 15 October 1887, p. 6a-c.
73. *Labour Tribune*, 6 April 1889, p. 5b; Arnot, *Miners, 1889–1910*, p. 103.
74. Welbourne, *Miners' Unions*, p. 286; *Newcastle Daily Chronicle*, 15 May 1891, pp. 4c, 5d-e.
75. Mitchell, *Economic Development*, p. 184.
76. Michael Barker, *Gladstone and Radicalism, the Reconstruction of Liberal Policy in Britain 1885–1894* (New York, 1975), pp. 144–53.
77. George Howell, *Trade Unionism New and Old* (Brighton, 1973, [4th rev. edn 1907]), pp. 178–9; *The Times*, 28 January 1890, p. 6c, 19 February, p. 8d-f, 17 June, p. 5e; *Newcastle Daily Leader*, 9 January 1891, p. 6b; B. McCormick and J. E. Williams, 'The Miners and the Eight-Hour Day, 1863–1910', *Economic History Review*, 12 (December 1959), 225; William D. Muller, *The Kept Men? The First Century of Trade Union Representation in the British House of Commons, 1874–1975* (Atlantic Highlands, NJ, 1977), pp. 17–18.
78. Watson, *Leader*, pp. 230–8.
79. Burt, 'Labour in Parliament', p. 690.
80. McCormick and Williams, 'Eight-Hour Day', pp. 225–6; Welbourne, *Miners' Unions*, pp. 243–5.
81. NMMCA Records, NRO 759/68, minutes, executive committee meetings, 19 September, 5 October 1889, pp. 59–64.
82. Ibid., minutes, delegate meetings, 16 November 1889, p. 28, and 17 February 1890, p. 9; results of voting, 4 March 1890, p. 9; report of committee to study the hours of boys, 28 January 1890, pp. 3–5.

Chapter 8

1. Evans, *Cremer*, pp. 124–31.
2. Annual Reports, International Arbitration and Peace Association; Proceedings of the Universal Peace Congress, 14–19 July 1890, 27 July–1 August 1908.
3. John Wilson, *CB: A Life of Sir Henry Campbell-Bannerman* (London, 1973), pp. 535–7.
4. Christian Lange *et al.*, *The Interparliamentary Union from 1889 to 1939* (Lausanne, 1939), pp. 8–10, 61; *Arbitrator*, November 1888, pp. 4–7, July and August 1889, pp. 1–9; Hayne Davis (ed.), *Among the World's Peacemakers* (New York, 1907), pp. 15–19; Evans, *Cremer*, pp. 134–49.

5. Lamar Cecil, *Wilhelm II* (Chapel Hill, NC, 1989), pp. 57–61.
6. For details of the conference, see Correspondence and Reports on the Berlin Labour Conference: 1890 (C. 5914), LXXXI; 1890 (C. 6042), LXXXI; 1890–91 (C. 6371), LXXXIII.
7. *Black and White*, 19 September 1891, p. 392.
8. Charles Lowe, *The German Emperor William II* (London, [1895]), p. 188.
9. Home Office Papers, HO 45/9806/B6239, Results of the Berlin Labour Conference, 1890; 3 *Hansard*, CCCL (26 February 1891), 1779–81, and CCCLIV (18 June 1891), 856–9, 860–3.
10. NMMCA Records, NRO 759/68, minutes, executive committee meetings, 1, 20 July 1889, pp. 44, 49, and report by Burt and Fenwick on Paris meetings, July 1889, pp. 22–8; Wilson, *Durham Miners*, p. 223.
11. NMMCA Records, NRO 759/68, Report on the International Conference by NMMCA delegation, 4 June 1890, pp. 16–23; Watson, *Leader*, pp. 209–12; *Newcastle Daily Chronicle*, 24 May 1890, p. 5d; *Newcastle Weekly Chronicle*, 24 May 1890, p. 7e.
12. *Justice*, 31 May 1890, p. 3c; *Commonweal*, 31 May 1890, p. 174a.
13. NMMCA Records, NRO 759/68, Monthly Report, April 1891, pp. 15–18; *Labour Tribune*, 4 April 1891, pp. 5b-d, 6a-b; *Newcastle Daily Leader*, 3 April 1891, p. 4c-d; *Newcastle Daily Chronicle*, 3 April 1891, p. 5c.
14. *Durham Chronicle*, 10 July 1891, p. 3d.
15. Douglas J. Newton, *British Labour, European Socialism, and the Struggle for Peace, 1889–1914* (Oxford, 1985), p. 87.
16. W. J. Davis, *The British Trades Union Congress: History and Recollections* (New York, 1984; first published 1910), pp. 6–9; Roberts, *TUC*, pp. 56–9.
17. NMMCA Records, NRO 759/68, Monthly Report, September 1891, pp. 41–2, September 1892, pp. 44–5.
18. Kenneth Morgan, *Keir Hardie: Radical and Socialist* (London, 1975), pp. 17–18; Kenneth Morgan, *Labour People: Leaders and Lieutenants, Hardie to Kinnock* (Oxford, 1987), pp. 23–38.
19. *Miner*, January 1887, pp. 1–2.
20. Joyce M. Belamy and John Saville (eds), *Dictionary of Labour Biography* (Clifton, NJ, 1972 –   ), vol. 1, p. 61; *Miner*, February 1887, pp. 17–18.
21. Morgan, *Hardie*, p. 18; Fred Reid, *Keir Hardie, The Making of a Socialist* (London, 1978), pp. 92–3.
22. *Miner*, July 1887, p. 97.
23. Reid, *Hardie*, pp. 102–4, 108–19.
24. William Stewart, *J. Keir Hardie* (London, 1921), p. 47.
25. TUC, minutes, annual meeting, 4 September 1890, pp. 50–3; Roberts, *TUC*, pp. 125–9; *Commonweal*, 13 September 1890, p. 294a; *The Times*, 9 September 1890, p. 6a-b.
26. *Newcastle Daily Chronicle*, 7 September 1891, p. 5d-e, 9 September, p. 5c.
27. Roberts, *TUC*, pp. 377–8; Watson, *Leader*, pp. 189–90.
28. TUC, minutes, annual meeting, 8 September 1891, pp. 32–5; text of most of the speech is found in Watson, *Leader*, pp. 185–9.
29. *Workman's Times*, 11 September 1891, p. 1a; *Newcastle Weekly Chronicle*, 12 September 1891, p. 4f; *Newcastle Daily Leader*, 9 September 1891, p. 4e; *Daily News*, 9 September 1891, p. 5a; *Northern*

Echo, 10 September 1981, p. 2g; *Labour Tribune*, 12 September 1891, p. 4b; *Spectator*, 12 September 1891, p. 338; William Hallam (ed.), *Miners' Leaders* (London, [1894]), pp. 25–6.
30. George Jacob Holyoake, *The Life of Thomas Burt, M.P.* (London, 1895), p. 15.
31. *Newcastle Daily Leader*, 9 September 1891, p. 4e-f.
32. *Black and White*, 19 September 1891, p. 392a.
33. *Newcastle Daily Chronicle*, 9 September 1891, p. 5a, 11 September, p. 4f; Watson, *Leader*, p. 192. A bell is included in the Burt memorabilia on display at the Woodhorn Colliery Museum in Northumberland.
34. *Newcastle Daily Leader*, 12 September 1891, p. 4f-g; TUC, minutes, annual meeting, 11 September 1891, p. 79.
35. Ibid., 11 September 1891, pp. 73–7; Arnot, *Miners, 1889–1910*, p. 178.
36. NMMCA Records, NRO 759/68, Monthly Report, September 1891, pp. 43–4, October 1891, pp. 46–7.
37. Ibid., minutes, executive committee meeting, 6 January 1892, pp. 5–6; Monthly Report, January 1892, p. 3; *Newcastle Daily Leader*, 14 December 1891, p. 5b-c, 28 December, pp. 4c-d, 8d.
38. *Newcastle Daily Chronicle*, 24 March 1892, p. 5d; 4 *Hansard*, II (23 March 1892), 1557–77.
39. Arnot, *Miners, 1889–1910*, pp. 178–83.
40. Heyck, *Dimensions*, pp. 172–4; Barker, *Gladstone*, p. 195.
41. Welbourne, *Miners' Unions*, p. 246.
42. Arnot, *Miners, 1889–1910*, pp. 91–116.
43. NMMCA Records, NRO 759/68, minutes, delegate meeting, 19 November 1887, p. 62; report from wage committee, 22 June 1891, pp. 19–23.
44. Ibid., addresses to members, 19, 26 November, 3 December 1888, pp. 32–43; *Newcastle Weekly Chronicle*, 13 February 1889, p. 4b.
45. NMMCA Records, NRO 759/68, Monthly Report, January 1892, p. 6, March 1892, pp. 14–16, August 1892, pp. 38–9; Arnot, *Miners, 1889–1910*, pp. 209–13; Cawley, 'Coal Owners', pp. 178–9.
46. Arnot, *Miners, 1889–1910*, p. 108.
47. NMMCA Records, NRO 759/68, Monthly Report, April 1892, pp. 20–2.
48. *Newcastle Daily Chronicle*, 9 April 1892, p. 4a-b. Craig Marshall, *Levels of Industrial Militancy and Political Radicalism of the Durham Miners, 1885–1914* (Durham, 1976), describes the radicalism of the Durham miners and their propensity to engage in wildcat strikes during this period.
49. W. R. Garside, 'Wage Determination and the Miners' Lockout of 1892', in Norman McCord (ed.), *Essays in Tyneside Labour History* (Newcastle upon Tyne Polytechnic, 1977), pp. 135–46; Welbourne, *Miners' Unions*, pp. 269–85; Arnot, *Miners, 1889–1910*, pp. 213–17.

Chapter 9

1. *Newcastle Daily Leader*, 11 July 1892, pp. 4g-5b.
2. 4 *Hansard*, VII (8 August 1892), 105–11; Watson, *Leader*, pp. 249–51.
3. Information from Dr Eric Wade, Open University, in personal interview

10 February 1992, and copy of Wade's interview on radio, in 1987, when he discussed the life of Thomas Burt; *Morpeth Herald*, 2 November 1907, p. 3a-c.

4. Copy of letter, Gladstone to Burt, 17 August 1892, Gladstone Papers, Add. MS 44515, fols. 185–6; Burt to Gladstone, 18 August 1892, fols. 213–14; copy of letter, Gladstone to Burt, 19 August 1892, fols. 221–2; Burt, *Autobiography*, pp. 276–7.

5. Burt to Trotter, 21 August 1892, Trotter Papers, NRO 1980/56; NMMCA Records, NRO 759/68, circular on Burt's appointment, 20 August 1892, pp. 14–15, and Monthly Report, September 1892, pp. 45–7.

6. Board of Trade Papers, BT 5/98, Minutes, Board of Trade, 24 August 1892.

7. NMMCA Records, NRO 759/68, wage committee report, 5 November 1892, pp. 22–3.

8. *Newcastle Daily Chronicle*, 26 December 1892, p. 6a-b; *Morpeth Herald*, 31 December 1892, p. 5b-f.

9. Henry Lucy, *A Diary of the Home Rule Parliament, 1892–1895* (London, 1896), p. 125; *The Times*, 30 June 1893, p. 10e.

10. Peter Marsh, *Joseph Chamberlain: Entrepreneur in Politics* (New Haven, 1994).

11. Burt, *Autobiography*, p. 264; Thomas Cox Meech, *From Mine to Ministry: The Life and Times of Thomas Burt, M.P.* ([1908]), pp. 105–6.

12. Joseph Chamberlain, 'The Labour Question', *The Nineteenth Century*, 32 (November 1892), 709.

13. Thomas Burt, 'Labour Leaders on the Labour Question: Mr. Chamberlain's Programme', *Nineteenth Century*, 32 (December 1892), 864–6.

14. Clegg *et al.*, *Unions*, p. 279.

15. George Howell, *Labour Legislation, Labour Leaders, and Labour Movements* (London, 1902), pp. 459–73.

16. Burt, 'Labour in Parliament', p. 679.

17. Ibid., pp. 678–91.

18. Cowen Papers, D 427, *Newcastle Daily Chronicle*, 29 June 1892, supplement, p. 1e-f. The list of the Cowen Papers indicates that the articles on Burt and other candidates were written by Cowen.

19. Burt, 'Labour in Parliament', p. 690.

20. Shepherd, 'Labour', pp. 187–213, especially recognizes the importance of the Lib-Labs. See also Clegg *et al.*, *Unions*, pp. 269–85.

21. Barker, *Gladstone*, pp. 137–8; Muller, *Kept Men*, pp. 16–17, 23–6; Shepherd, 'Labour', p. 197.

22. Armytage, *Mundella*.

23. Ibid., pp. 293–6; Sir Hurbert Llewellyn Smith, *The Board of Trade* (London, 1928), pp. 218–19.

24. Roger Davidson, *Whitehall and the Labour Problem in Late-Victorian and Edwardian Britain: A Study in Official Statistics and Social Control* (London, 1985), pp. 92–8; Alan Fox, *History and Heritage: The Social Origins of the British Industrial Relations System* (London, 1985), pp. 246–50.

25. Board of Trade Papers, BT 20/13, copy of letter, Burt to Treasury, 23 December 1892.

26. Burt to Mundella, 21 December 1892, Mundella Papers, 6P/25/40.
27. Board of Trade Papers, BT 13/22/E11367/94, on Home Office's Factories and Workshops Bill, 1894; Burt was appointed to a committee studying railway accidents, April 1894, BT 5/100; Burt was chairman of a parliamentary committee to provide transmission of a sailor's wages from ports in Europe to his home, BT 13/21 E10970/93.
28. See 4 *Hansard* for this period.
29. *Newcastle Daily Leader*, 5 April 1893, p. 8c-e; Final Report of the Royal Commission Appointed to Inquire into the Subject of Mining Royalties, 1893–4 (C. 6980), XLI.
30. Fox, *History and Heritage*, p. 252; Fifth and Final Report of the Royal Commission on Labour, 1894 (C. 7421), XXXV, pp. 35–6.
31. Magnus, *Edward*, pp. 199–200; Watson, *Leader*, p. 285.
32. NMMCA Records, NRO 759/68, Monthly Report, April 1892, pp. 20–2; Welbourne, *Miners' Unions*, p. 290.
33. *Labour Tribune*, 4 March 1893, p. 7d, 15 April, p. 3a; *Newcastle Daily Leader*, 12 April 1893, p. 6b-d, 13 April, p. 6a, 14 April, p. 8f.
34. NMMCA Records, NRO 759/68, minutes, executive committee meeting, 1 July 1893, p. 51, 7 July 1893, p. 55.
35. *Newcastle Daily Leader*, 26 June 1893, p. 8e.
36. Arnot, *Miners, 1889–1910*, pp. 227–8; NMMCA Records, NRO 759/68, minutes, executive committee meeting, 7, 22 July, 16 August 1893, pp. 56–9, 61–2, 70; report on MFGB meeting, 19–20 July 1893, pp. 18–21.
37. Welbourne, *Miners' Unions*, p. 291; NMMCA Records, NRO 759/68, minutes, executive committee meeting, 29 August 1893, p. 74; *Newcastle Daily Chronicle*, 21 August 1893, p. 4f, 28 August 1893, p. 8b, 27 March 1894, p. 3d.
38. Arnot, *Miners, 1889–1910*, pp. 219–65.
39. Henry Phelps Brown, *The Origin of Trade Union Power* (Oxford, 1983), pp. 43–4.
40. Robert Rhodes James, *Rosebery* (London, 1963), pp. 292–3; Marquess of Crewe, *Lord Rosebery* (London, 1931), vol. 2, p. 433; Smith, *Board of Trade*, p. 182; Armytage, *Mundella*, p. 298.
41. J. F. Clarke, 'Workers in the Tyneside Shipyards in the Nineteenth Century', in Norman McCord (ed.), *Essays in Tyneside Labour History* (Newcastle upon Tyne Polytechnic, 1977), pp. 120–2.
42. *Newcastle Daily Leader*, 22 January 1894, p. 8b-c.
43. See a series of interviews with labour and industrial leaders from the North East in the *Newcastle Daily Leader* beginning 7 December 1893; Ashton, *Adams*, p. 100.
44. Welbourne, *Miners' Unions*, p. 292; Burt, *Autobiography*, p. 202.
45. NMMCA Records, NRO 759/68, minutes, executive committee meetings, January–June 1894; circular by Young, 2 March 1894, pp. 13–17; *Newcastle Daily Chronicle*, 8 January 1894, p. 5d, 27 March, p. 3d; *Newcastle Daily Leader*, 31 January 1894, p. 8a-c; Colin McNiven, 'Ashington: The Growth of a Company Town', *Bulletin of North East Group for the Study of Labour History*, 12 (1978), 5–6.
46. NMMCA Records, NRO 759/68, minutes, executive committee meeting, pp. 29–30, 9 July 1894, p. 35.

47. Ibid., 30 July 1894, p. 42, 23 August, p. 55.
48. 4 *Hansard*, XI (3 May 1893); Arnot, *Miners, 1889–1910*, pp. 190–200; E. Porrit, 'English Labor in and out of Parliament in 1893', *Yale Review*, 2 (February 1894), 420–1; Barker, *Gladstone*, p. 255.
49. *Newcastle Daily Leader*, 26 May 1893, p. 8c-d; Report on the Strikes and Lock-outs of 1891, 1893–94 (C. 6890), LXXXIII, 75–78; NMMCA Records, NRO 759/68, report on the meeting held 14–20 May 1894, in Berlin, pp. 30–1.
50. Ibid., Circulars, 7 January 1895, p. 4, 6 April, p. 6, 5 October, p. 16; *Newcastle Daily Leader*, 22 April 1895, p. 8a.
51. NMMCA Records, NRO 759/68, Burt's address at NMA picnic, 6 July 1895, p. 27.
52. Edward Bristow, 'Profit-Sharing, Socialism and Labour Unrest', in Kenneth Brown (ed.), *Essays in Anti-Labour History* (Hamden, CT, 1974), p. 274.
53. *Newcastle Daily Leader*, 16 January 1895, p. 6c-e; David Powell, 'The Liberal Ministries and Labour, 1892–1895', *History*, 68 (October 1983), 408–26.
54. Burt to Mundella, 11 December 1893, Mundella Papers, 6P/26/28; Home Office Papers, HO 45/9865/B13816 and HO 45/9866/B13816, contain a large number of documents on the bill; 4 *Hansard*, XI (25 April 1893), 1210–13.
55. Bartrip and Burman, *Wounded Soldiers*, pp. 185, 190–8; *Newcastle Daily Leader*, 5 April 1893, p. 8c-d, 23 April 1894, p. 8a.
56. Thomas Burt, 'The House of Lords: A Dangerous Anachronism', *Nineteenth Century*, 35 (April 1894), 547–52.
57. Burt to Stead, 21 January 1895, Stead Papers, STED 1/12.
58. NMMCA Records, NRO 759/68, Celebration of Burt's Appointment, 28 October 1892, pp. 20–1; minutes, delegate meeting, 19 November 1892, p. 25.
59. *Newcastle Daily Chronicle*, 14 September 1895, p. 5c-d.
60. Ibid., 16 September 1895, pp. 4e-5b; *Newcastle Daily Leader*, 14 September 1895, p. 4c-d; *Newcastle Weekly Chronicle*, 21 September 1895, p. 4a-b; *Newcastle Courant*, 21 September 1895, p. 4e. NMMCA Records, NRO 759/68, contain a 32-page report on the opening of Burt Hall, which is taken from the *Newcastle Daily Leader*, 14 and 16 September 1895.
61. Matthew Tate, *Poems, Songs and Ballads* (Blyth, 1898), p. 173.

Chapter 10

1. J. T. Ward, 'Tory Socialist: A Preliminary Note on Michael Maltman Barry (1842–1909)', *Journal of the Scottish Labour History Society*, 2 (April 1970), 25-37; Paul Mertinez, 'The "People's Charter" and the Enigmatic Mr. Maltman Barry', *Bulletin of the Society for the Study of Labour History*, 41 (Autumn 1980), 34–45.
2. *Morpeth Herald*, 13 July 1895, p. 7d-e.
3. *Newcastle Daily Chronicle*, 13 July 1895, p. 5e; *Morpeth Herald*, 13 July 1895, p. 5b, f-g, and 20 July, p. 2c-d.
4. Burt to Mundella, 14 July 1895, Mundella Papers, 6P/28/18.

5. *Morpeth Herald*, 13 July 1895, p. 5g; *Blyth Bi-Weekly News*, 12 July 1895, p. 3c-d, 16 July, p. 3d.
6. *Morpeth Herald*, 20 July 1895, p. 7g.
7. D. A. Hamer, *John Morley, Liberal Intellectual in Politics* (Oxford, 1968), pp. 195–239, 254–80.
8. NMMCA Records, NRO 759/68, Burt speaking at picnic, 1896, pp. 3–5, and voting results, 18, 20 November 1899, p. 37; *Newcastle Daily Leader*, 26 June 1896, p. 8d.
9. NMMCA Records, NRO 759/68, minutes, delegate meeting, 23 June 1897, pp. 1–16.
10. Ibid, NRO 759/68, report on picnic, 3 July 1897, p. 10.
11. McNiven, 'Ashington', p. 9.
12. NMMCA Records, NRO 759/68, minutes, executive committee meeting, 20 September 1897, pp. 45–6; *Newcastle Daily Leader*, 27 August 1897, p. 8d-e, 28 August, p. 8e.
13. See, for example, the minutes of the six meetings of the Joint Committee for 1899, NMMCA Records, NRO 759/68, pp. 3–18; Burt, 'Conciliation in Industrial Disputes', *Trade Unionist*, October 1898, p. 13.
14. NMMCA Records, NRO 759/68, Monthly Circular, October 1898, pp. 49–53; Welbourne, *Miners' Unions*, p. 301.
15. *Trade Unionist*, February 1899, p. 204; NMMCA Records, NRO 759/68, Monthly Report, January 1899, pp. 7–8, September 1899; minutes, executive committee meeting, 11 April 1899, p. 25.
16. Ibid., Monthly Circular, January 1898, pp. 3–5.
17. *Newcastle Daily Leader*, 2 November 1896, p. 8f, 17 December 1896, p. 8c, 11 December 1897, p. 6b.
18. Ibid., 11 December 1897, p. 6c.
19. Ibid., 1 November 1898, p. 5c.
20. Newton, *British Labour*, p. 65; *Arbitrator*, April 1899, p. 87a-b.
21. Thomas Pakenham, *The Boer War* (New York, 1979).
22. *Newcastle Daily Leader*, 11 December 1897, p. 6c.
23. NMMCA Records, NRO 759/68, report on picnic, 1 July 1899, pp. 1–11.
24. Watson, *Leader*, pp. 196–200; *Newcastle Daily Chronicle*, 6 October 1899, p. 5a-b; *Newcastle Daily Leader*, 12 October 1899, p. 8a-d.
25. 4 *Hansard*, XCIII (2 May 1901), 527; Watson, *Leader*, p. 200.
26. Tsiang, *Labor and Empire*, pp. 77–83, 94–5; Newton, *British Labour*, pp. 101–3; Bernard Porter, *Critics of Empire: British Radical Attitudes to Colonialism in Africa, 1895–1914* (London, 1968), pp. 123–37.
27. Evans, *Cremer*, p. 216; I.A.L., 'Twelve Reasons Why War Is Hateful and Arbitration Is Preferable' [1900] and 'Now Tell Us All About the War', which was reissued under the title 'Labour Leaders and the War', of which one million copies were reportedly distributed to workmen, *Arbitrator*, January 1900, pp. 4–5, July 1900, p. 41.
28. *Arbitrator*, October 1899, p. 108.
29. Stephen Koss (ed.), *The Pro-Boers* (Chicago, 1973), pp. 38–45.
30. Ibid., pp. 99–100.
31. Ibid., pp. 176–7; *Reformers' Year Book*, 1902, p. 51, 1903, p. 115.
32. NMMCA Records, NRO 759/68, report on picnic, 21 July 1900, pp. 15–16.

33. *Newcastle Daily Chronicle*, 26 September 1900, p. 7e, 2 October, p. 6g, 3 October, pp. 6g-7a; *Morpeth Herald*, 29 September 1900, p. 5e; *Newcastle Daily Journal*, 29 September 1900, p. 8e.
34. *Blyth News*, 2 October 1900, p. 2h.
35. *Newcastle Daily Leader*, 1 October 1900, p. 6g, 27 September, p. 8a.
36. Ibid., 25 September 1900, p. 8g, 3 September, p. 5a; Hodgson, *Annand*, pp. 146–7.
37. *Newcastle Daily Leader*, 25 September 1900, p. 8g, 1 October, p. 7a, 3 October, p. 5g; *Newcastle Daily Chronicle*, 25 September 1900, p. 5f, 29 September, p. 7d.
38. Ibid. 26 September 1900, p. 7d-e; *Morpeth Herald*, 6 October 1900, p. 3d.
39. *Newcastle Daily Leader*, 26 September 1900, p. 7f, 1 October, p. 6g.
40. *Blyth News*, 28 September 1900, p. 2g.
41. *Newcastle Daily Leader*, 4 October 1900, p. 8e, 5 October, p. 8d.
42. Burt to Stead, 12 December 1900, Stead Papers, STED 1/12; NMMCA Records, NRO 759/68, Monthly Circular, September 1900, p. 54.
43. *Newcastle Daily Chronicle*, 4 October 1900, p. 7c-d; *Newcastle Daily Journal*, 4 October 1900, p. 4f; Henry Pelling, *Popular Politics and Society in Late Victorian Britain* (London, 1979; 2nd edn), p. 94.
44. *Newcastle Daily Leader*, 29 September 1900, p. 4g.
45. Martin Pugh, *The Tories and the People 1880–1935* (Oxford, 1985), p. 128.
46. NMMCA Records, NRO 759/68, report on picnic, July 1901, pp. 13–15.
47. Ibid., NRO 759/43, Young's diary, 13 July 1901.
48. *Newcastle Daily Leader*, 19 November 1901, p. 8d, 11 January 1902, p. 8c-d.
49. NMMCA Records, NRO 759/68, Monthly Circular, December 1900, pp. 65–7.
50. *Newcastle Daily Leader*, 21 July 1902, p. 8a.
51. NMMCA Records, NRO 759/68, minutes, executive committee meeting, 23 January 1900, p. 4; *Newcastle Daily Leader*, 29 January 1900, p. 8c.
52. *Newcastle Daily Leader*, 21 July 1902, p. 8a.
53. Jack Davison, *Northumberland Miners 1919–1939* (Newcastle upon Tyne, 1973), pp. 233–4.
54. NMMCA Records, NRO 759/68, Monthly Circular, August 1901, pp. 40–2; *Newcastle Daily Leader*, 2 September 1901, p. 5e-f.
55. NMMCA Records, NRO 759/A2/66, Jubilee Souvenir of Northumberland Aged Miners' Homes Association.
56. Elie Halevy, *Imperialism and the Rise of Labour* (London, 1961), pp. 318–21.
57. NMMCA Records, NRO 759/68, Monthly Circular, April and May 1901, pp. 22–4.
58. *Newcastle Daily Chronicle*, 26 April 1901, p. 5a–c; *Newcastle Daily Leader*, 20 April 1901, p. 8, 22 April, p. 5a-e; Miners' Federation of Great Britain Records [MFGB Records], minutes, Miners' National Conference, London, 25, 26, 29, 30 April, 1 May 1901; NMMCA Records, NRO 759/68, minutes, miners' deputation to Hicks Beach, 29 April 1901, pp. 1–23; report, delegate meeting, 4 May 1901, pp. 21–3, 28; *Manchester Guardian*, 1 May 1901, p. 5c.

59. 4 *Hansard*, XCIII (2 May 1901), 526–35.
60. NMMCA Records, NRO 759/68, Monthly Circular, June 1901, p. 31.
61. *Newcastle Daily Leader*, 24 June 1903, p. 5d; NMMCA Records, NRO 759/68, several of Burt's Monthly Circulars in 1904, and December 1905; 4 *Hansard*, CXXIV (23 June 1903), 301–3; CXXXVIII (20 July 1904), 624–5; CXLVII (29 May 1905), 138–9; Arnot, *Miners, 1889–1910*, p. 342.
62. NMMCA Records, NRO 759/68, Monthly Circular, June 1902, pp. 9–10; report, picnic, 19 July 1902; Burt to Harcourt, 3 March 1904, Harcourt Papers, MS 245/fols. 70–1.
63. NMMCA Records, NRO 759/68, Monthly Circular, June 1902, p. 13.
64. *Newcastle Daily Leader*, 9 October 1902, p. 8d-f.
65. Ibid., 22 January 1896, p. 8d.
66. Meech, *Burt*, pp. 95–8; *Newcastle Daily Chronicle*, 10 May 1904, p. 9a.
67. 4 *Hansard*, CXXXIV (9 May 1904), 778–87, quotations from 779, 784, 785.
68. A. M. Gollin, *Proconsul in Politics: A Study of Lord Milner in Opposition and in Power* (New York, 1964), pp. 53–75.
69. NMMCA Records, NRO 759/68, Monthly Circular, August 1903, pp. 39–41.
70. Ibid., January 1904, pp. 4–7.
71. Ibid., March 1904, pp. 16–19, April 1904, pp. 21–3.
72. *Newcastle Daily Chronicle*, 27 May 1904, p. 9b.
73. NMMCA Records, NRO 759/68, minutes, executive committee meeting, 31 August 1904, p. 40; Monthly Circular, September 1904, pp. 57–8; Watson, *Leader*, p. 201.
74. Thomas Burt, *A Visit to the Transvaal; Labour: White, Black, and Yellow* (Newcastle upon Tyne, 1905), quotations from pp. 13, 16, 30, 40, 66, 68.
75. Watson, *Leader*, p. 202; NMMCA Records, NRO 759/68, Monthly Circulars, June 1905, pp. 18–19, July 1906, pp. 23–5; 4 *Hansard*, CXLIX (13 July 1905), 549, and (18 July 1905), 1059–60; CL (27 July 1905), 686–8.
76. NMMCA Records, NRO 759/68, Monthly Circular, December 1905, pp. 60–2.

Chapter 11

1. Independent Labour Party, 'The Miners and Labour Representation' (n.d., c. 1906), p. 1.
2. Burt to Runciman, 15 February 1901, Walter Runciman Papers, WR 2; James Lemon to Runciman, 12 March 1906, WR 15.
3. *Blyth News*, 5 January 1906, p. 3f; G. O. Trevelyan to Runciman, 27 June 1905, Runciman Papers, WR 11.
4. A. W. Purdue, 'Jarrow Politics, 1885–1914: The Challenge to Liberal Hegemony', *Northern History*, 18 (1982), p. 182; Burt to Runciman, 17 January 1902, Runciman Papers, WR 5.
5. *Morpeth Herald*, 13 January 1906, p. 3b-c; *Newcastle Daily Journal*, 13 January 1906, p. 8c.

6. Burt, *Autobiography*, pp. 302–3; *Newcastle Daily Chronicle*, 3 January 1906, p. 7e; *Morpeth Herald*, 13 January 1906, p. 5a.
7. Burt to Greenwood, 29 March 1904, Weiss Papers.
8. Burt to Fred Burns, 17 January 1902, Runciman Papers, WR 5, and Burt to Runciman, 13 November 1905, WR 11.
9. *Morpeth Herald*, 13 January 1906, p. 3c-d, 20 January, p. 3a-b; *Newcastle Daily Chronicle*, 1 January 1906, p. 3b-c, 5 January, p. 12d, 9 January, p. 8d-e, 10 January, p. 9b.
10. *Blyth News*, 12 January 1906, p. 2d, 16 January, p. 2c; *Newcastle Daily Chronicle*, 15 January 1906, p. 7e-f.
11. Hodgson, *Annand*, p. 174.
12. NMMCA Records, NRO 759/68, executive committee meeting, 13 July 1906, pp. 49–50; result of vote on Federation question, 3 September 1907, pp. 43–4; Monthly Circular, September 1907, pp. 49–50.
13. R. M. Hodnett, *Politics and the Northumberland Miners: Liberals and Labour in Morpeth and Wansbeck, 1890–1922* (Cleveland, 1994), pp. 14–15.
14. Roy Gregory, *The Miners and British Politics 1906–1914* (London, 1968), p. 69; Frank Bealey and Henry Pelling, *Labour and Politics 1900–1906* (London, 1958), p. 163. Williamson, *Class*, pp. 69–72, describes how the village of Throckley gradually switched from Liberal to the ILP in the early 1900s.
15. *Blyth News*, 17 July 1906, p. 3c, 20 July, p. 3f; *Newcastle Daily Chronicle*, 16 July 1906, p. 8b.
16. NMMCA Records, NRO 759/68, article on Young's death, 17 December 1904, article on Boyle's death, 1907; Frederick Rogers, *Labour, Life and Literature* (London, 1913), pp. 230–3.
17. *Morpeth Herald*, 21 July 1906, p. 7d; *DLB*, II, 359–60; NMMCA Records, NRO 759/68, minutes, executive committee meeting, 29 April 1907, pp. 35–7.
18. Ashton, *Adams*, pp. 171, 172; *Morpeth Herald*, 13 October 1900, p. 2d; Todd, *Cowen*, p. 164.
19. For a review of this debate, especially as it applies to the North East, see Hodnett, *Politics*, pp. 3–6, and Duncan Tanner, *Political Change and the Labour Party, 1900–1918* (Cambridge, 1990), pp. 205–6.
20. *Labour Leader*, 20 July 1906, p. 133b.
21. *Morpeth Herald*, 14 July 1906, p. 5d, 28 July p. 3c-d, 1 September, p. 6g-h, 8 September, p. 2e-f.
22. *Northern Democrat*, August 1906, p. 1.
23. *Labour Leader*, 28 September 1906, p. 296c; *Morpeth Herald*, 6 October 1906, p. 2c.
24. ILP, 'Miners'; G. Jones to L.R.C., 26 July 1905, Labour Party Papers, LRC 24/399.
25. *Newcastle Daily Leader*, 29 December 1898, p. 6e.
26. Bealey and Pelling, *Labour*, p. 148.
27. *Newcastle Daily Chronicle*, 13 October 1906, p. 7f.
28. *Morpeth Herald*, 16 November 1907, p. 3b.
29. Ibid., 26 October 1907, p. 3a-d.
30. E. P. Hennock, *British Social Reforms and German Precedents: The Case of Social Insurance 1880–1914* (Oxford, 1987), pp. 118–19;

the Parliamentary Paper, known as 'Burt's Return', is 'Return ... of the Number of Persons ... in Receipt of In-door relief and of Out-door Relief Aged over 60 Returned in Quinquenniel Groups on 1st August 1890', 1890–1 (36), LXVIII.

31. Bentley B. Gilbert, *The Evolution of National Insurance in Great Britain: The Origins of the Welfare State* (London, 1966), pp. 188–90.

32. Pelling, *Popular Politics*, pp. 10–12.

33. 4 *Hansard*, XLIX (17 May 1897), 706; *Newcastle Daily Chronicle*, 29 July 1895, p. 5.

34. Quotation from *Newcastle Daily Leader*, 7 December 1898, p. 5c. See also ibid., 12 August 1895, p. 8c-d; NMMCA Records, NRO 759/68, Monthly Circular, July 1898, pp. 34–6.

35. Francis Herbert Stead, *How Old Age Pensions Began to Be* (London, [1909]), pp. 45–6, 63; Pat Thane, 'Non-Contributory Versus Insurance Pensions 1878–1908', in Pat Thane (ed.), *The Origins of British Social Policy* (Totowa, NJ, 1978), pp. 91–6; Gilbert, *National Insurance*, pp. 188–90.

36. Hennock, *British Social Reforms*, pp. 117–25.

37. Stead, *Old Age Pensions*, pp. 207–9, 213, 220–2; NMMCA Records, NRO 759/68, report on picnic, 14 July 1906, pp. 22–6; Monthly Circular, November 1906, pp. 62–5.

38. Thomas Burt, 'Old-Age Pensions', *Nineteenth Century and After*, 60 (September 1906), pp. 376–7.

39. *Newcastle Daily Chronicle*, 4 December 1907, p. 7.

40. NMMCA Records, NRO 759/68, Monthly Circular, May 1908, p. 31; 4 *Hansard*, CXC (16 June 1908), 744; *Newcastle Daily Chronicle*, 26 January 1909, p. 7d; Stead, *Old Age Pensions*, p. 259.

41. Ibid., p. 295; Rogers, *Labour*, p. 268.

42. Price, *Labour*, pp. 141–2; Norman McCord, 'Taff Vale Revisited', *History*, 78 (February 1993), 243–60.

43. NMMCA Records, NRO 759/68, Monthly Circular, August 1900, pp. 47–8, July 1901, pp. 33–6.

44. Ibid., January 1902, p. 8.

45. Ibid., August 1902, pp. 23–4, December 1902, pp. 48–53; Pelling, *Popular Politics*, pp. 74–9.

46. John Lovell, 'Trade unions and the development of independent labour politics 1889–1906', in Ben Pimlott and Chris Cook (eds), *Trade Unions in British Politics* (London, 1982), pp. 49–52; Bealey and Pelling, *Labour*, pp. 73–97.

47. Wilson, *CB*, pp. 504–5; David Powell, *British Politics and the Labour Question, 1868–1990* (New York, 1992), pp. 34–5.

48. NMMCA Records, NRO 759/68, minutes, delegate meeting, 21, 23, 28 March 1908, pp. 10–11; minutes, executive committee meeting, 13 May 1908, p. 49.

49. NMA members cast 14,331 votes in favour of the affiliation with the LRC, while 10,169 opposed it; MFGB members as a whole favoured joining by a vote of 213,137 to 168,446; Howell, *British Workers*, p. 51. Howell's numbers for NMA members voting 'against' affiliation is incorrect. NMMCA Records, NRO 759/68, minutes, executive committee meeting, 13 May 1908, pp. 49–51.

50. Ibid., Monthly Circular, October 1908, p. 69. For an explanation of the need for the pledge, see Gwyn, *Democracy*, pp. 173–7.
51. NMMCA Records, NRO 759/68, Monthly Circular, March 1908, p. 22.
52. *Newcastle Daily Chronicle*, 24 November 1908, p. 7e.
53. *Morpeth Herald*, 18 September 1909, p. 10a-b.
54. Ibid., 25 September 1909, p. 6a-c.
55. Ibid., 25 April 1908, pp. 7a-b, 10a, 9 October 1909, p. 10c-d.
56. Ibid., 16 October 1909, p. 4a-e.
57. Ibid., 30 October 1909, p. 10a-f; for an explanation of the differences between Burt and liberalism and the Labour Party, see *Blyth News*, 3 May 1910, p. 3e-f.
58. *Northern Democrat*, October 1909, p. 2; *Labour Leader*, 5 November 1909, p. 712c; *Manchester Guardian*, 27 October 1909, p. 10b, 1 November, p. 8f-g; *Daily News*, October–December 1909; *Pall Mall Gazette*, 25 October 1909, p. 1a; *Northern Echo*, 23 October 1909, p. 4c-d; *Newcastle Daily Chronicle*, 1 November 1909, p. 6a, 22 November, p. 12d; *Spectator*, 30 October 1909, p. 671.
59. Heatley's estimate is confirmed by Gregory, *Miners*, p. 96. Loss of some miners as Liberals probably explains why the number of members in the Liberal Club for the Borough of Morpeth dropped from 300 in 1907 to 150 in 1910, *Liberal Year Book* (London; reprint, Brighton, 1972), for year 1907, p. 169, for year 1910, p. 147.
60. *Morpeth Herald*, 6 November 1909, p. 6.
61. *Newcastle Daily Chronicle*, 15 November 1909, p. 7c. See several letters in 1909 over the Northumberland constituencies: Independent Labour Party [ILP] Collection, T. H. Baird, Secretary of the Northumberland District Council of ILP to Francis Johnson, General Secretary, ILP, 5 November 1909, ILP 4/1909/490; W. E. Moll to Johnson, 9 November, ILP 4/1909/497; Baird to Johnson, 15 November, ILP 4/1909/506; Baird to Johnson, 18 November, ILP 4/1909/513; M. T. Simm to Keir Hardie, 19 November, ILP 4/1909/520; Hardie to Simm, 23 November, ILP 4/1909/531; Walter M. Gillians, Ashington Colliery, to Johnson, 28 November, ILP 4/1909/528; Johnson to Baird, 29 November, ILP 4/1909/551.
62. Labour Party Papers, Minutes, National Executive Committee, 2 December 1909; Gregory, *Miners*, p. 76.
63. *Newcastle Daily Chronicle*, 30 December 1909, p. 5b.
64. Gregory, *Miners*, p. 76.
65. *Newcastle Daily Journal*, 15 December 1909, p. 3e.
66. A ballot of all the miners (13,374 to 11,696) confirmed that Burt and Fenwick had to sign the constitution of the Labour Party, but subsequently the NMA council (47 to 39) and the lodges (347 to 219) voted not to run candidates. *Morpeth Herald*, 4 December 1909, p. 10a-b, 18 December, p. 10f, 25 December, p. 4d. See also Hardie's comments on these developments, *Labour Leader*, 17 December 1909, p. 1.
67. *Newcastle Daily Chronicle*, 10 December 1909, p. 3f, 29 December, p. 7a-b; *Newcastle Daily Journal*, 14 December 1909, p. 7a-d, 23 December, p. 10e.
68. *Blyth News*, 7 January 1910, p. 4c; *Morpeth Herald*, 1 January 1910, p. 6c-d.

69. Ibid., p. 10c-d; Burt's election address of 1910, NRO 760; *Newcastle Daily Chronicle*, 5 January 1910, p. 16c.
70. *Morpeth Herald*, 8 January 1910, p. 10b; *Newcastle Daily Chronicle*, 13 January 1910, p. 11f, 17 January, p. 9f; *Blyth News*, 18 January 1910, p. 2e, 25 January, p. 3f.
71. Pugh, *British Politics*, p. 134; G. D. H. Cole, *British Working Class Politics 1832–1914* (London, 4th impression, 1965; first published 1941), p. 201.
72. Raymond Challinor, *The Origins of British Bolshevism* (London, 1977), pp. 73–4.
73. NMMCA Records, NRO 759/68, minutes, executive committee meeting, 25 April 1910, p. 45; proxy vote, May 1910, annual meeting, p. 54.
74. *Newcastle Daily Chronicle*, 22 November 1910, p. 3b-c.
75. Ibid., 23 May 1911, p. 8a.
76. Hodnett, *Politics*, pp. 23–4; Tanner, *Political Change*, pp. 214–15, 220, 222; A. W. Purdue, 'The Liberal and Labour Parties in North-East Politics, 1900–1914: The Struggle for Supremacy', *International Review of Social History*, 26 (1981), 15–23.
77. NMMCA Records, NRO 759/68, report on picnic, 20 August 1910, p. 21.
78. Lovell, 'Trade Unions', pp. 70–1.
79. NMMCA Records, NRO 759/68, Monthly Circular, March 1912, p. 18, and report on picnic, 15 July 1911, p. 20.
80. *Northern Democrat*, May 1912, p. 1.
81. NMMCA Records, NRO 759/68, Monthly Circular, March 1912, p. 18.
82. Ibid., Monthly Circular, December 1911, pp. 91–3.
83. *Morpeth Herald*, 3 October 1908, p. 3a-c.
84. NMMCA Records, NRO 759/68, Monthly Circular, May 1911, pp. 34–7.
85. *Newcastle Daily Chronicle*, 12 February 1912, p. 3c-e.
86. Burt, *Autobiography*, p. 313; NMMCA Records, NRO 759/68, Monthly Circulars for 1912, especially July, pp. 51–2.
87. Burt to Straker, 10 February 1913, NMMCA Records, NRO 759/28.
88. Ibid., NRO 759/68, minutes, annual meeting, 17 May 1913, pp. 24–5, also include Burt's letter of resignation. Burt's remark on 'advice' was recalled at his 80th birthday party, *Newcastle Weekly Chronicle*, 17 November 1917, p. 5d.
89. NMMCA Records, NRO 759/68, Monthly Circular, June 1913, p. 46.

Chapter 12

1. H. S. Jevons, *The British Coal Trade* (London, 1920; 2nd edn), p. 678; Mitchell, *Economic Development*, p. 18; Church, *British Coal Industry*, p. 189.
2. NMMCA Records, NRO 759/68, report on picnic, 22 July 1905, p. 2, and Compensation for Accidents for 1910, in 1911 minutes book, pp. 1–7; *Newcastle Daily Chronicle*, 16 July 1906, p. 8b.
3. NMMCA Records, NRO 759/52-53, English's diary, 1907–08.
4. Ibid., NRO 759/53, printed list included in loose paper file of English's diary, 1908.
5. *Newcastle Daily Chronicle*, 21 July 1913, p. 9a. Williamson, *Class*, pp. 85–9, discusses accidents in the Northumberland coal fields.

6. *Socialist*, April 1909, p. 1a-d.
7. Duckham, *Disasters*, pp. 202–9, for listing.
8. Watson, *Leader*, pp. 274–81; *Newcastle Weekly Chronicle*, 5 October 1907, p. 12c-d.
9. *Durham Chronicle*, 30 June 1911, p. 7c-d.
10. *Morpeth Herald*, 8 December 1911, p. 3a-d.
11. *Newcastle Daily Chronicle*, 20 January 1912, p. 7a-c; Burt, *Autobiography*, pp. 307–8.
12. *Daily Citizen*, 6 May 1913, pp. 1a-b, 2c; *Newcastle Daily Chronicle*, 6 May 1913, p. 5c; Burt, *Autobigraphy*, pp. 290–1.
13. *Labour Leader*, 22 May 1913, p. 14b.
14. NMMCA Records, NRO 759/68, Monthly Circular, January 1914, pp. 1–2.
15. Keith Robbins, *The Abolition of War: The 'Peace Movement' in Britain, 1914–1919* (Cardiff, 1976), pp. 8–12.
16. Burt, *Autobiography*, pp. 308–12; *The Times*, 18 June 1914, p. 10d.
17. *Arbitrator*, July 1914, p. 79b.
18. *Newcastle Daily Chronicle*, 5 August 1914, p. 6b.
19. Burt, *Autobiography*, p. 312; Burt's forward to Jonathan Dymond, *War: Its Causes, Consequences, Lawfulness, etc.* (London, 1915; first published 1823), p. iv.
20. NMMCA Records, NRO 759/68, Monthly Circular, December 1917, p. 118; Watson, in Burt, *Autobiography*, p. 312, states that Burt looked forward to a 'League of Nations ... to preserve and enforce peace'.
21. Tsiang, *Labor and Empire*, pp. 173–83.
22. 'Thomas Burt Album', Newcastle Public Central Library, Local Studies Department.
23. Interview with Peter Burt, Jr.
24. NMMCA Records, NRO 759/68, Monthly Circular, December 1917, p. 116.
25. *Morpeth Herald*, 8 December 1911, p. 3d-f.
26. *The Times*, 29 August 1919, p. 10d. Others who benefited were David Lloyd George, Lord Morley, John Wilson and John Burns.
27. Shepherd, 'Labour', p. 211.
28. Hodnett, *Politics*, pp. 25–31.
29. *Newcastle Daily Chronicle*, 15 April 1922, p. 2b-e.
30. *Illustrated Chronicle*, 20 April 1922, p. 16, includes photographs of the funeral; *Newcastle Daily Chronicle*, 20 April 1922, p. 10e-f.
31. *Colliery Guardian*, 21 April 1922, p. 985b-c; *Blyth News*, 18 April 1922, p. 3g; *Newcastle Daily Chronicle*, 15 April 1922, p. 2b-e; *Newcastle Daily Journal*, 15 April 1922, p. 6c; *Co-operative News*, 22 April 1922, p. 9c.
32. *Manchester Guardian*, 15 April 1922, p. 4e.
33. *Newcastle Daily Chronicle*, 15 April 1922, p. 4a.
34. *Daily News*, 15 April 1922, p. 4d.
35. *Durham Chronicle*, 21 April 1922, pp. 2c, 4g.
36. Information from Paul Talbot, curator of the museum.
37. Foundation stones for the homes were laid on 15 April 1922, two days after Burt died; *Newcastle Daily Chronicle*, 17 April 1922, p. 8b.

38. Towns with 'Burt' street names include North Shields, Peterlee, Newcastle, Cramlington, Morpeth, Bedlington, Blyth and Haswell.

Chapter 13

1. NMMCA Records, NRO 759/68, Monthly Circular, April 1922, pp. 50–3.
2. Fynes, *Miners*, p. 257.

BIBLIOGRAPHY

1. Manuscripts Consulted: Individuals

H. H. Asquith Papers. Bodleian Library
Benson (Newbrough) Papers. Northumberland Record Office
Charles Bradlaugh Papers. Bishopsgate Institute
Henry Broadhurst Papers. London School of Economics
John Burns Papers. British Library
Henry Campbell-Bannerman Papers. British Library
Joseph Cowen Papers. Tyne and Wear Archives
Charles Dilke Papers. British Library
Forster (Newcastle) Papers. Northumberland Record Office
William Gladstone Papers. British Library
Herbert Gladstone Papers. British Library
William Harcourt Papers. Bodleian Library
George Howell Papers. Microfilm, based on collection at Bishopsgate
    Institute, London
A. J. Mundella Papers. Sheffield University Library
Lord Rosebery Papers. National Library of Scotland
Walter Runciman Papers. University of Newcastle upon Tyne Library
W. T. Stead Papers. Churchill Archives Centre
Charles Philips Trevelyan Papers. University of Newcastle upon Tyne
    Library
James Trotter Papers. Northumberland Record Office
Webb Trade Union Collection. London School of Economics
M. I. Weiss Papers. Contain the R. Spence Watson MSS. Copies of letters
    provided by David Saunders, Newcastle

2. Manuscripts Consulted: Organizations

Ashington Mineworkers' Federation, Minutes. Northumberland Record
    Office
Church of Divine Unity, Newcastle, Papers. Tyne and Wear Archives
Durham Miners' Association Records. Durham County Record Office

Independent Labour Party Collection. London School of Economics

International Arbitration and Peace Association, Annual Reports. London
School of Economics

Labour Representation League, Minutes. London School of Economics

Labour Party Papers. National Museum of Labour History, Manchester

Labour Party Minutes, Letters, etc., 1900–1912. London School of Economics,
British Library of Political and Economic Science

Miners' Federation of Great Britain Records. National Union of Miners,
Sheffield

National Coal Board Records. Northumberland Record Office

National Union of Mineworkers, Burradon Branch, Minutes and Accounts.
Northumberland Record Office

Northumberland Aged Mineworkers' Homes Association Minute Book.
Northumberland Record Office

Northumberland & Durham Miners' Permanent Relief Fund Records. Tyne
and Wear Archives

Northumberland Coal Trade Arbitration Awards. Northumberland Record
Office

Northumberland and Durham Coal Owners' Association Records. Steam
Collieries' Association and Steam Collieries' Defence Association Minutes.
Northumberland Record Office

Northumberland Branch of the National Union of Miners Records.
Northumberland Record Office

Northumberland Miners' Mutual Confidence Association Records.
Northumberland Record Office

Northumberland Record Office [NRO]. Parish and other local records

Trades Union Congress, Annual Reports

Universal Peace Congress, Proceedings. London School of Economics

3. Government Collections and Publications: Great Britain

Board of Trade Papers

Home Office Papers

Hansard Parliamentary Debates

Sessional Papers:

First Report, Children's Employment Commission, 1842 (380), XV.
Appendix to First Report, Part I, 1842 (381), XVI

Report from the Commissioner ... Mining Districts, 1846 (737), XXIV;
1847 (844), XVI; 1849 (1109), XXII; 1850 (1248), XXIII; 1851 (1406),
XXIII; 1854 (1838), XIX

Report from the Select Committee on Mines, 1866 (431), XIV

Report from the Select Committee on Merchant Seamen Bill, 1878 (205),
XVI

Preliminary Report of Her Majesty's Commissioners Appointed to Inquire
into Accidents in Mines, 1881 (C. 3036), XXVI; Final Report, 1886 (C.
4699), XVI

Return ... of the Number of Persons ... in Receipt of In-door relief and of
Out-door Relief Aged over 60 Returned in Quinquenniel Groups on 1st
August 1890, 1890–1 (36), LXVIII

Correspondence Respecting the Proposed Labour Conference at Berlin, 1890 (C. 5914), LXXXI; Correspondence, 1890 (C. 6042), LXXXI; Reports on Recommendations, 1890–91 (C. 6371), LXXXIII

Report on the Strikes and Lock-outs of 1891, 1893–94 (C. 6890), LXXXIII

Final Report of the Royal Commission Appointed to Inquire into the Subject of Mining Royalties, 1893-4 (C. 6980), XLI

First Report of the Royal Commission on Labour, 1892 (C. 6708), XXXIV; Fifth and Final Report, 1894 (C. 7421), XXXV

4. Newspapers and Journals

Arbitrator
Bee-Hive
Biograph and Review
Birmingham Daily Post
Black and White
Blyth Weekly News, later *Blyth Bi-Weekly News* and *Blyth News*
British Miner & General Newsman
Capital and Labour
Colliery Guardian
Commonweal
Co-operative News
Daily Citizen
Daily News
Durham Chronicle
Englishwoman's Review
Illustrated Chronicle
Labour Leader
Labour Tribune
Manchester Guardian
Miner
Miner and Workman's Advocate, later *Workman's Advocate*
Miners' Advocate and Record
Miners' National Gazette
Miners' Watchman and Labour Sentinel
Morpeth Herald
Newcastle Courant
Newcastle Critic
Newcastle Daily Chronicle
Newcastle Daily Leader
Newcastle Guardian
Newcastle Journal
Newcastle Weekly Chronicle
Northern Democrat
Northern Echo
Pall Mall Gazette
Reynolds's Newspaper
St Helens Newspaper & Advertiser
Shields Evening News

Socialist
Spectator
The Times
Trade Unionist
Tyneside Daily Echo, later *Tyneside Echo*
Workman's Times

5. Contemporary Sources: Books, Articles, Collections of Letters, Autobiographies

Adams, W.E. *Memoirs of a Social Atom*. 2 vols. New York: Augustus M. Kelley, 1968; reprint of 1st edn of 1903.

[Addy, David]. *Dusty Diamonds*. [1910; Welbourne lists the publishing date as 1900, the author as David Addy].

Burt, Thomas. *An Autobiography* (With supplementary chapters by Aaron Watson). London: T. Fisher Unwin, 1924.

——. 'Conciliation in Industrial Disputes', *Trade Unionist* (October 1898), p. 13.

——. 'Forty Years in the House'. *Strand Magazine*, 50 (1915), 492–500.

——. 'The House of Lords: A Dangerous Anachronism'. *Nineteenth Century*, 35 (April 1894), 547–52.

——. 'Industrial Harmony: How Attained'. *Shipping World* (15 April 1908), pp. 434–6.

——. 'Labour in Parliament'. *Contemporary Review*, 55 (May 1889), 678–91.

——. 'Labour Leaders on the Labour Question: Mr. Chamberlain's Programme'. *Nineteenth Century*, 32 (December 1892), 864–74.

——. 'The Labour Party and the Books That Helped to Make It'. *Review of Reviews* (June 1906), pp. 569–70.

——. 'Methodism and the Northern Miners'. *Primitive Methodist Quarterly Review* (July 1882), pp. 385–97.

——. 'Old-Age Pensions'. *Nineteenth Century and After*, 60 (September 1906), 372–8.

——. 'The Thomas Burt Album' (letters and papers on the presentation of a bust of Burt unveiled 21 September 1915). Newcastle Public Central Library, Local Studies Department.

——. 'Thomas Burt Address at Bedlington'. *Shields Daily Gazette and Shipping Telegraph*, 10 November 1881.

——. 'Trade Unions and the Working Classes'. *Co-operative Wholesale Society Annual*, 1885, pp. 374–78.

——. *A Visit to the Transvaal; Labour: White, Black, and Yellow*. Newcastle upon Tyne: Co-operative Printing Society, 1905.

——. 'Working Men and the Political Situation'. *Nineteenth Century*, 9 (April 1881), 611–22.

——. 'Working Men and War'. *Fortnightly Review*, 32 (December 1882), 718–27.

Chamberlain, Joseph. 'The Labour Question'. *Nineteenth Century*, 32 (November 1892), 677–710.

Davis, Hayne (ed.). *Among the World's Peacemakers*. New York: Progressive Publishing, 1907.

Davis, W. J. *The British Trades Union Congress: History and Recollections*. New York: Garland, 1984; first published 1910.

Dymond, Jonathan (foreword by Thomas Burt). *War: Its Causes, Consequences, Lawfulness, etc.* London: Society of Friends, 1915; first published 1823.

Evans, Howard. *Sir Randal Cremer*. Boston: Ginn, 1910.

Freeland, Dr Alan (trans. and ed.). 'Letters of a Portuguese Consul, 1877–79'. *Bulletin of the North East Labour History Society*, no. 18 (1984), 29–40.

Fynes, Richard. *The Miners of Northumberland and Durham*. Newcastle: Davis Books, 1986; reprint, first published 1873.

Ginswick, Jules (ed.). *Labour and the Poor in England and Wales, 1849–1851*. Vol. 2. London: Frank Cass, 1983.

Greenwell, George Clemerson. *A Glossary of Terms Used in the Coal Trade of Northumberland and Durham*. 3rd edn. London: Bemrose & Sons, 1888.

Hallam, William (ed.). *Miners' Leaders*. London: Bemrose & Sons, [1894].

Healy, T. M. *Letters and Leaders of My Day*. Vol. 1. New York: Frederick A. Stokes, 1929.

Hodgson, Geo. B. *From Smithy to Senate: The Life Story of James Annand*. London: Cassell, 1908.

Holyoake, George Jacob. *The Life of Thomas Burt, M.P.* London: Walter Scott, 1895.

Howell, George. *Labour Legislation, Labour Leaders, and Labour Movements*. London: T. Fisher Unwin, 1902.

——. *Trade Unionism New and Old*. Brighton: Harvester Press, 1973; 4th rev. edn 1907, first published in 1891.

Independent Labour Party. 'The Miners and Labour Representation'. n.d., c. 1906. In John Burns Library, TUC.

International Arbitration League. 'Twelve Reasons Why War Is Hateful and Arbitration Is Preferable'. London [1900].

Leifchild, J.R. *Our Coal and Our Coal-Pits*. London: Frank Cass, 1968 (reprint); first published London: Longman, Brown, Green and Longmans, 1856.

Liberal Year Book 1905, 1907 and 1910. London: Liberal Publications Department; reprint, Brighton: Harvester Press, 1972.

Lucy, Henry W. *A Diary of the Home Rule Parliament, 1892–1895*. London: Cassell, 1896.

Mahon, J. L. *A Plea for Socialism. Delivered in the Course of a Socialist Campaign Amongst the Miners on Strike in Northumberland*. London: Commonweal Office, 1887.

Mann, Tom. *Memoirs*. London: Labour Publishing, 1923.

Martin, R.W. (collector). *An Interesting Collection Commencing in 1645 of the Freemen of Newcastle-upon-Tyne, down to 1928*. Newcastle Public Central Library, Local History Collection.

Meech, Thomas Cox. *From Mine to Ministry: The Life and Times of Thomas Burt, M.P.* [1908].

Mill, John Stuart. *Principles of Political Economy*. 2 vols. New York: Appleton, 1901 [from 5th London edn].

Porrit, E. 'English Labor in and out of Parliament in 1893'. *Yale Review*, 2 (February 1894), 418–34.

Price, L.L.F.R. *Industrial Peace*. London: Macmillan, 1887.

Reformers' Yearbook. London: 1902, 1903.

Rogers, Frederick. *Labour, Life and Literature*. London: Smith, Elder, 1913.

Ruskin, John. *'Unto This Last'*. London: Oxford University Press, 1934.

Smith, Adam. *An Inquiry into the Nature and Causes of the Wealth of Nations*. New York: Modern Library, 1937.

Stead, Francis Herbert. *How Old Age Pensions Began to Be*. London: Methuen, [1909].

Tate, Matthew. *Poems, Songs and Ballads*. Blyth: 1898.

Thornton, William T. *On Labour, Its Wrongful Claims and Rightful Dues, Its Actual Present and Possible Future*. Shannon: Irish University Press, 1971; reprint of 2nd edn, London, 1870, 1st edn 1869.

Watson, Aaron. *A Great Labour Leader*. London: Brown, Langham, 1908.

——. *A Newspaper Man's Memoirs*. London: Hutchinson, [1925].

Wilson, John. *A History of the Durham Miners' Association, 1870–1904*. Durham: J.H. Veitch and Sons, 1907

6. Secondary Sources: Books and Articles.

Alderman, Geoffrey. *The Railway Interest*. Leicester: Leicester University Press, 1973.

Allen, E. *The Durham Miners' Association*. Durham: National Union of Mineworkers, 1969.

—— et al. *The North-East Engineers' Strikes of 1871: The Nine Hours League*. Newcastle upon Tyne: Frank Graham, 1971.

Allen, V. L. *The Sociology of Industrial Relations*. London: Longman, 1971.

Armytage, W. H. G. *A. J. Mundella, 1825–1897: The Liberal Background to the Labour Movement*. London: Benn, 1951.

Arnot, R. Page. *The Miners: A History of the Miners' Federation of Great Britain, 1889–1910*. London: George Allen and Unwin, 1949.

Arnstein, Walter. *The Bradlaugh Case; A Study in Late Victorian Opinion and Politics*. Oxford: Clarendon Press, 1965.

Aronson, Theo. *Queen Victoria and the Bonapartes*. Indianapolis: Bobbs-Merrill, 1972.

Ashton, Owen R. *W. E. Adams: Chartist, Radical and Journalist 1832–1906*. Tyne and Wear: Bewick Press, 1991.

——. 'W. E. Adams and Working Class Opposition to Empire 1878–80: Cyprus and Afghanistan', *North East Labour History Bulletin*, No. 27 (1993), 49–74.

Barker, Michael. *Gladstone and Radicalism, the Reconstruction of Liberal Policy in Britain 1885–1894*. New York: Barnes and Noble, 1975.

Bartrip, P.W.J., and S.B. Burman. *The Wounded Soldiers of Industry: Industrial Compensation Policy, 1883–1897*. Oxford: Oxford University Press, 1983.

Baylen, Joseph, and Norbert Gossman (eds). *Biographical Dictionary of Modern British Radicals, Vol. 2, 1830–1870*. Atlantic Highlands: Humanities Press, 1982.

Bealey, Frank, and Henry Pelling. *Labour and Politics 1900–1906*. London: Macmillan, 1958.

Benson, John. *British Coalminers in the Nineteenth Century: A Social History*. Dublin: Gill and Macmillan, 1980.

Benson, John, Robert G. Neville and Charles H. Thompson (comps and eds). *Bibliography of the British Coal Industry*. Oxford: Oxford University Press, 1981.

Biagini, Eugenio F. 'British Trade Unions and Popular Political Economy'. *Historical Journal*, 30 (1987), 811–40.

——. *Liberty, Retrenchment and Reform: Popular Liberalism in the Age of Gladstone, 1860–1880*. Cambridge: Cambridge University Press, 1992.

Biagini, Eugenio, and Alastair J. Reid (eds). *Currents of Radicalism: Popular Radicalism, Organised Labour and Party Politics in Britain, 1850–1914*. Cambridge: Cambridge University Press, 1991.

Blake, Robert. *Disraeli*. New York: St Martin's Press, 1967.

Bristow, Edward. *Individualism Versus Socialism in Britain, 1880–1914*. New York: Garland, 1987.

——. 'Profit-Sharing, Socialism and Labour Unrest'. In Kenneth Brown (ed.), *Essays in Anti-Labour History*. Hamden, CN: Anchor Books, 1974, pp. 262–89.

Brown, Henry Phelps. *The Origin of Trade Union Power*. Oxford: Clarendon Press, 1983.

Brown, Kenneth. 'Trade Unions and the Law'. In Chris Wrigley (ed.), *A History of British Industrial Relations, 1875–1914*. Amherst: University of Massachusetts Press, 1982, pp. 116–34.

Buckle, George Earle. *The Life of Benjamin Disraeli*. Vol. 6. London: John Murray, 1920.

Burgess, K. *The Origins of British Industrial Relations: The Nineteenth Century Experience*. London: Croom Helm, 1975.

Cawley, Roger. 'British Coal Owners, 1881–1893: The Search for Structure'. Unpublished PhD dissertation, SUNY, Binghamton, 1984.

Cecil, Lamar. *Wilhelm II*. Chapel Hill: University of North Carolina Press, 1989.

Challinor, Raymond. *The Lancashire and Cheshire Miners*. Newcastle upon Tyne: Frank Graham, 1972.

——. *The Origins of British Bolshevism*. London: Croom Helm, 1977.

Challinor, Raymond, and Brian Ripley. *The Miners' Association: A Trade Union in the Age of the Chartists*. London: Lawrence and Wishart, 1968.

Chamberlain, Muriel. *'Pax Britannica'? British Foreign Policy, 1789–1914*. New York: Longman, 1988.

Chickering, Roger. *Imperial Germany and a World Without War: The Peace Movement and German Society, 1892–1914*. Princeton: Princeton University Press, 1975.

Church, Roy. *The History of the British Coal Industry*. Vol. 3. *1830–1913: Victorian Pre-eminence*. Oxford: Oxford University Press, 1986.

Clarke, J. F. 'Workers in the Tyneside Shipyards in the Nineteenth Century'. In Norman McCord (ed.), *Essays in Tyneside Labour History*. Newcastle upon Tyne Polytechnic, 1977, pp. 109–31.

Clegg, H. A., Alan Fox, and A. F. Thompson. *A History of the British Trade Unions Since 1889. Vol. 1, 1889–1910*. Oxford: Clarendon Press, 1964.

Cole, G.D.H. *British Working Class Politics 1832–1914*. London: Routledge and Kegan Paul, 4th impression, 1965, first published 1941.

——. *A Short History of the British Working Class Movement 1789–1937*. 3 vols. London: George Unwin [reprinted 1937].

Colls, Robert. *The Pitmen of the Northern Coalfield: Work, Culture and Protest, 1790–1850*. Manchester: Manchester University Press, 1987.

Crewe, Marquess of. *Lord Rosebery*. 2 vols. London: John Murray, 1931.

Curtis, L. P., Jr. *Coercion and Conciliation in Ireland, 1880–1892: A Study in Conservative Unionism*. Princeton: Princeton University Press, 1963.

Daunton, M. J. 'The Export Coalfields: South Wales and North East England, 1870–1914'. In R. W. Sturgess (ed.), *Pitmen, Viewers, and Coalmasters: Essays in North East Coal Mining in the Nineteenth Century*. North East Labour History, 1986, pp. 126–58.

Davey, Arthur. *The British Pro-Boers, 1877–1902*. Capetown: Tafelberg, 1978.

Davidson, Roger. *Whitehall and the Labour Problem in Late-Victorian and Edwardian Britain: A Study in Official Statistics and Social Control*. London: Croom Helm, 1985.

Davis, Hayne (ed.). *Among the World's Peacemakers*. New York: Progressive Publishing, 1907.

Dictionary of Labour Biography. Joyce M. Bellamy and John Saville (eds). Clifton, NJ: Augustus M. Kelley, 1972, multi-volume. Vol. 1, pp. 51–63, includes an entry on Burt.

Dictionary of National Biography. Oxford: Oxford University Press.

Dingle, A. E. *The Campaign for Prohibition in Victorian England*. New Brunswick: Rutgers University Press, 1980.

Douglass, David. 'The Durham Pitman'. In Raphael Samuel (ed.), *Miners, Quarrymen and Saltworkers*. London: Routledge and Kegan Paul, 1977, pp. 205–95.

Duckham, Helen and Baron Duckham *Great Pit Disasters*. Newton Abbot: David and Charles, 1973.

Fox, Alan. *History and Heritage: The Social Origins of the British Industrial Relations System*. London: George Allen & Unwin, 1985.

Fraser, W. Hamish. *Trade Unions and Society: The Struggle for Acceptance, 1850–1880*. Totowa, NJ: Rowman and Littlefield, 1974.

Gard, Robin. 'The Northumberland Pitman'. *Bulletin of the North East Group for the Study of Labour History*, 6 (1972), 17–22.

Garside, W.R. 'Wage Determination and the Miners' Lockout of 1892'. In Norman McCord (ed.), *Essays in Tyneside Labour History*. Newcastle upon Tyne Polytechnic, 1977, pp. 132–53.

Gash, Norman. *Politics in the Age of Peel*. London: Longmans, Green, 1953.

Gilbert, Bentley B. *The Evolution of National Insurance in Great Britain: The Origins of the Welfare State*. London: Michael Joseph, 1966.

Gollin, A. M. *Proconsul in Politics: A Study of Lord Milner in Opposition and in Power*. New York: Macmillan, 1964.

Gregory, Roy. *The Miners and British Politics 1906–1914*. London: Oxford University Press, 1968.

Gwyn, William. *Democracy and the Cost of Politics in Britain*. London: Athlone Press, 1962.

Halevy, Elie. *Imperialism and the Rise of Labour*. London: Earnest Benn, 1961.

Hamer, D.A. *John Morley, Liberal Intellectual in Politics*. Oxford: Oxford University Press, 1968.

Hanes, D.G. *The First British Workman's Compensation Act, 1897.* New Haven: Yale University Press, 1968.

Harrison, Royden. *Before the Socialists.* London: Routledge & Kegan Paul, 1965.

—— (ed.). *Independent Collier: The Coal Miner as Archtypal Proletarian Reconsidered.* New York: St Martin's Press, 1978.

Harrison, Royden, Gillian B. Woolven and Robert Duncan. *The Warwick Guide to British Labour Periodicals 1790–1970: A Checklist.* Chichester: Harvester Press, 1977.

Hearn, Francis. *Domination, Legislation, and Resistance: The Incorporation of the Nineteenth-Century English Working Class.* Westport, CT: Greenwood Press, 1978.

Hennock, E. P. *British Social Reforms and German Precedents: The Case of Social Insurance 1880–1914.* Oxford: Oxford University Press, 1987.

Heyck, Thomas William. *The Dimensions of British Radicalism: The Case of Ireland 1874–1895.* Urbana: University of Illinois Press, 1974.

Hobsbawm, E. J. *Worlds of Labour: Further Studies in the History of Labour.* London: Weidenfeld and Nicolson, 1984.

Hodnett, R. M. *Politics and the Northumberland Miners: Liberals and Labour in Morpeth and Wansbeck, 1890–1922.* Cleveland: University of Teesside, 1994.

Howell, David. *British Workers and the Independent Labour Party, 1888–1906.* New York: St Martin's Press, 1983.

A Howky Gan Te Parliement. Northumberland County Council, [1987].

Hunter, Ian. 'Labour in Local Government on Tyneside, 1883–1921'. In Maureen Callcott and Raymond Challinor (eds), *Working Class Politics in North East England.* Newcastle upon Tyne: North East Labour History Society, 1983, pp. 23–37.

Hurt, J. S. *Elementary Schooling and the Working Class 1860–1918.* London: Routledge and Kegan Paul, 1979.

Jaffe, J.A. 'The "Chiliasm of Despair" Reconsidered: Revivalism and Working-Class Agitation in County Durham'. *Journal of British Studies,* 28 (January 1989), 23–42.

——. 'Competition and the Size of Firms in the North-East Coal Trade, 1800–1850'. *Northern History,* 25 (1989), 235–55.

——. *The Struggle for Market Power: Industrial Relations in the British Coal Industry, 1800–1840.* Cambridge: Cambridge University Press, 1991.

James, Robert Rhodes. *Rosebery.* London: Weidenfeld and Nicolson, 1963.

Jenkins, Roy. *Sir Charles Dilke: A Victorian Tragedy.* London: Collins, 1958.

Jenkins, T. A. *The Liberal Ascendancy, 1830–86.* New York: St Martin's Press, 1994.

Jevons, H.S. *The British Coal Trade,* 2nd edn. London: Kegan Paul, Trench, Trubner, 1920.

John, Angela. *By the Sweat of Their Brow.* London: Croom Helm, 1980.

Jones, Carol. 'Experiences of a Strike: The North East Coalowners and the Pitmen, 1831–1832'. In R. W. Sturgess (ed.), *Pitmen, Viewers, and Coalmasters: Essays in North East Coal Mining in the Nineteenth Century.* North East Labour History, 1986, pp. 27–54.

Kadish, Alon. 'University Extension and the Working Classes: The Case of the Northumberland Miners'. *Historical Research*, 60 (June 1987), 188–207.

Koss, Stephen (ed.). *The Pro-Boers*. Chicago: University of Chicago Press, 1973.

Lange, Christian, *et al. The Interparliamentary Union from 1889 to 1939*. Lausanne: Payot, 1939.

Lawson, John, and Harold Silver. *A Social History of Education in England*. London: Methuen, 1973.

Lee, Alan. 'Ruskin and Political Economy: *Unto This Last*'. In Robert Hewison (ed.), *New Approaches to Ruskin*. London: Routledge and Kegan Paul, 1981, pp. 68–88.

Longford, Elizabeth. *Victoria R. I.* London: Weidenfeld and Nicolson, 1964.

Lovell, John. 'Trade Unions and the Development of Independent Labour Politics 1889–1906'. In Ben Pimlott and Chris Cook (eds), *Trade Unions in British Politics*. London: Longman, 1982, pp. 38–57.

Lowe, Charles. *The German Emperor William II*. London: Bliss, Sands and Foster, [1895].

Lyons, F.S.L., Jr. *Charles Stuart Parnell*. New York: Oxford University Press, 1977.

Maehl, William H. 'The Northeastern Miners' Struggle for the Franchise, 1872–74'. *International Review of Social History*, 20 (1975), 198–219.

Magnus, Philip. *Gladstone*. New York: E. P. Dutton, 1964.

——. *King Edward the Seventh*. New York: E. P. Dutton, 1964.

Marsh, Peter. *Joseph Chamberlain: Entrepreneur in Politics*. New Haven: Yale University Press, 1994.

Marshall, Craig. *Levels of Industrial Militancy and Political Radicalism of the Durham Miners, 1885–1914*. Durham, 1976.

McCord, Norman. 'Taff Vale Revisited'. *History*, 78 (February 1993), 243–60.

McCormick, B., and J. E. Williams. 'The Miners and the Eight-Hour Day, 1863–1910'. *Economic History Review*, 12 (December 1959), 222–38.

McCutcheon, John Elliott. *The Hartley Colliery Disaster, 1862*. Seaham, County Durham: E. McCutcheon, 1963.

McIvor, Arthur J. 'Employers' Organisation and Strikebreaking in Britain, 1880–1914'. *International Review of Social History*, 29 (1984), 1–33.

McNiven, Colin. 'Ashington: The Growth of a Company Town'. *Bulletin of the North East Group for the Study of Labour History*, 12 (1978), 1–20.

Mertinez, Paul. 'The "People's Charter" and the Enigmatic Mr. Maltman Barry'. *Bulletin of the Society for the Study of Labour History*, 41 (Autumn 1980), 34–45.

Milne, Maurice. *The Newspapers of Northumberland and Durham*. Newcastle upon Tyne: Frank Graham, [1971].

Mitchell, B. R. *Economic Development of the British Coal Industry 1800–1914*. New York: Cambridge University Press, 1984.

Morgan, Kenneth. *Keir Hardie, Radical and Socialist*. London: Weidenfeld and Nicolson, 1975.

——. *Labour People: Leaders and Lieutenants, Hardie to Kinnock*. Oxford: Oxford University Press, 1987.

Muller, William D. *The Kept Men? The First Century of Trade Union Representation in the British House of Commons, 1874–1975*. Atlantic Highlands, NJ: Humanities Press, 1977.

191

Newton, Douglas J. *British Labour, European Socialism, and the Struggle for Peace, 1889–1914*. Oxford: Oxford University Press, 1985.

Northumberland Miners' Mutual Confidence Association. *Northumberland Miners' Union Centenary Brochure, 1863–1963*. 1963.

Nossiter, T. J. *Influence, Opinion and Political Idioms in Reformed England: Case Studies from the North East 1832–1874*. Hassocks: Harvester Press, 1974.

O'Brien, Conor Cruise. *Parnell and His Party, 1880–90*. Oxford: Oxford University Press, 1957.

O'Day, Alan. *The English Face of Irish Nationalism. Parnellite Involvement in British Politics 1880–86*. Toronto: Macmillan, 1977.

Pakenham, Thomas. *The Boer War*. New York: Random House, 1979.

Pelling, Henry. *Popular Politics and Society in Late Victorian Britain*. 2nd edn London: Macmillan, 1979.

Porter, Bernard. *Critics of Empire: British Radical Attitudes to Colonialism in Africa, 1895–1914*. London: Macmillan, 1968.

Porter, Jeffrey Harvey. 'Wage Bargaining under Conciliation Agreements, 1860–1914'. *Economic History Review*, 2nd ser., 23 (1970), 460–75.

Potts, A. and E. Wade. *Stand True*. Blyth, Northumberland: National Union of Mineworkers, Northumberland Mechanics, 1975.

Powell, David. *British Politics and the Labour Question, 1868–1990*. New York: St Martin's Press, 1992.

——. 'The Liberal Ministries and Labour, 1892–1895'. *History*, 68 (October 1983), 408–26.

Price, Richard. *Labour in British Society: An Interpretative History*. London: Croom Helm, 1986.

Pugh, Martin. *The Making of Modern British Politics*. New York: St Martin's Press, 1982.

——. *The Tories and the People 1880–1935*. Oxford: Blackwell, 1985.

Purdue, A.W. 'Jarrow Politics, 1885–1914: The Challenge to Liberal Hegemony'. *Northern History*, 18 (1982), 182–98.

——. 'The Liberal and Labour Parties in North-East Politics, 1900–1914: The Struggle for Supremacy'. *International Review of Social History*, 26 (1981), 1–24.

Reid, Fred. *Keir Hardie: The Making of a Socialist*. London: Croom Helm, 1978.

Robbins, Keith. *The Abolition of War: The 'Peace Movement' in Britain, 1914–1919*. Cardiff: University of Wales Press, 1976.

Roberts, B. C. *The Trades Union Congress, 1868–1921*. Cambridge, MA: Harvard University Press, 1958.

Royle, Edward. *Radicals, Secularists and Republicans: Popular Free Thought in Britain, 1866–1915*. Manchester: Manchester University Press, 1980.

Saab, Ann Pottinger. *Reluctant Icon: Gladstone, Bulgaria, and the Working Classes, 1856–1878*. Cambridge, MA: Harvard University Press, 1991.

Satre, Lowell J. 'Education and Religion in the Shaping of Thomas Burt, Miners' Leader'. *North East Labour History Society Bulletin*, 26 (1992), 87–104.

——. 'Thomas Burt'. In Joseph O. Baylen and Norbert J. Gossman (eds), *Biographical Dictionary of Modern British Radicals, Vol. 2, 1830–1870*. Atlantic Highlands, NJ: Humanities Press, 1982, pp. 111–15.

——. 'Thomas Burt and the Crisis of Late-Victorian Liberalism in the North-East'. *Northern History*, 23 (1987), 174–93.

Shepherd, John. 'Labour and Parliament: The Lib.-Labs. as the First Working-class MPs, 1885–1906'. In Eugenio Biagini and Alastair J. Reid (eds), *Currents of Radicalism: Popular Radicalism, Organised Labour and Party Politics in Britain, 1850–1914*. Cambridge: Cambridge University Press, 1991, pp. 187–213.

Shiman, Lilian Lewis. *Crusade against Drink in Victorian England*. New York: St Martin's Press, 1988.

Smith, Paul. *Disraelian Conservatism and Social Reform*. London: Routledge & Kegan Paul, 1967.

Smith, Sir Hurbert Llewellyn. *The Board of Trade*. London: G.P. Putnam's Sons, 1928.

Soldon, Norbert C. 'Laissez-Faire as Dogma: The Liberty and Property Defence League, 1882–1914'. In Kenneth D. Brown (ed.), *Essays in Anti-Labour History*. Hamden, CT: Archon Books, 1974, pp. 208–33.

Stewart, William. *J. Keir Hardie*. London: ILP Edition, 1921.

Stigant, P. 'Wesleyan Methodism and Working-class Radicalism in the North, 1792–1821'. *Northern History*, 6 (1971), 98–116.

Sturgess, R. W. (ed.). *Pitmen, Viewers, and Coalmasters: Essays in North East Coal Mining in the Nineteenth Century*. North East Labour History, 1986.

Tanner, Duncan. *Political Change and the Labour Party, 1900–1918*. Cambridge: Cambridge University Press, 1990.

Thane, Pat. 'Non-Contributory Versus Insurance Pensions 1878–1908'. In Pat Thane (ed.), *The Origins of British Social Policy*. Totowa, NJ: Rowman and Littlefield, 1978, pp. 84–106.

Thompson, E. P. *William Morris, Romantic to Revolutionary*. New York: Pantheon Books, 1977, rev. edn.

Todd, Nigel. *The Militant Democracy: Joseph Cowen and Victorian Radicalism*. Tyne & Wear: Bewick Press, 1991.

Torr, Dona. *Tom Mann and His Times*. Vol. 1. London: Lawrence and Wishart, 1956.

Treble, John G. 'Sliding Scales and Conciliation Boards: Risk-Sharing in the Late 19th Century British Coal Industry'. *Oxford Economic Papers*, 39 (December 1987), 679–98.

Tsiang, Tingfu F. *Labor and Empire: A Study of the Reaction of British Labor, Mainly as Represented in Parliament, to British Imperialism Since 1880*. New York: Columbia University Press, 1923.

Tsuzuki, Chushichi. *Tom Mann, 1856–1941*. Oxford: Oxford University Press, 1991.

Waitt, E. I. 'John Morley, Joseph Cowen and Robert Spence Watson: Liberal Divisions in Newcastle Politics, 1873–1895'. Unpublished PhD dissertation, University of Manchester, 1972.

Ward, J. T. 'Tory Socialist: A Preliminary Note on Michael Maltman Barry (1842–1909)'. *Journal of the Scottish Labour History Society*, 2 (April 1970), 25–37.

Wearmouth, R.F. *Methodism and the Working-Class Movements of England, 1800–1850*. Clifton, NJ: Augustus M. Kelley, 1972; reprint, originally published 1937.

Welbourne, E. *The Miners' Unions of Northumberland and Durham.* Cambridge: Cambridge University Press, 1923.

Werner, Julia Stewart. *The Primitive Methodist Connexion: Its Background and Early History.* Madison: University of Wisconsin Press, 1984.

Wigley, John. *The Rise and Fall of the Victorian Sunday.* Manchester: Manchester University Press, 1980.

Williamson, Bill. *Class, Culture and Community: A Biographical Study of Social Change in Mining.* London: Routledge & Kegan Paul, 1982.

——. 'The 1887 Lock-out and Strike in the Northumberland Coalfield'. In R. W. Sturgess (ed.), *Pitmen, Viewers, and Coalmasters: Essays in North East Coal Mining in the Nineteenth Century.* North East Labour History, 1986, pp. 105–25.

Wilson, Gordon M. *Alexander McDonald, Leader of the Miners.* Aberdeen: Aberdeen University Press, 1982.

Wilson, John. *CB: A Life of Sir Henry Campbell-Bannerman.* London: Constable, 1973.

Wirthwein, Walter. *Britain and the Balkan Crisis, 1875–1878.* New York: AMS Press, 1966; first published 1935..

World Encyclopedia of Peace. 4 vols. Oxford: Pergamon Press, 1986.

Wrigley, Chris (ed.). *A History of British Industrial Relations, 1875–1914.* Amherst: University of Massachusetts Press, 1982

Index